Vital Readings in American Politics

Second Edition

Edited by

M. Jeffrey Colbert

University of North Carolina—Greensboro

KENDALL/HUNT PUBLISHING COMPANY
4050 Westmark Drive   Dubuque, Iowa 52002

CONTENTS

ACKNOWLEDGMENTS

In my acknowledgment to the first edition of this book, I likened myself to an Academy Award winner—rushing up on stage, they are breathless and, out of fear they will never win again, proceed to thank everyone they've ever known in their entire life! Having no idea that I would ever edit a text, much less do a second edition, the analogy was not all that far from the truth. While, in this second edition, I can adapt, modify, or completely rewrite my earlier acknowledgments, I find that I really only want to update my initial sentiments. Those who were significant to me several years ago still are today. We're all a little older, hopefully a bit wiser, and there are more grandchildren!! So, here's my updated shot at acknowledging those who have been instrumental in this process.

First and foremost, I must thank the God who made me, His Son who died for me, and His Spirit that lives in me. For me to fail to publicly recognize Him would be a gross injustice. Anything good in my life I have ever done, I have done because of His grace. The errors were completely and totally mine!

The most human expression of God's love expressed to me has been my Mother. No one has sacrificed more, forgiven more and loved more than she. I have tried to learn from her the art of selfless living and giving. On my absolute best days, I am a poor imitation of her.

For the past twenty seven years, the most constant human ray of sunshine in my life has been my daughter, Genny. I learned from her the complete trust that only children seem to possess in useful amounts. I also learned the ultimate aggravation that only a teenage daughter can give! Though, through the years, we were not always able to spend all the time together I would have liked, I have treasured every moment we have ever shared and treasure today the Godly woman she is becoming.

My wife of better than seventeen years, Sherry, has taught me that true love comes from an inexhaustible source. Over our years of dating and marriage, she has given to me and to others in ways I never thought possible. She is the ultimate Mom and daughter, and I will never do enough to deserve her as my wife. In addition, she gave me two wonderful step kids, Mike and Melissa, their respective spouses, Candy and Doug, and their respective kids (our grandkids!), Charlie, Sarah and Mikey, and Megan and Jackson.

More traditionally, I must thank my colleagues at UNC Greensboro, my alma mater and my home, and at Elon University, my adopted home. I have had excellent friends and colleagues and the secretarial staff (Maggie and Pat) make every day on either campus a pleasure. With great affection, I must acknowledge my long time colleague, Leigh Sink. Without her encouragement, it's doubtful this project would have been undertaken, much less completed.

From the moment this project began, I received nothing but support from my friends at Kendall-Hunt. Thank you for all your patience!

I would be completely remiss if I didn't thank Jim Svara, currently at NC State University. As the MPA program head at UNCG many years ago, he asked a first year graduate student to help him research, write and present a paper at the SPSA Conference in Nashville in 1985. It was there I learned I was supposed to teach, and I can't imagine anyone happier in their job that I am in mine.

Finally, to Brandy, Bill, Tiffany and Jen–you were the first to teach me how much more teaching could be, what good friends your students could become, and how we teachers can affect lives, if we'll only try.

Technically, the reader should be aware that I have removed virtually all notes and references from the articles and chapters in this text. Should you need that information, the reference pages should give sufficient information. Further, large omissions of material are noted by (* * *), smaller ones by (. . .). As always, all errors in the text are my responsibility and mine alone. Neither my family, friends, colleagues at UNCG and Elon University nor my valuable associates at Kendall Hunt can be held responsible for all the errors I make!

CHAPTER 1

INTRODUCTION

This reader begins with undoubtedly the two indispensable documents of any American Government reader: The Declaration of Independence and the Constitution of the United States. These documents obviously were and have been instrumental in the creation and sustenance of our nation for well over 200 years. The Declaration and the Constitution, both with multiple writers but significantly the documents of two different men, are not the same. A careful reading of the two, as I expect you will do, allows you to see different perspectives and viewpoints. Obviously, their purposes were not the same. One was a declaratory statement of separation from England and a listing of the grievances and expectations of citizens. The other became the foundational document of our governmental structure. As you read them both, note the differences, think about them, and be prepared to discuss them.

Most of the remaining works of this chapter are from a series of writings known as the Federalist Papers. Written after the Constitution was drafted and sent to the states, the authors explained and supported the proposed Constitution. You will see Federalist Papers in most chapters of this book. They are not "light" reading. I highly recommend turning down your stereo and ingesting stimulants no stronger than caffeine (But I recommend a lot of caffeine!) while you read these.

The chapter closes with the minority report of the Pennsylvania constitutional convention. A common misconception is that the Constitution and the subsequent new government were universally approved, at least in the United States. In fact, there was considerable debate and discontent. Honestly, a number of the "dire" predictions offered by the Constitutional critics turned out to be well founded. A lesson for us to learn, perhaps?

Federalist #47 was written by James Madison, the author of many of the papers. In this paper, Madison attempted to counter the criticism of the Constitution which centered around the "sharing" of powers by the three branches of government. Many believed that in order to preserve the necessary balance of power and to avoid one branch dominating another, clear lines of demarcation had to be placed around each branch. To them the interweave of the three branches (i.e. the President can veto laws passed by Congress, the Senate approves presidential appointments, the Supreme court is appointed by the President and confirmed by the Senate) were clear threats to liberty. As Madison refutes this, find the answers to the following:

1   What is Madison's definition of tyranny?

2. How did the British Constitution separate or delineate power (have *specific* examples)?

3. How did Madison reinterpret Montesquieu's writings and apply them to the Constitution?

4. What practical examples did he note to support a government that had "encroachments"?

Federalist #48 continued Madison's examination of the relationship between the branches of government in the proposed system. Seek the answers to the questions below:

1. What did Madison mean by "parchment barriers"?

2. Why did he doubt their capacity to succeed?

3. Which branch of government did it appear most people feared? Did Madison share this opinion? Why or why not?

Federalist #51 is my personal favorite of the papers because of his "angels" passage (you'll know what I'm talking about when you get there). Madison continues to address the issue of the relationship between the branches and introduces the powers delegated to the states as a further security against tyranny. Examine this paper for the following:

1. How did Madison justify the Supreme Court being appointed by the President and confirmed by the Senate?

2. When Madison wrote "Ambition must be made to counteract ambition", what did he mean?

3. What other security existed in our society which Madison believed would help guard against tyranny and injustice?

As noted on the first page, not everyone thought this new Constitution was such a great idea! Examine carefully the "Minority Report". Find and be able to explain the reasons they opposed the Constitution.

THE DECLARATION OF INDEPENDENCE

IN CONGRESS, JULY 4, 1776

(The unanimous Declaration of the Thirteen United States of America)

Preamble

When, in the course of human events, it becomes necessary for one people to dissolve the political bands which have connected them with another, and to assume, among the powers of the earth, the separate and equal station to which the laws of nature and of nature's God entitle them, a decent respect to the opinions of mankind requires that they should declare the causes which impel them to the separation.

We hold these truths to be self-evident; that all men are created equal, that they are endowed by their Creator with certain unalienable rights, that among these are life, liberty and the pursuit of happiness.

That, to secure these rights, governments are instituted among men, deriving their just powers from the consent of the governed.

That whenever any form of government becomes destructive of these ends, it is the right of the people to alter or to abolish it, and to institute new government, laying its foundation on such principles, and organizing its powers in such form, as to them shall seem most likely to effect their safety and happiness. Prudence, indeed will dictate that governments long established should not be changed for light and transient causes; and accordingly all experience hath shown that mankind are more disposed to suffer while evils are sufferable, than to right themselves by abolishing the forms to which they are accustomed. But when a long train of abuses and usurpations, pursuing invariably the same object, evinces a design to reduce them under absolute despotism, it is their right, it is their duty, to throw off such government, and to provide new guards for their future security.

Such has been the patient sufferance of these colonies; and such is now the necessity which constrains them to alter their former systems of government. The history of the present king of Great Britain is a history of repeated injuries and usurpations, all having in direct object the establishment of an absolute tyranny over these states. To prove this, let facts be submitted to a candid world.

He has refused his assent to laws, the most wholesome and necessary for the public good.

He has forbidden his governors to pass laws of immediate and pressing importance unless suspended in their operation till his assent should be obtained; and when so suspended, he has utterly neglected to attend to them.

He has refused to pass other laws for the accommodation of large districts of people, unless those people would relinquish the right of representation in the legislature, a right inestimable to them, and formidable to tyrants only.

He has called together legislative bodies at places unusual, uncomfortable, and distant for the depository of their public records, for the sole purpose of fatiguing them into compliance with his measures.

He has dissolved representative houses repeatedly: for opposing, with manly firmness, his invasions on the rights of people.

He has refused, for a long time after such dissolutions, to cause others to be elected: whereby the legislative powers incapable of annihilation, have returned to the people at large for their exercise; the state remaining, in the meantime, exposed to all the dangers of invasion from without and convulsions within.

He has endeavored to prevent the population of these states; for that purpose obstructing the laws of naturalization of foreigners, refusing to pass others to encourage their migration hither, and raising the conditions of new appropriations of lands.

He has obstructed the administration of justice, by refusing his assent to laws for establishing judiciary powers.

He has made judges dependent on his will alone for the tenure of their offices, and the amount and payment of their salaries.

He has erected a multitude of new offices, and sent hither swarms of officers to harass our people and eat out their substance.

He has kept among us, in times of peace, standing armies, without the consent of our legislature.

He has affected to render the military independent of and superior to, the civil power.

He has combined with others to subject us to jurisdiction foreign to our constitution and unacknowledged by our laws, giving his assent to their acts of pretended legislation:

For quartering large bodies of armed troops among us;

For protecting them, by a mock trial, from punishment for any murders which they should commit on the inhabitants of these states;

For cutting off our trade with all parts of the world:

For imposing taxes on us without our consent;

For depriving us, in many cases, of the benefits of trial by jury;

For transporting us beyond seas, to be tried for pretended offenses;

For abolishing the free system of English laws in a neighboring province, establishing therein an arbitrary government, and enlarging its boundaries, so as to render it at once an example and fit instrument for introducing the same absolute rule into these colonies:

For taking away our charters, abolishing our most valuable laws, and altering, fundamentally, the forms of our governments;

For suspending our own legislatures, and declaring themselves invented with power to legislate for us in all cases whatsoever.

He has abdicated government here, by declaring us out of his protection and waging war against us.

He has plundered our seas, ravaged our coasts, burned our towns, and destroyed the lives of our people.

He is at this time transporting large armies of foreign mercenaries to complete the works of death, desolation, and tyranny already begun with circumstances of cruelty and perfidy scarcely paralleled in the most barbarous ages and totally unworthy of the head of a civilized nation.

He has constrained our fellow-citizens, taken captive on the high seas, to bear arms against their country, to become the executioners of their friends and brethren, or to fall themselves by their hands.

He has excited domestic insurrections among us, and has endeavored to bring on the inhabitants of our frontiers the merciless Indian savages, whose known rule of warfare is an undistinguished destruction of all ages, sexes, and conditions.

In every stage of these oppressions we have petitioned for redress in the most humble terms; our repeated petitions have been answered only by repeated injury. A prince whose character is thus marked by every act which may define a tyrant is unfit to be the ruler of a free people.

Nor have we been wanting in attention to our British brethren. We have warned them, from time to time, of attempts by their legislature to extend an unwarrantable jurisdiction over us. We have reminded them of the circumstances of our emigration and settlement here. We have appealed to their native justice and magnanimity; and we have conjured them, by the ties of our common kindred, to disavow these usurpations, which would inevitably interrupt our connections and correspondence. They, too, have been deaf to the voice of justice and of consanguinity. We must, therefore, acquiesce in the necessity which denounces our separation, and hold them, as we hold the rest of mankind, enemies in war, in peace, friends.

We, therefore, the representatives of the United States of America, in General Congress assembled, appealing to the Supreme Judge of the world for the rectitude of our intentions, do, in the name and by authority of the good people of these colonies, solemnly publish and declare, that these united colonies are, and of right ought to be, free and independent states; that they are absolved from all allegiance to the British crown, and that all political connection between them and the state of Great Britain is, and ought to be, totally dissolved; and that, as free and independent states, they have full power to levy war, conclude peace, contract alliances, establish commerce, and do all other acts and things which independent states may of a right do. And, for the support of this declaration, with a firm reliance on the protection of Divine Providence, we mutually pledge to each other our lives, our fortunes, and our sacred honor.

CONSTITUTION FOR THE UNITED STATES OF AMERICA

We the People of the United States, in Order to form a more perfect Union, establish Justice, insure domestic Tranquility, provide for the common defence, promote the general Welfare, and secure the Blessings of Liberty to ourselves and our Posterity, do ordain and establish this Constitution for the United States of America.

Article. I.

Section. 1. All legislative Powers herein granted shall be vested in a Congress of the United States, which shall consist of a Senate and House of Representatives.

Section. 2. The House of Representatives shall be composed of Members chosen every second Year by the People of the several States, and the Electors in each State shall have the Qualifications requisite for Electors of the most numerous Branch of the State Legislature.

No Person shall be a Representative who shall not have attained to the Age of twenty five Years, and been seven Years a Citizen of the United States, and who shall not, when elected, be an Inhabitant of that State in which he shall be chosen.

Representatives and *direct Taxes* (1) shall be apportioned among the several States which may be included within this Union, according to their respective Numbers, *which shall be determined by adding to the whole Number of free Persons, including those bound to Service for a Term of Years, and excluding Indians not taxed, three fifths of all other Persons.* (2) The actual Enumeration shall be made within three Years after the first Meeting of the Congress of the United States, and within every subsequent Term of ten Years, in such Manner as they shall by Law direct. The Number of Representatives shall not exceed one for every thirty Thousand, but each State shall have at Least one Representative; and until such enumeration shall be made, the State of New Hampshire shall be entitled to chuse three, Massachusetts eight, Rhode-Island and Providence Plantations one, Connecticut five, New-York six, New Jersey four, Pennsylvania eight, Delaware one, Maryland six, Virginia ten, North Carolina five, South Carolina five, and Georgia three.

When vacancies happen in the Representation from any State, the Executive Authority thereof shall issue Writs of Election to fill such Vacancies.

The House of Representatives shall chuse their Speaker and other Officers; and shall have the sole Power of Impeachment.

Section. 3. The Senate of the United States shall be composed of two Senators from each State, *chosen by the Legislature thereof*, (3) for six Years; and each Senator shall have one Vote.

Immediately after they shall be assembled in Consequence of the first Election, they shall be divided as equally as may be into three Classes. The Seats of the Senators of the first Class shall be vacated at the Expiration of the second Year, of the second Class at the Expiration of the fourth Year, and of the third Class at the Expiration of the sixth Year, so that one third may be chosen every second Year; *and if Vacancies happen by Resignation, or otherwise, during the Recess of the Legislature of any State, the Executive thereof may make temporary Appointments until the next Meeting of the Legislature, which shall then fill such Vacancies.* (4)

No Person shall be a Senator who shall not have attained to the Age of thirty Years, and been nine Years a Citizen of the United States, and who shall not, when elected, be an Inhabitant of that State for which he shall be chosen.

The Vice President of the United States shall be President of the Senate, but shall have no Vote, unless they be equally divided.

The Senate shall chuse their other Officers, and also a President pro tempore, in the Absence of the Vice President, or when he shall exercise the Office of President of the United States.

The Senate shall have the sole Power to try all Impeachments. When sitting for that Purpose, they shall be on Oath or Affirmation. When the President of the United States is tried, the Chief Justice shall preside: And no Person shall be convicted without the Concurrence of two thirds of the Members present.

Judgment in Cases of Impeachment shall not extend further than to removal from Office, and disqualification to hold and enjoy any Office of honor, Trust or Profit under the United States: but the Party convicted shall nevertheless be liable and subject to Indictment, Trial, Judgment and Punishment, according to Law.

Section. 4. The Times, Places and Manner of holding Elections for Senators and Representatives, shall be prescribed in each State by the Legislature thereof; but the Congress may at any time by Law make or alter such Regulations, except as to the Places of chusing Senators.

The Congress shall assemble at least once in every Year, *and such Meeting shall be on the first Monday in December unless they shall by Law appoint a different Day.* (5)

Section. 5. Each House shall be the Judge of the Elections, Returns and Qualifications of its own Members, and a Majority of each shall constitute a Quorum to do Business; but a smaller Number may adjourn from day to day, and may be authorized to compel the Attendance of absent Members, in such Manner, and under such Penalties as each House may provide.

Each House may determine the Rules of its Proceedings, punish its Members for disorderly Behaviour, and, with the Concurrence of two thirds, expel a Member.

Each House shall keep a Journal of its Proceedings, and from time to time publish the same, excepting such Parts as may in their Judgment require Secrecy; and the Yeas and Nays of the Members of either House on any question shall, at the Desire of one fifth of those Present, be entered on the Journal.

Neither House, during the Session of Congress, shall, without the Consent of the other, adjourn for more than three days, nor to any other Place than that in which the two Houses shall be sitting.

Section. 6. The Senators and Representatives shall receive a Compensation for their Services, to be ascertained by Law, and paid out of the Treasury of the United States. They shall in all Cases, except Treason, Felony and Breach of the Peace, be privileged from Arrest during their Attendance at the Session of their respective Houses, and in going to and returning from the same; and for any Speech or Debate in either House, they shall not be questioned in any other Place.

No Senator or Representative shall, during the Time for which he was elected, be appointed to any civil Office under the Authority of the United States, which shall have been created, or the Emoluments whereof shall have been encreased during such time; and no Person holding any Office under the United States, shall be a Member of either House during his Continuance in Office.

Section. 7. All Bills for raising Revenue shall originate in the House of Representatives; but the Senate may propose or concur with Amendments as on other Bills.

Every Bill which shall have passed the House of Representatives and the Senate, shall, before it become a Law, be presented to the President of the United States: If he approve he shall sign it, but if not he shall return it, with his Objections to that House in which it shall have originated, who shall enter the Objections at large on their Journal, and proceed to reconsider it. If after such Reconsideration two thirds of that House shall agree to pass the Bill, it shall be sent, together with the Objections, to the other House, by which it shall likewise be reconsidered, and if approved by two thirds of that House, it shall become a Law. But in all such Cases the Votes of both Houses shall be determined by yeas and Nays, and the Names of the Persons voting for and against the Bill shall be entered on the Journal of each House respectively. If any Bill shall not be returned by the President within ten Days (Sundays excepted) after it shall have been presented to him, the Same shall be a Law, in like Manner as if he had signed it, unless the Congress by their Adjournment prevent its Return, in which Case it shall not be a Law.

Every Order, Resolution, or Vote to which the Concurrence of the Senate and House of Representatives may be necessary (except on a question of Adjournment) shall be presented to the President of the United States; and before the Same shall take Effect, shall be approved by him, or being disapproved by him, shall be repassed by two thirds of the Senate and House of Representatives, according to the Rules and Limitations prescribed in the Case of a Bill.

Section. 8. The Congress shall have Power To lay and collect Taxes, Duties, Imposts and Excises, to pay the Debts and provide for the common Defence and general Welfare of the United States; but all Duties, Imposts and Excises shall be uniform throughout the United States;

To borrow Money on the credit of the United States;

To regulate Commerce with foreign Nations, and among the several States, and with the Indian Tribes;

To establish an uniform Rule of Naturalization, and uniform Laws on the subject of Bankruptcies throughout the United States;

To coin Money, regulate the Value thereof, and of foreign Coin, and fix the Standard of Weights and Measures;

To provide for the Punishment of counterfeiting the Securities and current Coin of the United States;

To establish Post Offices and post Roads;

To promote the Progress of Science and useful Arts, by securing for limited Times to Authors and Inventors the exclusive Right to their respective Writings and Discoveries;

To constitute Tribunals inferior to the supreme Court;

To define and punish Piracies and Felonies committed on the high Seas, and Offences against the Law of Nations;

To declare War, grant Letters of Marque and Reprisal, and make Rules concerning Captures on Land and Water;

To raise and support Armies, but no Appropriation of Money to that Use shall be for a longer Term than two Years;

To provide and maintain a Navy;

To make Rules for the Government and Regulation of the land and naval Forces;

To provide for calling forth the Militia to execute the Laws of the Union, suppress Insurrections and repel Invasions;

To provide for organizing, arming, and disciplining, the Militia, and for governing such Part of them as may be employed in the Service of the United States, reserving to the States respectively, the Appointment of the Officers, and the Authority of training the Militia according to the discipline prescribed by Congress;

To exercise exclusive Legislation in all Cases whatsoever, over such District (not exceeding ten Miles square) as may, by Cession of particular States, and the Acceptance of Congress, become the Seat of the Government of the United States, and to exercise like Authority over all Places purchased by the Consent of the Legislature of the State in which the Same shall be, for the Erection of Forts, Magazines, Arsenals, dock-Yards, and other needful Buildings; —And

To make all Laws which shall be necessary and proper for carrying into Execution the foregoing Powers, and all other Powers vested by this Constitution in the Government of the United States, or in any Department or Officer thereof.

Section. 9. The Migration or Importation of such Persons as any of the States now existing shall think proper to admit, shall not be prohibited by the Congress prior to the Year one thousand eight hundred and eight, but a Tax or duty may be imposed on such Importation, not exceeding ten dollars for each Person.

The Privilege of the Writ of Habeas Corpus shall not be suspended, unless when in Cases of Rebellion or Invasion the public Safety may require it.

No Bill of Attainder or ex post facto Law shall be passed.

No Capitation, or other direct, Tax shall be laid, unless in Proportion to the Census or Enumeration herein before directed to be taken. (6)

No Tax or Duty shall be laid on Articles exported from any State.

No Preference shall be given by any Regulation of Commerce or Revenue to the Ports of one State over those of another; nor shall Vessels bound to, or from, one State, be obliged to enter, clear, or pay Duties in another.

No Money shall be drawn from the Treasury, but in Consequence of Appropriations made by Law; and a regular Statement and Account of the Receipts and Expenditures of all public Money shall be published from time to time.

No Title of Nobility shall be granted by the United States: And no Person holding any Office of Profit or Trust under them, shall, without the Consent of the Congress, accept of any present, Emolument, Office, or Title, of any kind whatever, from any King, Prince, or foreign State.

Section. 10. No State shall enter into any Treaty, Alliance, or Confederation; grant Letters of Marque and Reprisal; coin Money; emit Bills of Credit; make any Thing but gold and silver Coin a Tender in Payment of Debts; pass any Bill of Attainder, ex post facto Law, or Law impairing the Obligation of Contracts, or grant any Title of Nobility.

No State shall, without the Consent of the Congress, lay any Imposts or Duties on Imports or Exports, except what may be absolutely necessary for executing it's inspection Laws; and the net Produce of all Duties and Imposts, laid by any State on Imports or Exports, shall be for the Use of the Treasury of the United States; and all such Laws shall be subject to the Revision and Controul of the Congress.

No State shall, without the Consent of Congress, lay any Duty of Tonnage, keep Troops, or Ships of War in time of Peace, enter into any Agreement or Compact with another State, or with a foreign Power, or engage in War, unless actually invaded, or in such imminent Danger as will not admit of delay.

Article. II.

Section. 1. The executive Power shall be vested in a President of the United States of America. He shall hold his Office during the Term of four Years, and, together with the Vice President, chosen for the same Term, be elected, as follows:

Each State shall appoint, in such Manner as the Legislature thereof may direct, a Number of Electors, equal to the whole Number of Senators and Representatives to which the State may be entitled in the Congress: but no Senator or Representative, or Person holding an Office of Trust or Profit under the United States, shall be appointed an Elector.

The Electors shall meet in their respective States, and vote by Ballot for two Persons, of whom one at least shall not be an Inhabitant of the same State with themselves. And they shall make a List of all the Persons voted for, and of the Number of Votes for each; which List they shall sign and certify, and transmit sealed to the Seat of the Government of the United States, directed to the President of the Senate. The President of the Senate shall, in the Presence of the Senate and House of Representatives, open all the Certificates, and the Votes shall then be counted. The Person having the greatest Number of Votes shall be the President, if such Number be a Majority of the whole Number of Electors appointed; and if there be more than one who have such Majority, and have an equal Number of Votes, then the House of Representatives shall immediately chuse by Ballot one of them for President; and if no Person have a Majority, then from the five highest on the List the said House shall in like Manner chuse the President. But in chusing the President, the Votes shall be taken by States, the Representation from each State having one Vote; a quorum for this Purpose shall consist of a Member or Members from two thirds of the States, and a Majority of all the States shall be necessary to a Choice. In every Case, after the Choice of the President, the Person having the greatest Number of Votes of the Electors shall be the Vice President. But if there should remain two or more who have equal Votes, the Senate shall chuse from them by Ballot the Vice President. (7)

The Congress may determine the Time of chusing the Electors, and the Day on which they shall give their Votes; which Day shall be the same throughout the United States.

No Person except a natural born Citizen, or a Citizen of the United States, at the time of the Adoption of this Constitution, shall be eligible to the Office of President; neither shall any Person be eligible to that Office who shall not have attained to the Age of thirty five Years, and been fourteen Years a Resident within the United States.

In Case of the Removal of the President from Office, or of his Death, Resignation, or Inability to discharge the Powers and Duties of the said Office, the Same shall devolve on the Vice President, and the Congress may by Law provide for the Case of Removal, Death, Resignation or Inability, both of the President and Vice President, declaring what Officer shall then act as President, and such Officer shall act accordingly, until the Disability be removed, or a President shall be elected. (8)

The President shall, at stated Times, receive for his Services, a Compensation, which shall neither be increased nor diminished during the Period for which he shall have been elected, and he shall not receive within that Period any other Emolument from the United States, or any of them.

Before he enter on the Execution of his Office, he shall take the following Oath or Affirmation: "I do solemnly swear (or affirm) that I will faithfully execute the Office of President of the United States, and will to the best of my Ability, preserve, protect and defend the Constitution of the United States."

Section. 2. The President shall be Commander in Chief of the Army and Navy of the United States, and of the Militia of the several States, when called into the actual Service of the United States; he may require the Opinion, in writing, of the principal Officer in each of the executive Departments, upon any Subject relating to the Duties of their respective Offices, and he shall have Power to grant Reprieves and Pardons for Offences against the United States, except in Cases of Impeachment.

He shall have Power, by and with the Advice and Consent of the Senate, to make Treaties, provided two thirds of the Senators present concur; and he shall nominate, and by and with the Advice and Consent of the Senate, shall appoint Ambassadors, other public Ministers and Consuls, Judges of the supreme Court, and all other Officers of the United States, whose

Appointments are not herein otherwise provided for, and which shall be established by Law: but the Congress may by Law vest the Appointment of such inferior Officers, as they think proper, in the President alone, in the Courts of Law, or in the Heads of Departments.

The President shall have Power to fill up all Vacancies that may happen during the Recess of the Senate, by granting Commissions which shall expire at the End of their next Session.

Section. 3. He shall from time to time give to the Congress Information of the State of the Union, and recommend to their Consideration such Measures as he shall judge necessary and expedient; he may, on extraordinary Occasions, convene both Houses, or either of them, and in Case of Disagreement between them, with Respect to the Time of Adjournment, he may adjourn them to such Time as he shall think proper; he shall receive Ambassadors and other public Ministers; he shall take Care that the Laws be faithfully executed, and shall Commission all the Officers of the United States.

Section. 4. The President, Vice President and all civil Officers of the United States, shall be removed from Office on Impeachment for, and Conviction of, Treason, Bribery, or other high Crimes and Misdemeanors.

Article. III.

Section. 1. The judicial Power of the United States shall be vested in one supreme Court, and in such inferior Courts as the Congress may from time to time ordain and establish. The Judges, both of the supreme and inferior Courts, shall hold their Offices during good Behaviour, and shall, at stated Times, receive for their Services a Compensation, which shall not be diminished during their Continuance in Office.

Section. 2. The judicial Power shall extend to all Cases, in Law and Equity, arising under this Constitution, the Laws of the United States, and Treaties made, or which shall be made, under their Authority; to all Cases affecting Ambassadors, other public Ministers and Consuls; to all Cases of admiralty and maritime Jurisdiction; to Controversies to which the United States shall be a Party; to Controversies between two or more States; *between a State and Citizens of another State; between Citizens of different States;* (9) between Citizens of the same State claiming Lands under Grants of different States, and between a State, or the Citizens thereof, and foreign States, Citizens or Subjects.

In all Cases affecting Ambassadors, other public Ministers and Consuls, and those in which a State shall be Party, the supreme Court shall have original Jurisdiction. In all the other Cases before mentioned, the supreme Court shall have appellate Jurisdiction, both as to Law and Fact, with such Exceptions, and under such Regulations as the Congress shall make.

The Trial of all Crimes, except in Cases of Impeachment, shall be by Jury; and such Trial shall be held in the State where the said Crimes shall have been committed; but when not committed within any State, the Trial shall be at such Place or Places as the Congress may by Law have directed.

Section. 3. Treason against the United States shall consist only in levying War against them, or in adhering to their Enemies, giving them Aid and Comfort. No Person shall be convicted of Treason unless on the Testimony of two Witnesses to the same overt Act, or on Confession in open Court.

The Congress shall have Power to declare the Punishment of Treason, but no Attainder of Treason shall work Corruption of Blood, or Forfeiture except during the Life of the Person attainted.

Article. IV.

Section. 1. Full Faith and Credit shall be given in each State to the public Acts, Records, and judicial Proceedings of every other State. And the Congress may by general Laws prescribe the Manner in which such Acts, Records and Proceedings shall be proved, and the Effect thereof.

Section. 2. The Citizens of each State shall be entitled to all Privileges and Immunities of Citizens in the several States.

A Person charged in any State with Treason, Felony, or other Crime, who shall flee from Justice, and be found in another State, shall on Demand of the executive Authority of the State from which he fled, be delivered up, to be removed to the State having Jurisdiction of the Crime.

No Person held to Service or Labour in one State, under the Laws thereof, escaping into another, shall, in Consequence of any Law or Regulation therein, be discharged from such Service or Labour, but shall be delivered up on Claim of the Party to whom such Service or Labour may be due. (10)

Section. 3. New States may be admitted by the Congress into this Union; but no new State shall be formed or erected within the Jurisdiction of any other State; nor any State be formed by the Junction of two or more States, or Parts of States, without the Consent of the Legislatures of the States concerned as well as of the Congress.

The Congress shall have Power to dispose of and make all needful Rules and Regulations respecting the Territory or other Property belonging to the United States; and nothing in this Constitution shall be so construed as to Prejudice any Claims of the United States, or of any particular State.

Section. 4. The United States shall guarantee to every State in this Union a Republican Form of Government, and shall protect each of them against Invasion; and on Application of the Legislature, or of the Executive (when the Legislature cannot be convened), against domestic Violence.

Article. V.

The Congress, whenever two thirds of both Houses shall deem it necessary, shall propose Amendments to this Constitution, or, on the Application of the Legislatures of two thirds of the several States, shall call a Convention for proposing Amendments, which, in either Case, shall be valid to all Intents and Purposes, as Part of this Constitution, when ratified by the Legislatures of three fourths of the several States, or by Conventions in three fourths thereof, as the one or the other Mode of Ratification may be proposed by the Congress; Provided that no Amendment which may be made prior to the Year One thousand eight hundred and eight shall in any Manner affect the first and fourth Clauses in the Ninth Section of the first Article; and that no State, without its Consent, shall be deprived of its equal Suffrage in the Senate.

Article. VI.

All Debts contracted and Engagements entered into, before the Adoption of this Constitution, shall be as valid against the United States under this Constitution, as under the Confederation.

This Constitution, and the Laws of the United States which shall be made in Pursuance thereof; and all Treaties made, or which shall be made, under the Authority of the United States, shall be the supreme Law of the Land; and the Judges in every State shall be bound thereby, any Thing in the Constitution or Laws of any State to the Contrary notwithstanding.

The Senators and Representatives before mentioned, and the Members of the several State Legislatures, and all executive and judicial Officers, both of the United States and of the several States, shall be bound by Oath or Affirmation, to support this Constitution; but no religious Test shall ever be required as a Qualification to any Office or public Trust under the United States.

Article. VII.

The Ratification of the Conventions of nine States, shall be sufficient for the Establishment of this Constitution between the States so ratifying the Same.

Done in Convention by the Unanimous Consent of the States present the Seventeenth Day of September in the Year of our Lord one thousand seven hundred and Eighty seven and of the Independence of the United States of America the Twelfth In witness whereof We have hereunto subscribed our Names.

BILL OF RIGHTS

(Ratified December 15, 1791)

Amendment I

Congress shall make no law respecting an establishment of religion, or prohibiting the free exercise thereof; or abridging the freedom of speech, or of the press; or the right of the people peaceably to assemble, and to petition the Government for a redress of grievances.

Amendment II

A well regulated Militia, being necessary to the security of a free State, the right of the people to keep and bear Arms, shall not be infringed.

Amendment III

No Soldier shall, in time of peace be quartered in any house, without the consent of the Owner, nor in time of war, but in a manner to be prescribed by law.

Amendment IV

The right of the people to be secure in their persons, houses, papers, and effects, against unreasonable searches and seizures, shall not be violated, and no Warrants shall issue, but upon probable cause, supported by Oath or affirmation, and particularly describing the place to be searched, and the persons or things to be seized.

Amendment V

No person shall be held to answer for a capital, or otherwise infamous crime, unless on a presentment or indictment of a Grand Jury, except in cases arising in the land or naval forces, or in the Militia, when in actual service in time of War or public danger; nor shall any person be subject for the same offence to be twice put in jeopardy of life or limb; nor shall be compelled in any criminal case to be a witness against himself, nor be deprived of life, liberty, or property, without due process of law; nor shall private property be taken for public use, without just compensation.

Amendment VI

In all criminal prosecutions, the accused shall enjoy the right to a speedy and public trial, by an impartial jury of the State and district wherein the crime shall have been committed, which district shall have been previously ascertained by law, and to be informed of the nature and cause of the accusation; to be confronted with the witnesses against him; to have compulsory process for obtaining witnesses in his favor, and to have the Assistance of Counsel for his defence.

Amendment VII

In Suits at common law, where the value in controversy shall exceed twenty dollars, the right of trial by jury shall be preserved, and no fact tried by a jury, shall be otherwise re-examined in any Court of the United States, than according to the rules of the common law.

Amendment VIII

Excessive bail shall not be required, nor excessive fines imposed, nor cruel and unusual punishments inflicted.

Amendment IX

The enumeration in the Constitution, of certain rights, shall not be construed to deny or disparage others retained by the people.

Amendment X

The powers not delegated to the United States by the Constitution, nor prohibited by it to the States, are reserved to the States respectively, or to the people.

(Additional Amendments to the Constitution)

Amendment XI.   (Ratified 1795)

The Judicial power of the United States shall not be construed to extend to any suit in law or equity, commenced or prosecuted against one of the United States by Citizens of another State, or by Citizens or Subjects of any Foreign State.

Amendment XII.   (Ratified 1804)

The Electors shall meet in their respective states, and vote by ballot for President and Vice-President, one of whom, at least, shall not be an inhabitant of the same state with themselves; they shall name in their ballots the person voted for as President, and in distinct ballots the person voted for as Vice-President, and they shall make distinct lists of all persons voted for as President, and of all persons voted for as Vice-President, and of the number of votes for each, which lists they shall sign and certify, and transmit sealed to the seat of the government of the United States, directed to the President of the Senate;— The President of the Senate shall, in the presence of the Senate and House of Representatives, open all the certificates and the votes shall then be counted;—The person having the greatest number of votes for President, shall be the President, if such number be a majority of the whole number of Electors appointed; and if no person have such majority, then from the persons having the highest numbers not exceeding three on the list of those voted for as President, the House of Representatives shall choose immediately, by ballot, the President. But in choosing the President, the votes shall be taken by states, the representation from each state having one vote; a quorum for this purpose shall consist of a member or members from two-thirds of the states, and a majority of all the states shall be necessary to a choice. And if the House of Representatives shall not choose a President whenever the right of choice shall devolve upon them, *before the fourth day of March next following,* (11) then the Vice-President shall act as President, as in the case of the death or other constitutional disability of the President.— The person having the greatest number of votes as Vice-President, shall be the Vice-President, if such number be a majority of the whole number of Electors appointed, and if no person have a majority, then from the two highest numbers on the list, the Senate shall choose the Vice-President; a quorum for the purpose shall consist of two-thirds of the whole number of Senators, and a majority of the whole number shall be necessary to a choice. But no person constitutionally ineligible to the office of President shall be eligible to that of Vice-President of the United States.

Amendment XIII.   (Ratified 1865)

Section 1. Neither slavery nor involuntary servitude, except as a punishment for crime whereof the party shall have been duly convicted, shall exist within the United States, or any place subject to their jurisdiction.

Section 2. Congress shall have power to enforce this article by appropriate legislation.

Amendment XIV.   (Ratified 1868)

Section 1. All persons born or naturalized in the United States, and subject to the jurisdiction thereof, are citizens of the United States and of the State wherein they reside. No State shall make or enforce any law which shall abridge the privileges or immunities of citizens of the United States; nor shall any State deprive any person of life, liberty, or property, without due process of law; nor deny to any person within its jurisdiction the equal protection of the laws.

Section 2. Representatives shall be apportioned among the several States according to their respective numbers, counting the whole number of persons in each State, excluding Indians not taxed. But when the right to vote at any election for the choice of electors for President and Vice President of the United States, Representatives in Congress, the Executive and Judicial officers of a State, or the members of the Legislature thereof, is denied to any of the male inhabitants of such State, being twenty-one years of age, (12) and citizens of the United States, or in any way abridged, except for participation in rebellion, or other crime, the basis of representation therein shall be reduced in the proportion which the number of such male citizens shall bear to the whole number of male citizens twenty-one years of age in such State.

Section 3. No person shall be a Senator or Representative in Congress, or elector of President and Vice President, or hold any office, civil or military, under the United States, or under any State, who, having previously taken an oath, as a member of Congress, or as an officer of the United States, or as a member of any State legislature, or as an executive or judicial officer of any State, to support the Constitution of the United States, shall have engaged in insurrection or rebellion against the same, or given aid or comfort to the enemies thereof. But Congress may by a vote of two-thirds of each House, remove such disability.

Section 4. The validity of the public debt of the United States, authorized by law, including debts incurred for payment of pensions and bounties for services in suppressing insurrection or rebellion, shall not be questioned. But neither the United States nor any State shall assume or pay any debt or obligation incurred in aid of insurrection or rebellion against the United States, or any claim for the loss or emancipation of any slave; but all such debts, obligations and claims shall be held illegal and void.

Section 5. The Congress shall have power to enforce, by appropriate legislation, the provisions of this article.

Amendment XV.   (Ratified 1870)

Section 1. The right of citizens of the United States to vote shall not be denied or abridged by the United States or by any State on account of race, color, or previous condition of servitude.

Section 2. The Congress shall have power to enforce this article by appropriate legislation.

Amendment XVI.   (Ratified 1913)

The Congress shall have power to lay and collect taxes on incomes, from whatever source derived, without apportionment among the several States, and without regard to any census or enumeration.

Amendment XVII.   (Ratified 1913)

The Senate of the United States shall be composed of two Senators from each State, elected by the people thereof, for six years; and each Senator shall have one vote. The electors in each State shall have the qualifications requisite for electors of the most numerous branch of the State legislatures.

When vacancies happen in the representation of any State in the Senate, the executive authority of such State shall issue writs of election to fill such vacancies: Provided, That the legislature of any State may empower the executive thereof to make temporary appointments until the people fill the vacancies by election as the legislature may direct.

This amendment shall not be so construed as to affect the election or term of any Senator chosen before it becomes valid as part of the Constitution.

Amendment XVIII. (Ratified 1919)

Section 1. After one year from the ratification of this article the manufacture, sale, or transportation of intoxicating liquors within, the importation thereof into, or the exportation thereof from the United States and all territory subject to the jurisdiction thereof for beverage purposes is hereby prohibited.

Section 2. The Congress and the several States shall have concurrent power to enforce this article by appropriate legislation.

Section 3. This article shall be inoperative unless it shall have been ratified as an amendment to the Constitution by the legislatures of the several States, as provided in the Constitution, within seven years from the date of the submission hereof to the States by the Congress. (13)

Amendment XIX. (Ratified 1920)

The right of citizens of the United States to vote shall not be denied or abridged by the United States or by any State on account of sex.

Congress shall have power to enforce this article by appropriate legislation.

Amendment XX. (Ratified 1933)

Section 1. The terms of the President and Vice President shall end at noon on the 20th day of January, and the terms of Senators and Representatives at noon on the 3d day of January, of the years in which such terms would have ended if this article had not been ratified; and the terms of their successors shall then begin.

Section 2. The Congress shall assemble at least once in every year, and such meeting shall begin at noon on the 3d day of January, unless they shall by law appoint a different day.

Section 3. If, at the time fixed for the beginning of the term of the President, the President elect shall have died, the Vice President elect shall become President. If a President shall not have been chosen before the time fixed for the beginning of his term, or if the President elect shall have failed to qualify, then the Vice President elect shall act as President until a President shall have qualified; and the Congress may by law provide for the case wherein neither a President elect nor a Vice President elect shall have qualified, declaring who shall then act as President, or the manner in which one who is to act shall be selected, and such person shall act accordingly until a President or Vice President shall have qualified.

Section 4. The Congress may by law provide for the case of the death of any of the persons from whom the House of Representatives may choose a President whenever the right of choice shall have devolved upon them, and for the case of the death of any of the persons from whom the Senate may choose a Vice President whenever the right of choice shall have devolved upon them.

Section 5. Sections 1 and 2 shall take effect on the 15th day of October following the ratification of this article.

Section 6. This article shall be inoperative unless it shall have been ratified as an amendment to the Constitution by the legislatures of three-fourths of the several States within seven years from the date of its submission.

Amendment XXI. (Ratified 1933)

Section 1. The eighteenth article of amendment to the Constitution of the United States is hereby repealed.

Section 2. The transportation or importation into any State, Territory, or possession of the United States for delivery or use therein of intoxicating liquors, in violation of the laws thereof, is hereby prohibited.

Section 3. This article shall be inoperative unless it shall have been ratified as an amendment to the Constitution by conventions in the several States, as provided in the Constitution, within seven years from the date of the submission hereof to the States by the Congress.

Amendment XXII.   (Ratified 1951)

Section 1. No person shall be elected to the office of the President more than twice, and no person who has held the office of President, or acted as President, for more than two years of a term to which some other person was elected President shall be elected to the office of the President more than once. But this Article shall not apply to any person holding the office of President when this Article was proposed by the Congress, and shall not prevent any person who may be holding the office of President, or acting as President, during the term within which this Article becomes operative from holding the office of President or acting as President during the remainder of such term.

Section 2. This article shall be inoperative unless it shall have been ratified as an amendment to the Constitution by the legislatures of three-fourths of the several States within seven years from the date of its submission to the States by the Congress.

Amendment XXIII.   (Ratified 1961)

Section 1. The District constituting the seat of Government of the United States shall appoint in such manner as the Congress may direct:

A number of electors of President and Vice President equal to the whole number of Senators and Representatives in Congress to which the District would be entitled if it were a State, but in no event more than the least populous State; they shall be in addition to those appointed by the States, but they shall be considered, for the purposes of the election of President and Vice President, to be electors appointed by a State; and they shall meet in the District and perform such duties as provided by the twelfth article of amendment.

Section 2. The Congress shall have power to enforce this article by appropriate legislation.

Amendment XXIV.   (Ratified 1964)

Section 1. The right of citizens of the United States to vote in any primary or other election for President or Vice President, for electors for President or Vice President, or for Senator or Representative in Congress, shall not be denied or abridged by the United States or any State by reason of failure to pay any poll tax or other tax.

Section 2. The Congress shall have power to enforce this article by appropriate legislation.

Amendment XXV.   (Ratified 1967)

Section 1. In case of the removal of the President from office or of his death or resignation, the Vice President shall become President.

Section 2. Whenever there is a vacancy in the office of the Vice President, the President shall nominate a Vice President who shall take office upon confirmation by a majority vote of both Houses of Congress.

Section 3. Whenever the President transmits to the President pro tempore of the Senate and the Speaker of the House of Representatives his written declaration that he is unable to discharge the powers and duties of his office, and until he transmits to them a written declaration to the contrary, such powers and duties shall be discharged by the Vice President as Acting President.

Section 4. Whenever the Vice President and a majority of either the principal officers of the executive departments or of such other body as Congress may by law provide, transmit to the President pro tempore of the Senate and the Speaker of the House of Representatives their written declaration that the President is unable to discharge the powers and duties of his office, the Vice President shall immediately assume the powers and duties of the office as Acting President.

Thereafter, when the President transmits to the President pro tempore of the Senate and the Speaker of the House of Representatives his written declaration that no inability exists, he shall resume the powers and duties of his office unless the Vice President and a majority of either the principal officers of the executive department or of such other body as Congress may by law provide, transmit within four days to the President pro tempore of the Senate and the Speaker of the House of Representatives their written declaration that the President is unable to discharge the powers and duties of his office. Thereupon Congress shall decide the issue, assembling within forty-eight hours for that purpose if not in session. If the Congress, within twenty-one days after receipt of the latter written declaration, or, if Congress is not in session, within twenty-one days after Congress is required to assemble, determines by two-thirds vote of both Houses that the President is unable to discharge the powers and duties of his office, the Vice President shall continue to discharge the same as Acting President; otherwise, the President shall resume the powers and duties of his office.

Amendment XXVI.   (Ratified 1971)

Section 1. The right of citizens of the United States, who are eighteen years of age or older, to vote shall not be denied or abridged by the United States or by any State on account of age.

Section 2. The Congress shall have power to enforce this article by appropriate legislation.

Amendment XXVII.   (Ratified 1992)

No law, varying the compensation for the services of the Senators and Representatives, shall take effect, until an election of Representatives shall have intervened.

1. Modified by the 16th Amendment

2. Replaced by Section 2, 14th Amendment

3. Repealed by the 17th Amendment

4. Modified by the 17th Amendment

5. Changed by the 20th Amendment

6. Modified by the 16th Amendment

7. Changed by the 12th and 20th Amendments

8. Modified by the 25th Amendment

9. Modified by the 11th Amendment

10. Repealed by the 13th Amendment

11. Changed by the 20th Amendment

12. Changed by the 26th Amendment

13. Repealed by the 21st Amendment

THE FEDERALIST NO. 47: MADISON

January 30, 1788

To the People of the State of New York.

Having reviewed the general form of the proposed government, and the general mass of power allotted to it: I proceed to examine the particular structure of this government, and the distribution of this mass of power among its constituent parts.

One of the principal objections inculcated by the more respectable adversaries to the constitution, is its supposed violation of the political maxim, that the legislative, executive and judiciary departments ought to be separate and distinct. In the structure of the federal government, no regard, it is said, seems to have been paid to this essential precaution in favor of liberty. The several departments of power are distributed and blended in such a manner, as at once to destroy all symmetry and beauty of form; and to expose some of the essential parts of the edifice to the danger of being crushed by the disproportionate weight of other parts.

No political truth is certainly of greater intrinsic value or is stamped with the authority of more enlightened patrons of liberty than that on which the objection is founded. The accumulation of all powers legislative, executive and judiciary in the same hands, whether of one, a few or many, and whether hereditary, self appointed, or elective, may justly be pronounced the very definition of tyranny. Were the federal constitution therefore really chargeable with this accumulation of power or with a mixture of powers having a dangerous tendency to such an accumulation, no further arguments would be necessary to inspire a universal reprobation of the system. I persuade myself however, that it will be made apparent to every one, that the charge cannot be supported, and that the maxim on which it relies, has been totally misconceived and misapplied. . . .

The oracle who is always consulted and cited on this subject, is the celebrated Montesquieu. If he be not the author of this invaluable precept in the science of politics, he has the merit at least of displaying, and recommending it most effectually to the attention of mankind. Let us endeavour in the first place to ascertain his meaning on this point.

The British constitution was to Montesquieu, what Homer has been to the didactic writers on epic poetry. As the latter have considered the work of the immortal Bard, as the perfect model from which the principles and rules of the epic art were to be drawn, and by which all similar works were to be judged; so this great political critic appears to have viewed the constitution of England, as the standard, or to use his own expression, as the mirrour of political liberty; and to have delivered in the form of elementary truths, the several characteristic principles of that particular system. That we may be sure then not to mistake his meaning in this case, let us recur to the source from which the maxim was drawn.

On the slightest view of the British constitution we must perceive, that the legislative, executive and judiciary departments are by no means totally separate and distinct from each other. The executive magistrate forms an integral part of the legislative authority. He alone has the prerogative of making treaties with foreign sovereigns, which when made have, under certain limitations, the force of legislative acts. All the members of the judiciary department are appointed by him; can be removed by him on the address of the two Houses of Parliament, and form, when he pleases to consult them, one of his constitutional councils. One branch of the legislative department forms also, a great constitutional council to the executive chief; as on another hand, it is the sole depositary of judicial power in cases of impeachment, and is invested with the supreme appellate jurisdiction, in all other cases. The judges again are so far connected with the legislative department, as often to attend and participate in its deliberations, though not admitted to a legislative vote.

From these facts by which Montesquieu was guided it may clearly be inferred, that in saying "there can be no liberty where the legislative and executive powers are united in the same person, or body of magistrates," or "if the power of judging be not separated from the legislative and executive powers," he did not mean that these departments ought to have no *partial agency* in, or no *controul* over the acts of each other. His meaning, as his own words import, and still more conclusively as illustrated by the example in his eye, can amount to no more than this, that where the *whole* power of one department is exercised by the same hands which possess the *whole* power of another department, the fundamental principles of a free constitution, are subverted. This would have been the case in the constitution examined by him, if the King who is the sole executive magistrate, had possessed also the compleat legislative power, or the supreme administration of justice; or if the entire legislative body, had possessed the supreme judiciary, or the supreme executive authority. This however is not among the vices of that constitution. The magistrate in whom the whole executive power resides cannot of himself make a law, though he can put a negative on every law, nor administer justice in person, though he has the appointment of those who do administer it. The judges can exercise no executive prerogative, though they are shoots from the executive stock, nor any legislative function, though they may be advised with by the legislative councils. The entire legislature, can perform no judiciary act, though by the joint act of two of its branches, the judges may be removed from their offices; and though one of its branches is possessed of the judicial power in the last resort. The entire legislature again can exercise no executive prerogative, though one of its branches constitutes the supreme executive magistracy; and another, on the empeachment of a third, can try and condemn all the subordinate officers in the executive department.

The reasons on which Montesquieu grounds his maxim are a further demonstration of his meaning. "When the legislative and executive powers are united in the same person or body" says he, "there can be no liberty, because apprehensions may arise lest *the same* monarch or senate should *enact* tyrannical laws, to *execute* them in a tyrannical manner." Again "Were the power of judging joined with the legislative, the life and liberty of the subject would be exposed to arbitrary controul, for *the judge* would then be *the legislator*. Were it joined to the executive power, *the judge* might behave with all the violence of *an oppressor*." Some of these reasons are more fully explained in other passages; but briefly stated as they are here, they sufficiently establish the meaning which we have put on this celebrated maxim of this celebrated author.

If we look into the constitutions of the several states we find that notwithstanding the emphatical, and in some instances, the unqualified terms in which this axiom has been laid down, there is not a single instance in which the several departments of power have been kept absolutely separate and distinct. New Hampshire, whose constitution was the last formed, seems to have been fully aware of the impossibility and inexpediency of avoiding any mixture whatever of these departments; and has qualified the doctrine by declaring "that the legislative, executive and judiciary powers ought to be kept as separate from, and independent of each other *as the nature of a free government will admit; or as is consistent with that chain of connection, that binds the whole fabric of the constitution in one indissoluble bond of unity and amity.*" Her constitution accordingly mixes these departments in several respects. The senate which is a branch of the legislative department is also a judicial tribunal for the trial of empeachments. The president who is the head of the executive department, is the presiding member also of the senate; and besides an equal vote in all cases, has a casting vote in case of a tie. The executive head is himself eventually elective every year by the legislative department; and his council is every Year chosen by and from the members of the same department. Several of the officers of state are also appointed by the legislature. And the members of the judiciary department are appointed by the executive department.

* * *

(At this point, Madison continues the examination of almost all of the state constitutions to further illustrate his point. I included New Hampshire because it was the first he cited and I include North Carolina because, well, I'm a North Carolinian!)

The constitution of North-Carolina, which declares, "that the legislative, executive and supreme judicial powers of government, ought to be forever separate and distinct from each other," refers at the same time to the legislative department, the appointment not only of the executive chief, but all the principal officers within both that and the judiciary department. . . .

In citing these cases in which the legislative, executive and judiciary departments, have not been kept totally separate and distinct, I wish not to be regarded as an advocate for the particular organizations of the several state governments. I am fully aware that among the many excellent principles which they exemplify, they carry strong marks of the haste, and still stronger of the inexperience, under which they were framed. It is but too obvious that in some instances, the fundamental principle under consideration has been violated by too great a mixture, and even an actual consolidation of the different powers; and that in no instance has a competent provision been made for maintaining in practice the separation delineated on paper. What I have wished to evince is, that the charge brought against the proposed constitution, of violating a sacred maxim of free government, is warranted neither by the real meaning annexed to that maxim by its author; nor by the sense in which it has hitherto been understood in America. This interesting subject will be resumed in the ensuing paper.

PUBLIUS.

THE FEDERALIST NO. 48: MADISON

February 1, 1788

To the People of the State of New York.

It was shewn in the last paper, that the political apothegm there examined, does not require that the legislative, executive and judiciary departments should be wholly unconnected with each other. I shall undertake in the next place, to shew that unless these departments be so far connected and blended, as to give to each a constitutional controul over the others, the degree of separation which the maxim requires as essential to a free government, can never in practice, be duly maintained.

It is agreed on all sides, that the powers properly belonging to one of the departments, ought not to be directly and compleatly administered by either of the other departments. It is equally evident, that neither of them ought to possess directly or indirectly, an overruling influence over the others in the administration of their respective powers. It will not be denied, that power is of an encroaching nature, and that it ought to be effectually restrained from passing the limits assigned to it. After discriminating therefore in theory, the several classes of power, as they may in their nature be legislative; executive, or judiciary; the next and most difficult task, is to provide some practical security for each against the invasion of the others. What this security ought to be, is the great problem to be solved.

Will it be sufficient to mark with precision the boundaries of these departments in the Constitution of the government, and to trust to these parchment barriers against the encroaching spirit of power? This is the security which appears to have been principally relied on by the compilers of most of the American Constitutions. But experience assures us, that the efficacy of the provision has been greatly over-rated; and that some more adequate defence is indispensibly necessary for the more feeble, against the more powerful members of the government. The legislative department is every where extending the sphere of its activity, and drawing all power into its impetuous vortex.

The founders of our republics have so much merit for the wisdom which they have displayed, that no task can be less pleasing than that of pointing out the errors into which they have fallen. A respect for truth however obliges us to remark, that they seem never for a moment to have turned their eyes from the danger to liberty from the overgrown and all-grasping prerogative of an hereditary magistrate, supported and fortified by an hereditary, branch of the legislative authority. They seem never to have recollected the danger from legislative usurpations; which by assembling all power in the same hands, must lead to the same tyranny as is threatened by executive usurpations.

In a government, where numerous and extensive prerogatives are placed in the hands of a hereditary monarch, the executive department is very justly regarded as the source of danger, and watched with all the jealousy which a zeal for liberty ought to inspire. In a democracy, where a multitude of people exercise in person the legislative functions, and are continually exposed by their incapacity for regular deliberation and concerted measures, to the ambitious intrigues of their executive magistrates, tyranny may well be apprehended on some favorable emergency, to start up in the same quarter. But in a representative republic, where the executive magistracy is carefully limited both in the extent and the duration of its power; and where the legislative power is exercised by an assembly, which is inspired by a supposed influence over the people with an intrepid confidence in its own strength; which is sufficiently numerous to feel all the passions which actuate a multitude; yet not so numerous as to be incapable of pursuing the objects of its passions, by means which reason prescribes; it is against the enterprising ambition of this department, that the people ought to indulge all their jealousy and exhaust all their precautions.

The legislative department derives a superiority in our governments from other circumstances. Its constitutional powers being at once more extensive and less susceptible of precise limits, it can with the greater facility, mask under complicated and indirect measures, the encroachments which it makes on the co-ordinate departments. It is not unfrequently a question of real-nicety in legislative bodies, whether the operation of a particular measure, will, or will not extend beyond the legislative sphere. On the other side, the executive power being restrained within a narrower compass, and being more simple in its nature; and the judiciary being described by land marks, still less uncertain, projects of usurpation by either of these departments, would immediately betray and defeat themselves. Nor is this all: As the legislative department alone has access to the pockets of the people, and has in some Constitutions full discretion, and in all, a prevailing influence over the pecuniary rewards of those who fill the other departments, a dependence is thus created in the latter, which gives still greater facility to encroachments of the former.

I have appealed to our own experience for the truth of what I advance on this subject. Were it necessary to verify this experience by particular proofs, they might be multiplied without end. I might find a witness in every citizen who has shared in, or been attentive to, the course of public administrations. I might collect vouchers in abundance from the records and archieves of every State in the Union.

* * *

The conclusion which I am warranted in drawing from these observations is, that a mere demarkation on parchment of the constitutional limits of the several departments, is not a sufficient guard against those encroachments which lead to a tyrannical concentration of all the powers of government in the same hands.

PUBLIUS.

THE FEDERALIST NO. 51: MADISON

February 6, 1788

To the People of the State of New York.

To what expedient then shall we finally resort for maintaining in practice the necessary partition of power among the several departments, as laid down in the constitution? The only answer that can be given is, that as all these exterior provisions are found to be inadequate, the defect must be supplied, by so contriving the interior structure of the government, as that its several constituent parts may, by their mutual relations, be the means of keeping each other in their proper places. Without presuming to undertake a full developement of this important idea, I will hazard a few general observations, which may perhaps place it in a clearer light, and enable us to form a more correct judgment of the principles and structure of the government planned by the convention.

In order to lay a due foundation for that separate and distinct exercise of the different powers of government, which to a certain extent, is admitted on all hands to be essential to the preservation of liberty, it is evident that each department should have a will of its own; and consequently should be so constituted, that the members of each should have as little agency as possible in the appointment of the members of the others. Were this principle rigorously adhered to, it would require that all the appointments for the supreme executive, legislative, and judiciary magistracies, should be drawn from the same fountain of authority, the people, through channels, having no communication whatever with one another. Perhaps such a plan of constructing the several departments would be less difficult in practice than it may in contemplation appear. Some difficulties however, and some additional expence, would attend the execution of it. Some deviations therefore from the principle must be admitted. In the constitution of the judiciary department in particular, it might be inexpedient to insist rigorously on the principle; first, because peculiar qualifications being essential in the members, the primary consideration ought to be to select that mode of choice, Which best secures these qualifications; secondly, because the permanent tenure by which the appointments are held in that department, must soon destroy all sense of dependence on the authority conferring them.

It is equally evident that the members of each department should be as little dependent as possible on those of the others, for the emoluments annexed to their offices. Were the executive magistrate, or the judges, not independent of the legislature in this particular, their independence in every other would be merely nominal.

But the great security against a gradual concentration of the several powers in the same department, consists in giving to those who administer each department, the necessary constitutional means, and personal motives, to resist encroachments of the others. The provision for defence must in this, as in all other cases, be made commensurate to the danger of attack. Ambition must be made to counteract ambition. The interest of the man must be connected with the constitutional rights of the place. It may be a reflection on human nature, that such devices should be necessary to controul the abuses of government. But what is government itself but the greatest of all reflections on human nature? If men were angels, no government would be necessary. If angels were to govern men, neither external nor internal controuls on government would be necessary. In framing a government which is to be administered by men over men, the great difficulty lies in this: You must first enable the government to controul the governed; and in the next place, oblige it to controul itself. . . .

But it is not possible to give to each department an equal power of self defence. In republican government the legislative authority, necessarily, predominates. The remedy for this inconveniency is, to divide the legislature into different branches; and to render them by different modes of election, and different principles of action, as little connected with each other, as the nature of their common functions, and their common dependence on the society, will admit. It may even be necessary to guard against dangerous encroachments by still further precautions. As the weight of the legislative authority requires that it should be thus divided, the weakness of the executive may require, on the other hand, that it should be fortified. An absolute negative, on the legislature, appears at first view to be the natural defence with which the executive magistrate should be armed. But perhaps it would be neither altogether safe, nor alone sufficient. On ordinary occasions, it might not be exerted with the requisite firmness; and on extraordinary occasions, it might be perfidiously abused. May not this defect of an absolute negative be supplied, by some qualified connection between this weaker department, and the weaker branch of the stronger department, by which the latter may be led to support the constitutional rights of the former, without being too much detached from the rights of its own department?

If the principles on which these observations are founded be just, as I persuade myself they are, and they be applied as a criterion, to the several state constitutions, and to the federal constitution, it will be found, that if the latter does not perfectly correspond with them, the former are infinitely less able to bear such a test.

There are moreover two considerations particularly applicable to the federal system of America, which place that system in a very interesting point of view.

First. In a single republic, all the power surrendered by the people, is submitted to the administration of a single government; and usurpations are guarded against by a division of the government into distinct and separate departments. In the compound republic of America, the power surrendered by the people, is first divided between two distinct governments, and then the portion allotted to each, subdivided among distinct and separate departments. Hence a double security arises to the rights of the people. The different governments will controul each other; at he same time that each will be controuled by itself.

Second. It is of great importance in a republic, not only to guard the society against the oppression of its rulers; but to guard one part of the society against the injustice of the other part. Different interests necessarily exist in different classes of citizens. If a majority be united by a common interest, the rights of the minority will be insecure. There are but two methods of providing against this evil: The one by creating a will in the community independent of the majority, that is, of the society itself; the other by comprehending in the society so many separate descriptions of citizens, as will render an unjust combination of a majority of the whole, very improbable, if not impracticable. The first method prevails in all governments possessing an hereditary or self appointed authority. This at best is but a precarious security; because a power independent of the society may as well espouse the unjust views of the major, as the rightful interests, of the minor party, and may possibly be turned against both parties. The second method will be exemplified in the federal republic of the United States. Whilst all authority in it will be derived from and dependent on the society, the society itself will be broken into so many parts, interests and classes of citizens, that the rights of individuals or of the minority, will be in little danger from interested combinations of the majority. In a free government, the security for civil rights must be the same as for religious rights. It consists in the one case in the multiplicity of interests, and in the other, in the multiplicity of sects. The degree of security in both cases will depend on the number of interests and sects; and this may be presumed to depend on the extent of country and number of people comprehended under the same government. This view of the subject must particularly recommend a proper federal system to all the sincere and considerate friends of republican government: Since it shews that in exact proportion as the territory of the union may be formed into more circumscribed confederacies or states, oppressive combinations of a majority will be facilitated, the best security under the republican form, for the rights of every class of citizens, will be diminished; and consequently, the stability and independence of some member of the government, the only other security, must be proportionally increased. Justice is the end of government. It the end of civil society. It ever has been, and ever will be pursued, until it be obtained, or until liberty be lost in the pursuit. . . .

In the extended republic of the United States, and among the great variety of interests, parties and sects which it embraces, a coalition of a majority of the whole society could seldom take place on any other principles than those of justice and the general good; and there being thus less danger to a minor from the will of the major party, there must be less pretext also, to provide for the security of the former, by introducing into the government a will not dependent on the latter; or in other words, a will independent of the society itself. It is no less certain than it is important, notwithstanding the contrary opinions which have been entertained, that the larger the society, provided it lie within a practicable sphere, the more duly capable it will be of self government. And happily for the *republican cause*, the practicable sphere may be carried to a very great extent, by a judicious modification and mixture of the *federal principle*.

PUBLIUS.

ADDRESS AND REASONS OF DISSENT OF THE MINORITY OF THE CONVENTION OF PENNSYLVANIA TO THEIR CONSTITUENTS

(December 18, 1787)

. . . We dissent, first, because it is the opinion of the most celebrated writers on government, and confirmed by uniform experience, that a very extensive territory cannot be governed on the principles of freedom, otherwise than by a confederation of republics, possessing all the powers of internal government; but united in the management of their general, and foreign concerns. . . .

We dissent, secondly, because the powers vested in Congress by this constitution, must necessarily annihilate and absorb the legislative, executive, and judicial powers of the several states and produce from their ruins one consolidated government, which from the nature of things will be an *iron handed despotism*, as nothing short of the supremacy of despotic sway could connect and govern these United States under one government.

As the truth of this position is of such decisive importance, it ought to be fully investigated, and if it is founded to be clearly ascertained; for, should it be demonstrated, that the power vested by this constitution in Congress, will have such an effect as necessarily to produce one consolidated government, the question then will be reduced to this short issue, viz., whether satiated with the blessings of liberty; whether repenting of the folly of so recently asserting their unalienable rights, against foreign despots at the expence of so much blood and treasure, and such painful and arduous struggles, the people of America are not willing to resign every privilege of freemen, and submit to the dominion of an absolute government, that will embrace all America in one chain of despotism: or whether they will with virtuous indignation, spurn at the shackles prepared for them, and confirm their liberties by a conduct becoming freemen.

That the new government will not be a confederacy of states, as it ought, but one consolidated government, founded upon the destruction of the several governments of the states, we shall now shew.

The powers of Congress under the new constitution, are complete and unlimited over the *purse* and the *sword*, and are perfectly independent of, and supreme over, the state governments; whose intervention in these great points is entirely destroyed. By virtue of their power of taxation, Congress may command the whole, or any part of the property of the people. They may impose what imposts upon commerce; they may impose what land taxes, poll taxes, excises, duties on all written instruments, and duties on every other article that they may judge proper; in short, every species of taxation, whether of an external or internal nature is comprised in section the 8th, of Article the 1st, viz., "The Congress shall have power to lay and collect taxes, duties, imposts, and excises, to pay the debts, and provide for the common defence and general welfare of the United States."

As there is no one article of taxation reserved to the state governments, the Congress may monopolise every source of revenue, and thus indirectly demolish the state governments, for without funds they could not exist, . . .

The new constitution, consistently with the plan of consolidation, contains no reservation of the rights and privileges of the state governments, which was made in the confederation of the year 1778, by article the 2d, viz., "That each state retains its sovereignty, freedom and independence, and every power, jurisdiction and right, which is not by this confederation expressly delegated to the United States in Congress assembled."

The legislative power vested in Congress by the foregoing recited sections, is so unlimited in its nature; may be so comprehensive and boundless in its exercise, that this alone would be amply sufficient to annihilate the state governments, and swallow them up in the grand vortex of general empire. . . .

The first consideration that this review suggests, is the omission of a BILL of RIGHTS, ascertaining and fundamentally establishing those unalienable and personal rights of men, without the full, free, and secure enjoyment of which there can be no liberty, and over which it is not necessary for a good government to have the control. The principal of which are the rights of conscience, personal liberty by the clear and unequivocal establishment of the writ of *habeas corpus*, jury trial in criminal and civil cases, by an impartial jury of the vicinage or county, with the common-law proceedings, for the safety of the accused in criminal prosecutions; and the liberty of the press, that scourge of tyrants, and the grand bulwark of every other liberty and privilege; the stipulations heretofore made in favor of them in the state constitutions are entirely superceded by this constitution. . . .

We will now bring the legislature under this constitution to the test of the foregoing principles, which will demonstrate, that it is deficient in every essential quality of a just and safe representation.

The house of representatives is to consist of 65 members; that is one for about every 50,000 inhabitants, to be chosen every two years. Thirty-three members will form a quorum for doing business; and 17 of these, being the majority, determine the sense of the house.

The senate, the other constituent branch of the legislature, consists of 26 members being *two* from each state, appointed by their legislatures every six years--fourteen senators make a quorum; the majority of whom, eight, determines the sense of that body; except in judging on impeachments, or in making treaties, or in expelling a member, when two thirds of the senators present, must concur.

The president is to have the control over the enacting of laws, so far as to make the concurrence of two thirds of the representatives and and senators present necessary, if he should object to the laws.

Thus it appears that the liberties, happiness, interests, and great concerns of the whole United States, may be dependent upon the integrity, virtue, wisdom, and knowledge of 25 or 26 men—How unadequate and unsafe a representation! . . .

The number of members in the house of representatives *may* be encreased to one for every 30.000 inhabitants. But when we consider, that this cannot be done without the consent of the senate, who from their share in the legislative, in the executive and judicial departments, and permanency of appointment, will be the great efficient body in this government, and whose weight and predominancy would be abridged by an increase of the representatives, we are persuaded that this is a circumstance that cannot be expected. On the contrary, the number of representatives will probably be continued at 65, although the population of the country may swell to treble what it now is; unless a revolution should effect a change. . . .

The next consideration that the constitution presents, is the undue and dangerous mixture of the powers of government; the same body possessing legislative, executive, and judicial powers. The senate is a constituent branch of the legislature, it has judicial power in judging on impeachments, and in this case unites in some measure the characters of judge and party, as all the principal officers are appointed by the president-general, with the concurrence of the senate and therefore they derive their offices in part from the senate. This may bias the judgments of the senators and tend to screen great delinquents from punishment. And the senate has, moreover, various and great executive powers, viz., in concurrence with the president-general, they form treaties with foreign nations, that may control and abrogate the constitutions and laws of the several states. Indeed, there is no power, privilege or liberty of the state governments, or of the people, but what may be affected by virtue of this power. For all treaties, made by them, are to be the "supreme law of the land, any thing in the constitution or laws of any state, to the contrary notwithstanding."

And this great power may be exercised by the president and 10 senators (being two thirds of 14, which is a quorum of that body). What an inducement would this offer to the ministers of foreign powers to compass by bribery *such concessions* as could not otherwise be obtained. . . .

The president general is dangerously connected with the senate; his coincidence with the views of the ruling junto in that body, is made essential to his weight and importance in the government, which will destroy all independency and purity in the executive department, and having the power of pardoning without the concurrence of a council, he may screen from punishment the most treasonable attempts that may be made on the liberties of the people, when instigated by his coadjutors in the senate. Instead of this dangerous and improper mixture of the executive with the legislative and judicial, the supreme executive powers ought to have been placed in the president, with a small independent council, made personally responsible for every appointment to office or other act, by having their opinions recorded; and that without the concurrence of the majority of the quorum of this council, the president should not be capable of taking any step.

We have before considered internal taxation, as it would effect the destruction of the state governments, and produce one consolidated government. We will now consider that subject as it affects the personal concerns of the people.

The power of direct taxation applies to every individual, as congress, under this government, is expressly vested with the authority of laying a capitation or poll tax upon every person to any amount. . . .

The power of direct taxation will further apply to every individual, as congress may tax land, cattle, trades, occupations, etc. in any amount, and every object of internal taxation is of the nature, that however oppressive, the people will have but this alternative, except to pay the tax, or let their property be taken, for all resistance will be in vain. The standing army and select militia would enforce the collection.

For the moderate exercise of this power, there is no control left in the state governments, whose intervention is destroyed. No relief, or redress of grievances can be extended, as heretofore by them. There is not even a declaration of RIGHTS to which the people may appeal for the vindication of their wrongs in the court of justice. They must therefore, implicitly obey the most arbitrary laws, as the worst of them will be pursuant to the principles and form of the constitution, and that strongest of all checks upon the conduct of administration, *responsibility to the people*, will not exist in this government. . . .

From the foregoing investigation, it appears that the Congress under this constitution will not possess the confidence of the people, which is an essential requisite in a good government; for unless the laws command the confidence and respect of the great body of the people, so as to induce them to support them, when called on by the civil magistrate, they must be executed by the aid of a numerous standing army, which would be inconsistent with every idea of liberty; for the same force that may be employed to compel obedience to good laws, might and probably would be used to wrest from the people their constitutional liberties. The framers of this constitution appear to have been aware of this great deficiency; to have been sensible that no dependence could be placed on the people for their support: but on the contrary, that the government must be executed by force. They have therefore made a provision for this purpose in a permanent STANDING ARMY, and a MILITIA that may be subjected to as strict discipline and government.

A standing army in the hands of a government placed so independent of the people, may be made a fatal instrument to overturn the public liberties; it may be employed to enforce the collection of the most oppressive taxes, and to carry into execution the most arbitrary measures. An ambitious man who may have the army at his devotion, may step up into the throne, and seize upon absolute power.

The absolute unqualified command that Congress have over the militia may be made instrumental to the destruction of all liberty, both public and private; whether of a personal, civil religious nature.

First, the personal liberty of every man probably from sixteen to sixty years of age, may be destroyed by the power Congress have in organizing and governing of the militia. . . .

Secondly, the rights of conscience may be violated, as there is no exemption of those persons who are conscientiously scrupulous of bearing arms. These compose a respectable proportion of the community in the state. This is the more remarkable, because even when the distresses of the late war, and the evident disaffection of many citizens of that description, inflamed our passions, and when every person, who was obliged to risque his own life, must have been exasperated against such as on any account kept back from the common danger, yet even then, when outrage and violence might have been expected, the rights of conscience were held sacred. . . .

Thirdly, the absolute command of Congress over the militia may be destructive of public liberty; for under the guidance of an arbitrary government, they may be made the unwilling instruments of tyranny. . . .

As this government will not enjoy the confidence of the people, but be executed by force, it will be a very expensive and burthensome government. The standing army must be numerous, and as a further support, it will be the policy of this government to multiply officers in every department: judges, collectors, tax gatherers, excisemen and the whole host of revenue officers will swarm over the land, devouring the hard earnings of the industrious. Like the locusts of old, impoverishing and desolating all before them.

   We have not noticed the smaller, nor many of the considerable blemishes, but have confined our objections to the great and essential defects; the main pillars of the constitution; which we have shewn to be inconsistent with the liberty and happiness of the people, as its establishment will annihilate the state governments, and produce one consolidated government that will eventually and speedily issue in the supremacy of despotism.

   In this investigation, we have not confined our views to the interests or welfare of this state, in preference to the others. We have overlooked all local circumstances--we have considered this subject on the broad scale of the general good; we have asserted the cause of the present and future ages; the cause of liberty and mankind.

CHAPTER 2

INTRODUCTION

Forrest MacDonald and Ellen Shapiro MacDonald, the authors of the third selection in this chapter, wrote that "federalism is the greatest contribution of the Founding Fathers to the science of government." While some might disagree with the superlative nature of their comment, it's probably equally fair to say that most political scientists would agree that it was a truly significant contribution. But, is the federalism of today the federalism envisioned by the men who met in Philadelphia? Again, most would say "no". This realization then calls us to ask three questions:

1. What did the "founding fathers" mean for the relationship to be between the states and the national government (since the Constitution never mentions local government)?

2. What is the current relationship between the myriad levels and numbers of governments that exist in the United States today?

3. What effected the change between the answers to questions 1 and 2?

The three components of this chapter, hopefully, will give you some insight into the answers.

Federalist #45, written by Madison, attempted to respond to those who argued for a return to the pre-eminence of the states and opposed the increased powers of the national government. In both passionate and sarcastic tones, he challenged those who attacked the proposed Constitution. Important questions to note are:

1. How did Madison use the American Revolution to make his opponents look petty and power hungry?

2. Do you believe Madison genuinely believed the states would be superior to the states? If so, what were his reasons for thinking so?

3. When did Madison believe the national government would have dominance over the states?

McCulloch v. Maryland is considered one of the landmark court cases in American history. In the early years of our country's history, power struggles ensued between the states and the national government. The Constitution, by design, is a document largely devoid of details. Hence, many of the actions of the national government were challenged by the states. In this case, look for the answers to the following questions:

1. Does Congress have the power to incorporate a bank? Why or why not?

2. Find the "Supremacy Clause" in the Constitution. Explain what it means and its importance.

3. Why did the Court argue a state could not be allowed to tax the national government?

Next is an article written by the previously mentioned MacDonalds. They explain what they see as the essential elements of federalism, as created 200+ years ago, and then walk the reader through the reasons it "no longer exists on its native shores." While I may not agree with all their arguments and I have a hard time accepting that federalism is dead, it is also undeniable that what we have today is not what we had, and likely not what the early leaders of our republic intended.   Important points to consider from this article are:

1. What do the MacDonald's see as the three dimensions of federalism?

2. Who ratified the Constitution–the people or the states?

3. They wrote that the framers "did something that political theorists since ancient times had insisted could not be done". What did they do and how did they do it?

4. How did fiscal changes and the doctrine of incorporation change federalism?

Finally is an article from the "New Federalist Papers." Kathleen Sullivan essentially writes that the concerns or objections of people like the McDonalds are overdrawn and overstated. She contends that the balance today is acceptable and that states are well suited to protect themselves when the federal government encroaches on areas of power normally reserved to the states. So, consider these questions:

1. Why does Sullivan reject the concept of "states rights"?

2. What powers are left to the states?

3. By what means does Sullivan believe states can protect themselves from an overreaching federal government?

THE FEDERALIST NO. 45: MADISON

January 26, 1788

To the People of the State of New York.

Having shewn that no one of the powers transferred to the federal Government is unnecessary or improper, the next question to be considered is whether the whole mass of them will be dangerous to the portion of authority left in the several States.

The adversaries to the plan of the Convention instead of considering in the first place what degree of power was absolutely necessary for the purposes of the federal Government, have exhausted themselves in a secondary enquiry into the possible consequences of the proposed degree of power, to the Governments of the particular States. But if the Union, as has been shewn, be essential, to the security of the people of America against foreign danger; if it be essential to their security against contentions and wars among the different States; if it be essential to guard them against those violent and oppressive factions which embitter the blessings of liberty, and against those military establishments which must gradually poison its very fountain; if, in a word the Union be essential to the happiness of the people of America, is it not preposterous, to urge as an objection to a government without which the objects of the Union cannot be attained, that such a Government may derogate from the importance of the Governments of the individual States? Was then the American revolution effected, was the American confederacy formed, was the precious blood of thousands spilt, and the hard earned substance of millions lavished, not that the people of America should enjoy peace, liberty and safety; but that the Governments of the individual States, that particular municipal establishments, might enjoy a certain extent of power, and be arrayed with certain dignities and attributes of sovereignty? We have heard of the impious doctrine in the old world that the people were made for kings, not kings for the people. Is the same doctrine to be revived in the new, in another shape, that the solid happiness of the people is to be sacrificed to the views of political institutions of a different form? It is too early for politicians to presume on our forgetting that the public good, the real welfare of the great body of the people is the supreme object to be pursued; and that no form of Government whatever, has any other value, than as it may be fitted for the attainment of this object. Were the plan of the Convention adverse to the public happiness, my voice would be, reject the plan. Were the Union itself inconsistent with the public happiness, it would be, abolish the Union. In like manner as far as the sovereignty of the States cannot be reconciled to the happiness of the people, the voice of every good citizen must be, let the former be sacrificed to the latter. How far the sacrifice is necessary, has been shewn. How far the unsacrificed residue will be endangered, is the question before us.

Several important considerations have been touched in the course of these papers, which discountenance the supposition that the operation of the federal Government will by degrees prove fatal to the State Governments. The more I revolve the subject the more fully I am persuaded that the balance is much more likely to be disturbed by the preponderancy of the last than of the first scale.

* * *

The State Governments will have the advantage of the federal Government, whether we compare them in respect to the immediate dependence of the one or the other; to the weight of personal influence which each side will possess; to the powers respectively vested in them; to the predilection and probable support of the people; to the disposition and faculty of resisting and frustrating the measures of each other.

The State Governments may be regarded as constituent and essential parts of the federal Government; whilst the latter is nowise essential to the operation or organisation of the former. Without the intervention of the State Legislatures, the President of the United States cannot be elected at all. They must in all cases have a great share in his appointment, and will perhaps in most cases of themselves determine it. The Senate will be elected absolutely and exclusively by the State Legislatures. Even the House of Representatives, though drawn immediately from the people, will be chosen very much under the influence of that class of men, whose influence over the people obtains for themselves an election into the State Legislatures. Thus each of the principal branches of the federal Government will owe its existence more or less to the favor of the State Governments, and must consequently feel a dependence, which is much more likely to beget a disposition too obsequious, than too overbearing towards them. On the other side, the component parts of the State Governments will in no instance be indebted for their appointment to the direct agency of the federal government, and very little if at all, to the local influence of its members.

The number of individuals employed under the Constitution of the United States, will be much smaller, than the number employed under the particular States. There will consequently be less of personal influence on the side of the former, than of the latter. The members of the legislative, executive and judiciary departments of thirteen and more States; the justices of peace, officers of militia, ministerial officers of justice, with all the county corporation and town-officers, for three millions and more of people, intermixed and having particular acquaintance with every class and circle of people, must exceed beyond all proportion, both in number and influence, those of every description who will be employed in the administration of the federal system. Compare the members of the three great departments, of the thirteen States, excluding from the judiciary department the justices of peace, with the members of the corresponding departments of the single Government of the Union; compare the militia officers of three millions of people, with the military and marine officers of any establishment which is within the compass of probability, or I may add, of possibility, and in this view alone, we may pronounce the advantage of the States to be decisive. If the federal Government is to have collectors of revenue, the State Governments will have theirs also. And as those of the former will be principally on the sea-coast, and not very numerous; whilst those of the latter will be spread over the face of the country, and will be very numerous, the advantage in this view also lies on the same side. It is true that the confederacy is to possess, and may exercise, the power of collecting internal as well as external taxes throughout the States: But it is probable that this power will not be resorted to, except for supplemental purposes of revenue; that an option will then be given to the States to supply their quotas by previous collections of their own; and that the eventual collection under the immediate authority of the Union will generally be made by the officers, and according to the rules, appointed by the several States. Indeed it is extremely probable that in other instances, particularly in the organisation of the judicial power, the officers of the States will be cloathed with the correspondent authority of the Union. Should it happen however that separate collectors of internal revenue should be appointed under the federal Government, the influence of the whole number would not be a comparison with that of the multitude of State officers in the opposite scale. Within every district, to which a federal collector would be allotted, there would not be less than thirty or forty or even more officers of different descriptions and many of them persons of character and weight, whose influence would lie on the side of the State.

The powers delegated by the proposed Constitution to the Federal Government, are few and defined. Those which are to remain in the State Governments are numerous and indefinite. The former will be exercised principally on external objects, as war, peace, negociation, and foreign commerce; with which last the power of taxation will for the most part be connected. The powers reserved to the several States will extend to all the objects, which, in the ordinary course of affairs, concern the lives, liberties and properties of the people; and the internal order, improvement, and prosperity of the State.

The operations of the Federal Government will be most extensive and important in times of war and danger; those of the State Governments, in times of peace and security. As the former periods will probably bear a small proportion to the latter, the State Governments will here enjoy another advantage over the Federal Government. The more adequate indeed the federal powers may be rendered to the national defence, the less frequent will be those scenes of danger which might favour their ascendency over the governments of the particular States. . . .

PUBLIUS.

McCulloch v. The State of Maryland

Supreme Court of the United States
February, 1819 Term

OPINION BY: MARSHALL

OPINION: Mr. Chief Justice MARSHALL delivered the opinion of the Court.

In the case now to be determined, the defendant, a sovereign State, denies the obligation of a law enacted by the legislature of the Union, and the plaintiff, on his part, contests the validity of an act which has been passed by the legislature of that State. The constitution of our country, in its most interesting and vital parts, is to be considered; the conflicting powers of the government of the Union and of its members, as marked in that constitution, are to be discussed; and an opinion given, which may essentially influence the great operations of the government. No tribunal can approach such a question without a deep sense of its importance, and of the awful responsibility involved in its decision. But it must be decided peacefully, or remain a source of hostile legislation, perhaps of hostility of a still more serious nature; and if it is to be so decided, by this tribunal alone can the decision be made. On the Supreme Court of the United States has the constitution of our country devolved this important duty.

The first question made in the cause is, has Congress power to incorporate a bank? . . .

The power now contested was exercised by the first Congress elected under the present constitution. The bill for incorporating the bank of the United States did not steal upon an unsuspecting legislature, and pass unobserved. Its principle was completely understood, and was opposed with equal zeal and ability. After being resisted, first in the fair and open field of debate, and afterwards in the executive cabinet, with as much persevering talent as any measure has ever experienced, and being supported by arguments which convinced minds as pure and as intelligent as this country can boast, it became a law. The original act was permitted to expire; but a short experience of the embarrassments to which the refusal to revive it exposed the government, convinced those who were most prejudiced against the measure of its necessity, and induced the passage of the present law. It would require no ordinary share of intrepidity to assert that a measure adopted under these circumstances was a bold and plain usurpation, to which the constitution gave no countenance. . . .

The government of the Union, then, (whatever may be the influence of this fact on the case,) is, emphatically, and truly, a government of the people. In form and in substance it emanates from them. Its powers are granted by them, and are to be exercised directly on them, and for their benefit.

This government is acknowledged by all to be one of enumerated powers. The principle, that it can exercise only the powers granted to it, would seem too apparent to have required to be enforced by all those arguments which it enlightened friends, while it was depending before the people, found it necessary to urge. That principle is now universally admitted. But the question respecting the extent of the powers actually granted, is perpetually arising, and will probably continue to arise, as long as our system shall exist.

In discussing these questions, the conflicting powers of the general and State governments must be brought into view, and the supremacy of their respective laws, when they are in opposition, must be settled.

If any one proposition could command the universal assent of mankind, we might expect it would be this — that the government of the Union, though limited in its powers, is supreme within its sphere of action. This would seem to result necessarily from its nature. It is the government of all; its powers are delegated by all; it represents all, and acts for all. Though any one State may be willing to control its operations, no State is willing to allow others to control them. The nation, on those subjects on which it can act, must necessarily bind its component parts. But this question is not left to mere reason: the people have, in express terms, decided it, by saying, "this constitution, and the laws of the United States, which shall be made in pursuance thereof," "shall be the supreme law of the land," and by requiring that the members of the State legislatures, and the officers of the executive and judicial departments of the States, shall take the oath of fidelity to it.

The government of the United States, then, though limited in its powers, is supreme; and its laws, when made in pursuance of the constitution, form the supreme law of the land, "any thing in the constitution or laws of any State to the contrary notwithstanding."

Among the enumerated powers, we do not find that of establishing a bank or creating a corporation. But there is no phrase in the instrument which, like the articles of confederation, excludes incidental or implied powers; and which requires that every thing granted shall be expressly and minutely described. Even the 10th amendment, which was framed for the purpose of quieting the excessive jealousies which had been excited, omits the word "expressly," and declares only that the powers "not delegated to the United States, nor prohibited to the States, are reserved to the States or to the people;" thus leaving the question, whether the particular power which may become the subject of contest has been delegated to the one government, or prohibited to the other, to depend on a fair construction of the whole instrument. The men who drew and adopted this amendment had experienced the embarrassments resulting from the insertion of this word in the articles of confederation, and probably omitted it to avoid those embarrassments. A constitution, to contain an accurate detail of all the subdivisions of which its great powers will admit, and of all the means by which they may be carried into execution, would partake of the prolixity of a legal code, and could scarcely be embraced by the human mind. It would probably never be understood by the public. Its nature, therefore, requires, that only its great outlines should be marked, its important objects designated, and the minor ingre- dients which compose those objects be deduced from the nature of the objects themselves. . . .

Although, among the enumerated powers of government, we do not find the word "bank" or "incorporation," we find the great powers to lay and collect taxes; to borrow money; to regulate commerce; to declare and conduct a war; and to raise and support armies and navies. The sword and the purse, all the external relations, and no inconsiderable portion of the industry of the nation, are entrusted to its government. It can never be pretended that these vast powers draw after them others of inferior importance, merely because they are inferior. Such an idea can never be advanced. But it may with great reason be contended, that a government, entrusted with such ample powers, on the due execution of which the happiness and prosperity of the nation so vitally depends, must also be entrusted with ample means for their execution.

* * *

But the constitution of the United States has not left the right of Congress to employ the necessary means, for the execution of the powers conferred on the government, to general reasoning. To its enumeration of powers is added that of making "all laws which shall be necessary and proper, for carrying into execution the foregoing powers, and all other powers vested by this constitution, in the government of the United States, or in any department thereof." . . .

But the argument on which most reliance is placed, is drawn from the peculiar language of this clause. Congress is not empowered by it to make all laws, which may have relation to the powers conferred on the government, but such only as may be "necessary and proper" for carrying them into execution. The word "necessary," is considered as controlling the whole sentence, and as limiting the right to pass laws for the execution of the granted powers, to such as are indispensable, and without which the power would be nugatory. That it excludes the choice of means, and leaves to Congress, in each case, that only which is most direct and simple.

Is it true, that this is the sense in which the word "necessary" is always used? Does it always import an absolute physical necessity, so strong, that one thing, to which another may be termed necessary, cannot exist without that other? We think it does not. If reference be had to its use, in the common affairs of the world, or in approved authors, we find that it frequently imports no more than that one thing is convenient, or useful, or essential to another. To employ the means necessary to an end, is generally understood as employing any means calculated to produce the end, and not as being confined to those single means, without which the end would be entirely unattainable.

* * *

After this declaration, it can scarcely be necessary to say, that the existence of State banks can have no possible influence on the question. No trace is to be found in the constitution of an intention to create a dependence of the government of the Union on those of the States, for the execution of the great powers assigned to it. Its means are adequate to its ends; and on those means alone was it expected to rely for the accomplishment of its ends. To impose on it the necessity of resorting to means which it cannot control, which another government may furnish or withhold, would render its course precarious, the result of its measures uncertain, and create a dependence on other governments, which might disappoint its most important desigue, and is incompatible with the language of the constitution. But were it otherwise, the choice of means implies a right to choose a national bank in preference to State banks, and Congress alone can make the election.

After the most deliberate consideration, it is the unanimous and decided opinion of this Court, that the act to incorporate the Bank of the United States is a law made in pursuance of the constitution, and is a part of the supreme law of the land.

The branches, proceeding from the same stock, and being conducive to the complete accomplishment of the object, are equally constitutional. It would have been unwise to locate them in the charter, and it would be unnecessarily inconvenient to employ the legislative power in making those subordinate arrangements. The great duties of the bank are prescribed; those duties require branches; and the bank itself may, we think, be safely trusted with the selection of places where those branches shall be fixed; reserving always to the government the right to require that a branch shall be located where it may be deemed necessary.

It being the opinion of the Court, that the act incorporating the bank is constitutional; and that the power of establishing a branch in the State of Maryland might be properly exercised by the bank itself, we proceed to inquire–

Whether the State of Maryland may, without violating the constitution, tax that branch?

That the power of taxation is one of vital importance; that it is retained by the States; that it is not abridged by the grant of a similar power to the government of the Union; that it is to be concurrently exercised by the two governments: are truths which have never been denied. But, such is the paramount character of the constitution, that its capacity to withdraw any subject from the action of even this power, is admitted. The States are expressly forbidden to lay any duties on imports or exports, except what may be absolutely necessary for executing their inspection laws. If the obligation of this prohibition must be conceded — if it may restrain a State from the exercise of its taxing power on imports and exports; the same paramount character would seem to restrain, as it certainly may restrain, a State from such other exercise of this power, as is in its nature incompatible with, and repugnant to, the constitutional laws of the Union. A law, absolutely repugnant to another, as entirely repeals that other as if express terms of repeal were used.

On this ground the counsel for the bank place its claim to be exempted from the power of a State to tax its operations. There is no express provision for the case, but the claim has been sustained on a principle which so entirely pervades the constitution, is so intermixed with the materials which compose it, so interwoven with its web, so blended with its texture, as to be incapable of being separated from it, without rending it into shreds.

This great principle is, that the constitution and the laws made in pursuance thereof are supreme; that they control the constitution and laws of the respective States, and cannot be controlled by them. From this, which may be almost termed an axiom, other propositions are deduced as corollaries, on the truth or error of which, and on their application to this case, the cause has been supposed to depend. These are, 1st. that a power to create implies a power to preserve. 2nd. That a power to destroy, if wielded by a different hand, is hostile to, and incompatible with these powers to create and to preserve. 3d. That where this repugnancy exists, that authority which is supreme must control, not yield to that over which it is supreme.

These propositions, as abstract truths, would, perhaps, never be controverted. Their application to this case, however, has been denied; and, both in maintaining the affirmative and the negative, a splendor of eloquence, and strength of argument, seldom, if ever, surpassed, have been displayed.

The power of Congress to create, and of course to continue, the bank, was the subject of the preceding part of this opinion; and is no longer to be considered as questionable.

That the power of taxing it by the States may be exercised so as to destroy it, is too obvious to be denied. But taxation is said to be an absolute power, which acknowledges no other limits than those expressly prescribed in the constitution, and like sovereign power of every other description, is trusted to the discretion of those who use it. But the very terms of this argument admit that the sovereignty of the State, in the article of taxation itself, is subordinate to, and may be controlled by the constitution of the United States. How far it has been controlled by that instrument must be a question of construction. In making this construction, no principle not declared, can be admissible, which would defeat the legitimate operations of a supreme government. It is of the very essence of supremacy to remove all obstacles to its action within its own sphere, and so to modify every power vested in subordinate governments, as to exempt its own operations from their own influence. This effect need not be stated in terms. It is so involved in the declaration of supremacy, so necessarily implied in it, that the expression of it could not make it more certain. We must, therefore, keep it in view while construing the constitution.

* * *

That the power to tax involves the power to destroy; that the power to destroy may defeat and render useless the power to create; that there is a plain repugnance, in conferring on one government a power to control the constitutional measures of another, which other, with respect to those very measures, is declared to be supreme over that which exerts the control, are propositions not to be denied. But all inconsistencies are to be reconciled by the magic of the word CONFIDENCE. Taxation, it is said, does not necessarily and unavoidably destroy. To carry it to the excess of destruction would be an abuse, to presume which, would banish that confidence which is essential to all government.

But is this a case of confidence? Would the people of any one State trust those of another with a power to control the most insignificant operations of their State government? We know they would not. Why, then, should we suppose that the people of any one State should be willing to trust those of another with a power to control the operations of a government to which they have confided their most important and most valuable interests? In the legislature of the Union alone, are all represented. The legislature of the Union alone, therefore, can be trusted by the people with the power of controlling measures which concern all, in the confidence that it will not be abused. This, then, is not a case of confidence, and we must consider it as it really is.

If we apply the principle for which the State of Maryland contends, to the constitution generally, we shall find it capable of changing totally the character of that instrument. We shall find it capable of arresting all the measures of the government, and of prostrating it at the foot of the States. The American people have declared their constitution, and the laws made in pursuance thereof, to be supreme; but this principle would transfer the supremacy, in fact, to the States.

If the States may tax one instrument, employed by the government in the execution of its powers, they may tax any and every other instrument. They may tax the mail; they may tax the mint; they may tax patent rights; they may tax the papers of the custom-house; they may tax judicial process; they may tax all the means employed by the government, to an excess which would defeat all the ends of government. This was not intended by the American people. They did not design to make their government dependent on the States.

* * *

The Court has bestowed on this subject its most deliberate consideration. The result is a conviction that the States have no power, by taxation or otherwise, to retard, impede, burden, or in any manner control, the operations of the constitutional laws enacted by Congress to carry into execution the powers vested in the general government. This is, we think, the unavoidable consequence of that supremacy which the constitution has declared.

We are unanimously of opinion, that the law passed by the legislature of Maryland, imposing a tax on the Bank of the United States, is unconstitutional and void.

FEDERALISM IN AMERICA: AN OBITUARY

Forrest McDonald and Susan McDonald

A Central feature of the new order that was created in Philadelphia in 1787—perhaps the central feature—was federalism, which in America has historically had three distinct dimensions. The first is the representation of the states as states in the national government: what James Madison had in mind when he wrote in Federalist number 39 that the Constitution established a system that was partly national and partly federal. The second involves the source of sovereignty in America and the nature of the constitutional union. The third, and ultimately the most important, has to do with the division of the powers of sovereignty between national and state governments.

In each of these dimensions federalism has a separate history, but the end result has been the same. For many years, the system served as a protector of liberty and a preserver of local autonomy, as the authors of the Constitution intended. Over the course of time, however, federalism in each of its aspects has been undermined, eroded, or destroyed.

Under the Articles of confederation the Congress had been a purely federal body. Its members were elected by the state legislatures, the states had one vote apiece, and Congress could act only through the agency of the state governments. The Constitution wrought a fundamental change by vesting the national government with power to act directly upon individuals in certain limited and specified areas, but it retained the federal principle in three of the four branches of the government it established. The Senate continued the old system, its members being elected directly by the state legislatures, and the states continued to be equally represented in it, though with two votes apiece instead of one. The president was to be elected by electors, who were to be chosen in such manner as the several state legislatures should determine; in the early elections the legislatures themselves often chose the electors and thus indirectly elected the president. Judges, being appointed by the president with the approval of the Senate, were likewise indirectly the creatures of the state legislatures, though at yet another stage of remove.

These arrangements were undone by the growth of democracy. The popular election of presidential electors was a matter of evolution: one by one the states changed their election laws until, by 1836, only the legislature of South Carolina continued to choose the electors. The popular election of senators was slower in coming: it was adopted by a number of states late in the nineteenth century and early in the twentieth, and it became a part of the Constitution upon the ratification of the Seventeenth Amendment in 1913.

The second dimension of federalism—that relating to the source of sovereignty and the nature of the union—was considerably more complex. At the time of the Revolution, there had been some disagreement as to where sovereignty devolved upon the severance of America's ties with Britain, but the matter was resolved by the way in which the Constitution was established. The Articles of Confederation had been ratified by the state legislatures, but as Madison pointed out during the Federal Convention, a constitution ratified by the legislatures could be construed as being a treaty "among the Governments of Independent States," and thus it could be held that "a breach of any one article, by any of the parties, absolved the other parties" from any further obligation.

To avoid that construction, Madison continued, it was necessary to submit the Constitution to "the supreme authority of the people themselves." Yet it could not be submitted to the people of the United States as a whole, because the Constitution amended each of the state constitutions in various ways, and if it were adopted by majority vote of the whole people, the people in some states would be altering the constitutions of other states. This, in the nature of things, they could not have the authority to do. Accordingly, the Constitution was submitted for ratification by conventions in each of the states, delegates to which were elected by the people of the several states in their capacities as people of the several states. Madison put it thus in Federalist number 39: "Ratification is to be given by the people, not as individuals

From *Requiem: Variations on Eighteenth-Century Themes* by Forrest McDonald and Ellen Shapiro McDonald. Lawrence: University Press of Kansas, 1988. Copyright © 1988 University Press of Kansas. Used with permission of the publisher.

composing one entire nation, but as composing the distinct and independent States to which they respectively belong. It is to be the assent and ratification of the several States, derived from the supreme authority in each State, —the authority of the people themselves" This procedure unmistakably implied that the source of sovereignty was the people of the states, severally, and that the residue of sovereignty which was not committed by them to either the national government or the state governments remained in them—an implication that was subsequently made explicit by the Tenth Amendment. The process of ratification also indicated that the Union was a compact among political societies, which is to say among the people of Virginia with the people of Massachusetts with the people of Georgia, and so on.

Now, though the nature of the compact was perfectly understood at the time, it was both subtle and unprecedented; and it is scarcely a source of wonderment that alternative formulations of what had happened were soon forthcoming. Nor is it surprising that those alternative formulations had profoundly different implications.

One of the formulations was the juristic, which was first suggested by Chief Justice John Jay but given its fullest expression by John Marshall, both as historian (in his five-volume, highly partisan biography of Washington) and as chief justice in his decision in M'Culloch v. Maryland (1819). The juristic view was that the Constitution had been created by the people as a whole, that the process of ratification by states had been resorted to only as a matter of convenience, and thus that any claims to state sovereignty or states' rights were unfounded.

The opposite view was formulated by James Madison in 1798 and was adopted by the legislature of Virginia in protest against the Alien and Sedition Acts. Conveniently forgetting what he had said earlier, Madison wrote that the federal government had resulted "from the compact to which the states are parties." From that premise it followed that when Congress enacts statutes that exceed its constitutional authority, the state governments "have the right and are in duty bound to interpose" their own authority between their citizens and the federal government, to prevent the unconstitutional enactments from being enforced. Thomas Jefferson, in the counterpart Kentucky Resolutions, referred to the federal compact as being among "sovereign and independent states. . . .

Meanwhile, the original, compact-among-peoples understanding was not entirely forgotten, but it was rarely appealed to because its implications were so radical. It was brought up in New England in 1805 and again in 1814, amidst talk of and as a justification for secession—a justification that no less ardent a nationalist than Gouverneur Morris declared to be sound. It arose again during the nullification controversy of 1832/33, with more ominous portents.

That controversy is remembered as a conflict between South Carolina and the national government and between John C. Calhoun and Andrew Jackson; the procedures that were followed, though of crucial importance, are often forgotten. Late in 1832 Governor James Hamilton called the state legislature into special session, and the legislature passed a law calling for a popularly elected state convention. The maneuver was carefully chosen. As the Constitution had been ratified in South Carolina by a popularly elected convention, the state was now returning to such a convention as the ultimate source of sovereignty. The convention met and adopted ordinances declaring the tariff acts of 1828 and 1832 null and void, forbidding appeal to the Supreme Court in cases arising under the ordinances, and asserting that the state would have just cause for seceding from the Union if the national government should attempt to use force to collect the tariff.

The outcome of the confrontation was indecisive. Congress backed down, passing Henry Clay's compromise tariff; but it also enacted Jackson's Force Bill, which authorized the president to use the army against South Carolina if it continued to defy the law. The state, for its part, rescinded its nullification ordinances, but it also formally nullified the Force Bill.

South Carolina's position was what in the eighteenth century was called a "return to first principles" and when it was adopted, it could be refuted only by the sword. And it was adopted during the winter of 1860/61: each of the eleven seceding states left the Union the way the original thirteen states had entered into it, by means of conventions elected by the people for the purpose. The defeat of the Confederacy in the Civil War resolved the issue for all time, though not immediately. Radicals in Congress first insisted that the southern states had committed political suicide by seceding and that they were therefore to be treated as "conquered provinces." Subsequently, however, the Radicals realized that the votes of the southern states would probably be necessary to ensure the ratification of the Fourteenth Amendment. Accordingly, they reversed themselves and—on condition that the amendment be ratified—now held that the states had never left the Union. The Supreme Court confirmed that interpretation in the case of Texas v. White (1869). Disregarding the fact that Virginia had been dismembered, in palpable violation of the Constitution, by the creation of West Virginia in 1863, the Court ruled that the Constitution "looks to an indestructible Union, composed of indestructible states." . . .

The third dimension of federalism arose from the fact that the Framers of the Constitution did something that political theorists since ancient times had insisted could not be done, which is to say, divide sovereignty. In the eighteenth century, sovereignty was defined as the supreme law-making power; as Blackstone said, "Sovereignty and legislature are indeed convertible terms. Having two sovereignties in the same territory was obviously impossible. The Framers worked their way around that stumbling block by attacking the problem in an ingenious way. Conceiving of sovereignty, not as a single power, but as an aggregate of many specific powers, they could allocate those specific powers among different governments and among different branches of the same government. Each government or branch of government had, in Hamilton's words, "sovereign power as to certain things, and not as to other things."

The Constitution bestowed sovereign powers upon the national government only in regard to a handful of general objects. All other powers, except those that were forbidden to both national and state governments, remained in the hands of the states. . . .

Despite Article VI, which declares the Constitution and congressional enactments passed in pursuance thereof to be the supreme law of the land, the preponderance of powers thus lay with the states, and most states insisted from the outset that all disputes about which governments could do what should be decided in favor of the states. As early as 1790, Virginia was challenging what it saw as congressional usurpation of powers reserved to the states, provoking Alexander Hamilton to declare that this was "the first symptom of a spirit which must either be killed or will kill the constitution." The very first decision in which the Supreme Court ruled against a state—that in Chisholm v. Georgia (1793)—resulted in a constitutional amendment curtailing the Court's jurisdiction and protecting the sovereignty of the states against suits by foreigners or citizens of other states. Repeatedly during Marshall's tenure (1801-35) the Court ruled that the states could not constitutionally do one thing or another, and the states did them anyway. Under Chief Justice Roger Brooke Taney (1836-64) the Court erected a virtual wall of separation around the states. The adoption of the Fourteenth Amendment in 1868 provided features that might have been employed to curtail state power, but apart from the relatively minor restrictions imposed under the doctrine of substantive due process, the states continued to be the principal units of government until well into the twentieth century. . . .

The process by which the balance of federal and state powers was overturned was long and involved, but the major phases can be described under three broad headings. First came the evolution of a national police power. The police power had resided exclusively in the states, and it had been consistently upheld by the Court even when there were conflicts with other constitutional provisions, as there were, for example, in Stone v. Mississippi (1880) and Holden v. Hardy (1898). But just after the turn of the century, Congress passed an act prohibiting the interstate transportation of lottery tickets and an act imposing a tax on oleomargarine, the latter on the pretext that margarine was dangerous to the health. In upholding these acts in 1903 and 1904, the Supreme Court ruled for the first time that the national government does in fact have a police power. The passage of the Pure Food and Drug Act and the Meat Inspection Act soon followed. Other such legislation steadily accumulated, and between 1937 and 1957—during which period the Court declared only one act of Congress unconstitutional—the whole range of police-power legislation was invaded by Congress.

A second group of developments was fiscal. The adoption of the Sixteenth Amendment, authorizing taxes on incomes; the passage of the Glass-Steagall Act of 1932, basing federal-reserve note currency upon governmental debt; and the abandonment of the gold standard; all these combined to make possible virtually unlimited and uncontrollable spending by the national government. Closely related to that development and in part growing out of it was the emergence of revenue sharing in one form and another—

the subsidization of state and local governments by the national government and the ever-increasing dependence of the first two upon the last. It is to be observed that southerners, despite their traditional adherence to federalism and states' rights, did not resist this turn of events and were indeed in the vanguard of bringing it about. As the Bible puts it, they proved willing to sell their birthright for a mess of pottage. (A very large mess, but a mess nonetheless.)

The final blows were wielded by the Supreme Court, largely through the doctrine of incorporation, which runs roughly as follows. The Bill of Rights, as originally passed and as interpreted by the courts for 134 years, restricted the federal government but did not apply to the state governments. Then in 1925 the Court declared, in its decision in the case of Gitlow v. New York, that the Fourteenth Amendment's protection of liberty against state interference extended some of the fundamental liberties guaranteed by the Bill of Rights to apply to the states. For a time, the consequences of that declaration were minimal; the Court was loath to determine just what was a "fundamental" liberty. The conviction of Gitlow for publishing Communist propaganda in violation of a New York law, for instance, was upheld on the ground that freedom of speech is not an absolute right. A number of other cases were settled in similar fashion during the next dozen years; they culminated in a case in which the Court ruled that the Fifth Amendment's protection against double jeopardy was not a fundamental liberty. The Court continued to be cautious about applying the doctrine of incorporation throughout the 1940s and the 1950s. Indeed, it was not until 1961 that incorporation began to be applied on a grand scale, but since that time the Court has manufactured "fundamental rights" with reckless abandon. The result has been that control over matters of local concern has been transferred from local and state governments to the national government in Washington.

Constitutional traditionalists, especially in the South, have been incensed by most of this, and much of the relevant litigation has arisen in the South. The rights of accused criminals were established in suits originating in Arizona and Illinois; but both pioneering abortion cases, many of the landmark cases concerning school prayer, some of the most important affirmative-active cases, and all of the major legislative-reapportionment cases were southern in origin.

There are some ironies in all this. Among the foremost apostles of the doctrine of incorporation, especially in regard to First Amendment rights, was the next-to-the-last southerner to sit on the Supreme Court, Hugo Black of Alabama. But Black, toward the end of his long and distinguished career, at last came to recognize the dangers inherent in carrying the principle too far. In a dissenting opinion in 1968 he pointed out that the nation had always understood "that it could be more tranquil and orderly if it functioned on the principle that the local communities should control their own peculiar affairs under their own particular rules." In 1970, the year before he died, he warned that if the Court did not exercise restraint, it would destroy the federal system created by the Constitution by reducing the state governments to "impotent figureheads."

The larger irony is this. Political scientists and historians are in agreement that federalism is the greatest contribution of the Founding Fathers to the science of government. It is also the only feature of the Constitution that has been successfully exported, that can be employed to protect liberty elsewhere in the world. Yet what we invented, and others imitate, no longer exists on its native shores.

THE BALANCE OF POWER BETWEEN THE FEDERAL GOVERNMENT AND THE STATES

Kathleen M. Sullivan

The antifederalists opposed the Constitution out of fear that it would give too much power to the federal government. Contemporary antifederalists claim their intellectual ancestors were right, and they seek to roll federal power back in a variety of ways. Governors and new members of Congress ally to devolve welfare policy to the fifty states. State and local law enforcement officers refuse to perform the background checks on handgun purchasers required by the federal Brady law in order to keep guns out of criminal hands. State motor vehicle bureaus try to resist a federal "motor voter" law requiring them to offer to register citizens to vote at the same time as they license them to drive. Criminal defendants, newly emboldened as states' rights advocates, argue that Congress lacks power to regulate local crimes. Governors seek legislation providing that Congress will pay for any mandates with which it might burden the states.

These modern antifederalists invoke the structure of the Constitution, which gave limited powers to the federal government, and the text of the Tenth Amendment, which reiterated that all other powers were reserved to the states. On the antifederalists' view, the peoples of the various states, not "We the People of the United States," are the ultimate source of constitutional authority. They argue that "We the People" have engaged in a power grab, tilting the balance of power too far in favor of the federal government. They demand that the courts should right that balance, as Congress is unlikely to restrain itself. In short, they have developed a modern ideology of states' "rights" against federal laws.

The framers of the Constitution would hardly recognize such an ideology. In their view, the Constitution was not a winner-take-all contest for sovereignty between the federal government and the states. It sought instead, in Justice Anthony Kennedy's words, to "split the atom of sovereignty" in two. The United States is neither a centralized nation-state like France nor a loose confederation of independent, sovereign entities like the European Union. Rather, it is what Madison called a "compound republic": "We the People of the United States" ordained the Constitution, but it was ratified only by the consent of the peoples of the several states. And while it strengthened the federal government, the Constitution contemplated a robust state governmental role.

Thus, in our constitutional system, the question of state versus federal power is not a question of "rights." States do not have rights as individuals do. Nor is it a question of inviolable principles. It is instead a practical question: what allocation of power between the states and the federal government best serves our ends? In the framers' view, the federal system served two ends: liberty and the public good. People would be freer, they predicted, under two levels of government rather than just one. In *The Federalist* No. 51, for example, Madison argued that the division of power between "two distinct governments" would allow the state and federal governments to check each other, providing security to the "rights of the people." The framers also reasoned that each level of government has distinctive contributions to make to the public good. The states are better at some things; the federal government at others. The trick is to allocate responsibility for the right things to the appropriate level of government.

In their pursuit of states' "rights," modern antifederalists lose sight of the important reasons why some policies are better handled at the federal level. To begin with, the federal government is better at providing public goods whose benefits transcend state boundaries. The best example is national defense. Missiles siloed in Texas will also protect the citizens of Connecticut and California from attack by a foreign enemy. The other states might be happy to let Texas pay for the missiles itself since they would then get the benefits of protection without the cost. But in that case, Texas might well not furnish the missiles in the first place, as it would not want to give the rest of the nation a free ride. Thus, as Hamilton pointed out in *The Federalist* No. 25, only the federal government can be relied upon to provide the level of defense needed for the entire nation. Because enemies "encircle the union from Maine to Georgia," he wrote, the common danger ought to be defended against by "a common treasury," lest "the security of all . . . , be subjected to the parsimony, improvidence or inability of a part."

The same argument holds true for many other public goods that benefit broad segments of the national population and hence are likely to be underproduced by any individual state. For example, the federal government provides, through federal taxation and borrowing, for interstate highways, national parks, space exploration, the Post Office, the Coast Guard, air traffic control, and the bulk of medical research, to name a few. Some have suggested that some of these goods would be provided more efficiently by private businesses than by government, but such arguments for privatization offer no support for devolution to the states.

The federal government also has a distinct advantage over the states in policing goods, persons, and businesses that move across state lines. For that reason, the Constitution makes explicit Congress's power to regulate "interstate commerce." Federal laws ensure, for example, that apple juice shipped across the country is safe to drink, that offers of securities on national markets rest on truthful information, and that deadbeat dads cannot evade one state's child-support obligations by moving to another.

Federal intervention may also be called for when an activity in one state causes more harm to residents of other states than to its own residents. For example, a state with coal-burning industries might not take adequate account of the cost of acid rain caused by their pollution in states downwind. A tobacco-growing state might downplay the health care costs associated with smoking nationwide. Interstate agreements are one solution, but the political obstacles to such bargains are often daunting. In cases like these, setting policy at the national level can break the logjam.

Federal action can also correct the problem of "races to the bottom" among the states. Each state has an interest in attracting the rich, who will pay taxes and create employment, and deflecting the poor, who will impose net costs. Thus each state has an incentive to compete with other states to attract businesses by relaxing regulations that would otherwise be in their citizens' best interests. Each state likewise has an incentive to avoid becoming a "welfare magnet" by reducing its level of social services below those offered by competing states, even if its citizens would prefer to be more generous. Any agreement among a few states to do otherwise is likely to be undercut by others. National programs or minimum federal standards can stop such destructive competition. Child labor laws, Social Security, and unemployment insurance are some examples that originated with the New Deal.

Finally, there are enormous disparities in wealth and income among the states, and only the federal government can effectively collect revenue and redistribute it from rich states to poor. A state too poor to fund minimally equipped schools, or a state that has been hit by a sudden disaster—earthquake, fire, hurricane, tornado, or flood—will be grateful for federal education aid or federal emergency relief subsidized by the citizens of other states.

What is left for the state governments to do? Almost anything they wish. As Madison noted in *The Federalist* No. 45, while federal powers are "few and defined," the powers of the states "are numerous and indefinite." Although the enumerated federal powers have of course been construed more expansively than the framers anticipated, the powers of the states remain unbounded in scope and variety. So long as they do not enter into treaties, coin money, grant titles of nobility, pass bills of attainder, ex post facto laws, or laws impairing obligations of contract, or violate individual rights, states may regulate the health, safety, morals, and well-being of their citizens any way they see fit, subject only to their own state constitutions.

True, federal law is supreme over state law, and so Congress can preempt the states from enacting regulations that conflict with federal law. Modern antifederalists chafe at this federal supremacy. But they exaggerate the extent to which the federal government has displaced state policy-making. There are strong structural, political, and cultural limits on federalization.

First, the federal government can never set a ceiling for state policies; it can only set a floor. A state that wants to have more protection for individual liberties than the federal Constitution provides is free to so interpret its state constitution. A state that wants to have cleaner air than federal pollution standards require is not prevented from imposing stricter emission controls. Under uniform, national, minimal education standards, local school administrators could still set more ambitious performance goals. There is thus a structural limit to how far the federal government could homogenize the nation even if it wanted to.

Second, there are political limits on federalization. The state and local governments are a powerful lobbying force in their own right. They have proved capable of defending themselves politically when Congress steps too hard on their toes. For example, when the Supreme Court, reversing its own earlier states' rights ruling, upheld a federal statute telling municipalities how much to pay their police and fire-fighters, the National League of Cities and its allies persuaded Congress to rewrite the law. Such state and local governmental exemptions from generally applicable federal statutes are commonplace. More-over, various federal legislative initiatives originate with state and local government lobbies, from the welfare policy prescriptions of the National Governors' Council to the requests of state and local law enforcement organizations for greater federal funding of community police.

Finally, federalism is rooted in long tradition. Even if it is no longer true, as Madison once wrote, that "the first and most natural attachment of the people will be to the governments of their respective States," state identity remains a powerful part of our political culture. We never vote as members of an undifferentiated national electorate. We never go to a federal polling place or vote in a nationwide refer-endum. We vote for our federal representatives in the time, place, and manner set up by our state govern-ments. We elect two senators from every state, giving small states a disproportionate voice in national governance. And we vote for the president state by state through the electoral college rather than directly by popular vote. In such a system, the president and Congress ignore distinctive state concerns at their peril.

This tradition survives because it makes practical sense to leave many policy matters to the states. To the extent that conditions vary among states, decentralized approaches can tailor policy to local circum-stance. To the extent that preferences vary among states, decentralization fosters liberty. If citizens of one state feel tyrannized by its policies, they can vote with their feet by migrating freely across state lines. Hence the concentration of Mormons in Utah, libertarians in New Hampshire, environmentalists in Or-egon, or gay people in northern California. Even if the states share similar goals, they may act as what Justice Louis Brandeis called "laboratories for experiment," competing with one another to develop the best means for realizing social or economic policy. The more experiments, the greater the likelihood of a breakthrough, and if one state makes a breakthrough, others can follow suit. For example, Massachu-setts pioneered innovations in elementary and secondary education, California in public higher educa-tion, Wisconsin in industrial compensation and unemployment insurance, New York in community polic-ing, and Hawaii in universal health care, to name a few.

These structural, political, and cultural safeguards of federalism can be expected to protect state in-terests from the bottom up without frequent resort to judicial intervention or constitutional command. Of course, the courts should stand by to protect the states against any extreme federal incursions on their sovereignty: Congress could not tell a state where to locate its capital or how many chambers its legisla-ture should have. It also makes sense for the courts to police outright federal intervention in state law-making, just as they police transgressions of the separation of powers among the federal branches.

In one illustrative case, the Supreme Court has held that Congress may not order a state either to pass laws regulating disposal of low-level radioactive waste or else to take title to the waste itself. As Justice Sandra Day O'Connor wrote for the Court, such a federal law wrongly "commandeers" the state's legis-lative process. If Congress passes the buck to the states to solve a national problem, she explained, "state officials may bear the brunt of public disapproval" while federal lawmakers enjoy a free ride. Lines of electoral accountability are blurred; voters will not know which set of bums to throw out.

However sensible this principle might be, modern antifederalists exaggerate its reach. Some local sheriffs claim that the federal Brady law, which requires them to run background checks on handgun purchasers, "makes the states dance like marionettes on the fingers of the federal government," in Justice Antonin Scalia's words. But requiring local law enforcement officers to inspect state arrest records does not trench upon state legislative sovereignty. Congress has made all the hard policy choices on handgun control in the Brady law and bears the brunt of any public disapproval. When the local sheriff performs a background check, he or she is not being forced to make any policy judgments on behalf of the state. If a handgun purchaser does not like the background check, it is clear that Congress, not the sheriff, is to blame. For these reasons, the sheriffs' invocation of states' rights should be rejected.

Finally, there may be reason for the courts to draw outer limits to federal power when the structural, political, and cultural safeguards of federalism break down and the federal government encroaches needlessly upon areas traditionally and sensibly regulated by the states. The worst example in our recent politics is the overfederalization of crime. The Constitution names only three federal crimes: counterfeiting coin or securities, piracy on the high seas, and treason. But Congress has created more than three thousand federal crimes under the power to regulate interstate commerce. There are many crimes that should be federal, such as bombing federal buildings or sending explosives through the mail. But should it also be a federal crime to grow marijuana at home or to hijack a car around the corner? Federal crimes have proliferated not because it is good crime policy but because it is good politics: as Chief Justice William Rehnquist has observed, "the political combination of creating a federal offense and attaching a mandatory minimum sentence has become a veritable siren song for Congress," loud enough to drown out any careful consideration of the comparative advantages of state and federal crime control.

Shifting crime control from the states to the federal government in purely local cases diverts the work of federal investigators, prosecutors, and judges from areas of greater federal need. It also fills federal prisons with nonviolent and first-time offenders who occupy space that could better be used for violent, career criminals whose operations cross state lines. There is no reason why most of the new federal crimes could not be handled by the states, as they have been traditionally, unless they involve multistate enterprises or intrastate enterprises so vast as to overwhelm the resources of state authorities.

For such reasons, the Supreme Court recently struck down an act of Congress criminalizing possession of a handgun at school. Possession is not commerce, the gun had not been shown to have traveled across state lines, and education and crime control are traditional local functions, held the Court. Congress's power over interstate commerce is broad, but not so broad as to amount to a national police power. The Court in effect directed Congress to consider the relative merits of state and local governance before legislating—an appropriate and not excessive burden.

Contemporary antifederalists are mistaken, however, when they read this decision as a declaration of open season on federal law. Some courts have invalidated federal laws against rape and other violence against women. Others have invalidated federal laws making it a crime to fail to pay child support. These laws, though, involve subjects quite different from gun possession at school. Stopping sexual and other battery of women may not implicate interstate commerce, but it may well implicate Congress's power to enforce federal civil rights. Congress has long had expansive power not only to stop invidious discrimination in the states but also to eliminate conditions in which it might flourish. While it is a close question, a high incidence of private violence against women might amount to such a regulable condition. Child-support evasion is an easier case, for it involves a classic problem warranting federal intervention, the problem of mobility across state lines. In enacting both these laws, unlike the gun possession law, Congress paid more than lip service to the balance of federal and state power.

Against this backdrop, there is little warrant for an antifederalist revival. If power has flowed to the center since the nation's founding, that is in large part because federal power has served as a crucial check on local factionalism and as a source of ingenious solutions to coordination problems among the states. To the extent that imbalance of state and federal power is a problem, it is largely self-correcting because the states can protect themselves through politics. To the extent that it is not, the Supreme Court has supplied sensible but narrow outer limits. There is no need for greater judicial intervention on the states' behalf.

CHAPTER 3

INTRODUCTION

People debated throughout the Cold War whether the President of the United States was the most powerful man on earth. Obviously, during this time, comparisons were made with the Soviet Premier and debates involving unilateral power of the leader, military might, economic strength, etc. occupied hours of debate, pages of texts and no doubt lead to the loss of numerous brain cells. In the post Cold War era, the debate is barely even an argument. With no apparent rivals to the United States in the foreseeable future, it's hard to argue against the power of the Presidency. However, for decades, Presidents have decried their inability to shape agendas, to control their party, to see favorable legislation passed, to get appointments confirmed and treaties ratified. Does this sound like the most powerful man of the face of the earth? Perhaps this whole conversation says less about the power of the President and more about the lack of power of the other leaders in the world.

In the three selections for this chapter, the Presidency is examined in three different ways. In Federalist 70, Hamilton addressed the need for a single executive by emphasizing the importance of unity. Questions for you to consider are:

1. What are Hamilton's "ingredients which constitute energy in the executive"?

2. What are the multiple dangers Hamilton sees in a plural executive?

3. Specifically, why is it a benefit for the legislative branch to have larger numbers (and the naturally corresponding disagreements) but a detriment for the executive?

Hedrick Smith's time tested piece reminds us that modern presidents are required to be able to negotiate and compromise if they are to be effective in dealing with Congress. The questions to answer from this classic article are rather straightforward.

1. Why are some presidents more effective than others in the world of compromise and negotiation?

2. What are the rules of the "Coalition Game"?

The final article is by Godfrey Hodgson. Several political scientists in recent years have begun to write about the paradoxes of the American government, policy making and, of course, the Presidency. As noted in the two quotations from Harry Truman that start the article, there seems to be some inconsistency in the examination of this person–the most powerful person on the face of the earth. What are good questions to guide you in this excerpt?

1. What are examples of a president's power? What are examples of his lack of power?

2. What resources can a president use to get others to do what he wants them to do?

THE FEDERALIST NO. 70: HAMILTON

March 15, 1788

To the People of the State of New York.

There is an idea, which is not without its advocates, that a vigorous executive is inconsistent with the genius of republican government. The enlightened well wishers to this species of government must at least hope that the supposition is destitute of foundation; since they can never admit its truth, without at the same time admitting the condemnation of their own principles. Energy in the executive is a leading character in the definition of good government. It is essential to the protection of the community against foreign attacks: It is not less essential to the steady administration of the laws, to the protection of property against those irregular and high handed combinations, which sometimes interrupt the ordinary course of justice, to the security of liberty against the enterprises and assaults of ambition, of faction and of anarchy. Every man the least conversant in Roman story knows how often that republic was obliged to take refuge in the absolute power of a single man, under the formidable title of dictator, as well against the intrigues of ambitious individuals, who aspired to the tyranny, and the seditions of whole classes of the community, whose conduct threatened the existence of all government, as against the invasions of external enemies, who menaced the conquest and destruction of Rome.

There can be no need however to multiply arguments or examples on this head. A feeble executive implies a feeble execution of the government. A feeble execution is but another phrase for a bad execution: And a government ill executed, whatever it may be in theory, must be in practice a bad government.

Taking it for granted, therefore, that all men of sense will agree in the necessity of an energetic executive; it will only remain to inquire, what are the ingredients which constitute this energy—how far can they be combined with those other ingredients which constitute safety in the republican sense? And how far does this combination characterise the plan, which has been reported by the convention?

The ingredients which constitute energy in the executive, are first unity, secondly duration, thirdly an adequate provision for its support, fourthly competent powers.

The circumstances which constitute safety in the republican sense are, 1st. a due dependence on the people, secondly a due responsibility.

Those politicians and statesmen, who have been the most celebrated for the soundness of their principles, and for the justness of their views, have declared in favor of a single executive and a numerous legislature. They have with great propriety considered energy as the most necessary qualification of the former, and have regarded this as most applicable to power in a single hand; while they have with equal propriety considered the latter as best adapted to deliberation and wisdom, and best calculated to conciliate the confidence of the people and to secure their privileges and interests.

That unity is conducive to energy will not be disputed. Decision, activity, secrecy, and dispatch will generally characterise the proceedings of one man, in a much more eminent degree, than the proceedings of any greater number; and in proportion as the number is increased, these qualities will be diminished.

* * *

Wherever two or more persons are engaged in any common enterprize or pursuit, there is always danger of difference of opinion. If it be a public trust or office in which they are cloathed with equal dignity and authority, there is peculiar danger of personal emulation and even animosity. From either and especially from all these causes, the most bitter dissentions are apt to spring. Whenever these happen, they lessen the respectability, weaken the authority, and distract the plans and operations of those whom they divide. If they should unfortunately assail the supreme executive magistracy of a country, consisting of a plurality of persons, they might impede or frustrate the most important measures of the government, in the most critical emergencies of the state. And what is still worse, they might split the community into the most violent and irreconcilable factions, adhering differently to the different individuals who composed the magistracy.

Men often oppose a thing merely because they have had no agency in planning it, or because it may have been planned by those whom they dislike. But if they have been consulted and have happened to disapprove, opposition then becomes in their estimation an indispensable duty of self love. They seem to think themselves bound in honor, and by all the motives of personal infallibility to defeat the success of what has been resolved upon, contrary to their sentiments. Men of upright, benevolent tempers have too many opportunities of remarking with horror, to what desperate lengths this disposition is sometimes carried, and how often the great interests of society are sacrificed to the vanity, to the conceit and to the obstinacy of individuals, who have credit enough to make their passions and their caprices interesting to mankind. Perhaps the question now before the public may in its consequences afford melancholy proofs of the effects of this despicable frailty, or rather detestable vice in the human character.

Upon the principles of a free government, inconveniencies from the source just mentioned must necessarily be submitted to in the formation of the legislature; but it is unnecessary and therefore unwise to introduce them into the constitution of the executive. It is here too that they may be most pernicious. In the legislature, promptitude of decision is oftener an evil than a benefit. The differences of opinion, and the jarrings of parties in that department of the government, though they may sometime obstruct salutary plans, yet often promote deliberation and circumspection; and serve to check excesses in the majority. When a resolution too is once taken, the opposition must be at an end. That resolution is a law, and resistance to it punishable. But no favourable circumstances palliate or atone for the disadvantage of dissention in the executive department. Here they are pure and unmixed. There is no point at which they cease to operate. They serve to embarrass and weaken the execution of the plan or measure, to which they relate, from the first step to the final conclusion of it. They constantly counteract those qualities in the executive, which are the most necessary ingredients in its composition, vigour and expedition, and this without any counter ballancing good. In the conduct of war, in which the energy of the executive is the bulwark of the national security, every thing would be to be apprehended from its plurality.

It must be confessed that these observations apply with principal weight to the first case supposed, that is to a plurality of magistrates of equal dignity and authority; a scheme the advocates for which are not likely to form a numerous sect: But they apply, though not with equal, yet with considerable weight, to the project of a council, whose concurrence is made constitutionally necessary to the operations of the ostensible executive. An artful cabal in that council would be able to distract and to enervate the whole system of administration. If no such cabal should exist, the mere diversity of views and opinions would alone be sufficient to tincture the exercise of the executive authority with a spirit of habitual feebleness and dilatoriness.

But one of the weightiest objections to a plurality in the executive, and which lies as much against the last as the first plan, is that it tends to conceal faults, and destroy responsibility. Responsibility is of two kinds, to censure and to punishment. The first is the most important of the two; especially in an elective office. Man, in public trust, will much oftener act in such a manner as to render him unworthy of being any longer trusted, than in such a manner as to make him obnoxious to legal punishment. But the multiplication of the executive adds to the difficulty of detection in either case. It often becomes impossible, amidst mutual accusations, to determine on whom the blame or the punishment of a pernicious measure, or series of pernicious measures ought really to fall. It is shifted from one to another with so much dexterity, and under such plausible appearances, that the public opinion is left in suspense about the real author. The circumstances which may have led to any national miscarriage or misfortune are sometimes so complicated, that where there are a number of actors who may have had different degrees and kinds of agency, though we may clearly see upon the whole that there has been mismanagement, yet it may be impracticable to pronounce to whose account the evil which may have been incurred is truly chargeable. . . .

It is evident from these considerations, that the plurality of the executive tends to deprive the people of the two greatest securities they can have for the faithful exercise of any delegated power; first, the restraints of public opinion, which lose their efficacy as well on account of the division of the censure attendant on bad measures among a number, as on account of the uncertainty on whom it ought to fall; and secondly, the opportunity of discovering with facility and clearness the misconduct of the persons they trust, in order either to their removal from office, or to their actual punishment, in cases which admit of it.

* * *

I will only add, that prior to the appearance of the constitution, I rarely met with an intelligent man from any of the states, who did not admit as the result of experience, that the UNITY of the Executive of this state was one of the best of the distinguishing features of our constitution.

PUBLIUS

THE COALITION GAME: THE HEART OF GOVERNING

Hedrick Smith

"Putting a majority together is like a one-armed man wrapping cranberries: You can't get them all in the wrap."

—Senate Majority Leader Bob Dole

* * *

The coalition game—building coalitions and making coalitions work—is the heart of our system of government. Although the coalition game is usually ignored during the passions of American election campaigns, no president can succeed unless he can build a governing coalition. For limited periods, presidents can act on their own: devaluing the dollar as Nixon did, negotiating an arms treaty with Moscow as Carter did, sending American Marines into Lebanon or working secret arms deals with Iran as Reagan did. But eventually a president must come to Congress to fund his programs, approve his treaties, finance his wars, or sanction his secret diplomacy. If he cannot bring Congress along—cannot form a governing coalition—his programs founder, his treaty must be shelved, the Marines must come home, his diplomacy must halt. Coalitions are the necessary engines for sustaining policies.

Triumphant coalition makers are rare: Franklin Roosevelt at the start of the New Deal, Lyndon Johnson in the mid-1960s, and Ronald Reagan in the early 1980s. Other presidents, such as Richard Nixon, Jimmy Carter, John F. Kennedy, and Gerald Ford did pass pieces of legislation or got particular treaties ratified, but they did not pass their major programs because they could not make coalition government work. Solid congressional majorities eluded them. Over the past half century, with Congress usually in Democratic hands, Democratic presidents have had an advantage. Roosevelt and Johnson, for example, built their legislative achievements on big partisan Democratic coalitions. But Kennedy never managed that, and Carter labored like Sisyphus with precious little to show for it because he could not pull the Democrats together. Republican presidents, normally faced with a Democratic Congress, usually have to take the bipartisan route to coalition government. Eisenhower did that fairly effectively, but Nixon and Ford were hamstrung by divided government—Congress in the hands of the political opposition.

Reagan, in his first, most triumphant year, chose to build his coalition with partisan hardball, not with Eisenhower-style bipartisan compromise. In 1981, Reagan did woo conservative southern Democrats and get some to vote with him against their own congressional party leadership. But Republican unity was Reagan's Gibraltar. That is the primary lesson of American politics—rule number one of the coalition game: *Secure your political base first.* Much was required for Reagan's first-year coalition: the President's wide popular appeal, his knack for lobbying Congress, some tough grass-roots politicking, and of course a winning idea to rally a coalition. But Republican unity was the anchor. With unity forged by Howard Baker and House Republican Leader Bob Michel of Illinois, Reagan made his legislative mark. Without that unity, he would have been destined to one-term mediocrity. . . .

What is more, Republicans had been in the minority in both houses for so long that they had fallen into a "minority mentality." They were not trained or conditioned to govern. Instead, they had developed the habits of a permanent opposition. They were practiced in the arts of negative politics: how to stall, how to filibuster, how to resist, how to block. Newt Gingrich, a bright light among younger Reaganites, gloomily declared, "The House Republican party, as a culture, has a defeatist, minority mentality that either did nothing, or opposed for so long, that it has no internal habits of inventing a coherent strategy or following it through for any length of time."

When Orrin Hatch, a staunch Utah conservative, took over from Ted Kennedy, the Massachusetts liberal, as chairman of the Labor and Human Resources Committee, his staff had to train him to work legislation through his committee. "His mind-set of what you do in the Labor Committee is oppose Ted Kennedy," a senior Republican aide said. "Suddenly he had a big chunk of the Reagan program thrust on him, and he didn't know what to do." Other Republicans were accustomed to cutting personal deals with Democratic chairmen, but not to passing bills. Newcomers such as Alfonse D'Amato of New York, Robert Kasten of Wisconsin, or Paula Hawkins of Florida were suddenly thrust into being subcommittee chairs without a single day's experience in the Senate.

"The first thought on my personal agenda was whether or not we can turn these folks into a real majority, a functioning majority, instead of a numerical majority," Howard Baker told me later. "No single person in the Republican branch had ever been a committee chairman or a subcommittee chairman before. Brand new. We were going to have to reinvent the role of the majority party in the Senate. We were going to have to figure out if we have a permanent minority mind-set or whether we can pull together. . . . I perceived the greatest responsibility I had [was] to make the place work, because it could quickly have "devolved into chaos if we had two minority parties."

That is rule number two in forming a functioning coalition: *Inculcate the mind-set of governing.* It is a subtle, intangible notion ..one that comes naturally to parties long in power, but not to parties long out of power. Without that governing mind-set, little can be accomplished in our system; parties clash, factions stalemate each other, individual members of Congress push their agendas, selfish interests overwhelm the common interest, and the machinery of government is immobilized. . . .

It takes more than enthusiasm to consolidate power. In the king of the hill game, rule number three is: *Strike quickly for win, during the early rush of power.* That helps establish momentum and an aura of success. Lyndon Johnson had a colorful maxim for such moments. "Johnson operated under the philosophy with Congress—if you're not doing it to them, they're doing it to you. And frequently, he used a more vivid word than doing," recalled Douglass Cater, one of Johnson's White House advisers.

Winning is power, was the gut summation given me by Jim Baker. "I've always felt that it is extremely important in terms of a president's power—power as opposed to popularity—that presidents succeed on the Hill with what they undertake up there," Baker asserted. "And I really believe that one reason that Ronald Reagan has been so successful is that he succeeded in the high-profile issues that he jumped on in the first term. The way presidents govern is to translate their philosophy into policy by working with Congress. That's why Carter failed in my view. Because he never learned that lesson."

The image of success is crucial, as Dick Darman pointed out in a White House memo. On February 21, 1981, Darman told me that he had urged crafting a "plan for the preservation of the appearance of the president's continuing strength and effectiveness—the avoidance of association with 'losses,' the association with a planned string of 'successes.'"

* * *

Success in the coalition game depends enormously on presidential influence with the individual members of Congress; a president can pull enough reluctant votes his way if he has the right political touch. It is an old maxim of politics that an effective leader, mayor, governor, and above all, president, must be both loved and feared. That is how a president marshals support from his natural followers and deters attack from his natural enemies. Issues matter, of course, but so does human chemistry. A president has to make clear there are benefits for supporting him and consequences for opposing him.

No one understood this better than Lyndon Johnson, who was masterful at ferreting out the weak points and deepest hungers of other politicians. Yet Johnson was so blatantly Machiavellian that it hampered him. He made it hard for people to go along and still retain their dignity and independence. Carter had the opposite problem. Arm-twisting and deal-making were not his forte. When he tried to act strong, he often came across as mean and willful because exaggerated forcefulness was out of character.

At bottom, Carter seemed ill at ease with power, and ill at ease hobnobbing with other politicians. He immersed himself in substance but despised wheeling and dealing with Congress. Many a senator or House member told me that Carter was awkward or hesitant about asking directly for his or her vote. He frowned on horse-trading. Only from painful experience did he learn the value of doing little favors for other politicians. Both his intellect and his engineer's training at Annapolis made him impatient with that vital lubrication of the wheels of legislation: making other politicians feel important.

* * *

As Reagan roped together his first-year coalition, he profited greatly by striking contrasts with Jimmy Carter. It hardly requires much rehearsing of Reagan's Irish warmth and his love of personal banter to underscore the differences. Reagan is as comfortable shmoozing with other politicians as he is with power. He fitted the presidency easily, and that was reassuring to other politicians as well as to ordinary people. Reagan was far from perfect. I have heard Republicans such as Bob Packwood, Pete Domenici, and Warren Rudman bridling after a session with President Reagan because he read from his cue cards or, deflected serious discussion by repeating shopworn anecdotes about welfare queens supposedly defrauding tax-payers with high living. But in that first year, Reagan was in top form. He demonstrated rule number four in the coalition game: *Lavish attention on the Washington power structure.* Democrats were flattered to be courted. Republicans were tickled to walk away with a Reagan story to retell, or some Reagan cuff links, or tickets to the presidential box at the Kennedy Center. For a man who, like Carter, had run his campaign against Washington, Reagan did a quick 180-degree turn in catering to the Washington establishment. He mounted a mellow social and political campaign that set a Dale Carnegie (How to Win Friends and Influence People) standard. Shelving his campaign rhetoric, Reagan played the gracious outsider eager to win acceptance inside the beltway.

* * *

In the making of a majority coalition, a new president has the great advantage of casting his first major legislative proposal as a personal test of confidence in his presidency. The key to this strategy is rule number five of the coalition game: *Make the president himself the issue, as much as the substance of his proposals.* That strategy immediately puts the congressional opposition on the defensive. It makes voting against the new president almost like repudiating the results of the election just finished, which many politicians are loath to do.

Reagan was doubly armed for this strategy by his election victory and by surging public sympathy after the attempt on his life. Communications Director David Gergen shrewdly proposed that Reagan capitalize on the outpouring of public goodwill to make what amounted to a second Inaugural Address in 1981, to a joint session of Congress on April 28. It was a very powerful gambit. I remember Reagan that evening, striding confidently into the House, the picture of manly vigor and purpose, bathed in applause, acknowledging it with a frisky toss of his head. Democrats as well as Republicans were cheered by his recovery, warmed by his ruddy good humor. The country was so pro-Reagan then that it was easy for Reagan's lieutenants to frame virtually every vote for another hundred days on Reagan personally: Are you with Reagan or against him?

Republican control of the Senate in 1981 gave Reagan an excellent arena to work that strategy and an important advantage over Nixon, Ford, and Eisenhower, who had faced Democratic control of Congress except in Eisenhower's first two years.

In the Senate, it fell to Majority Leader Howard Baker to translate the "up-or-down strategy"—the strategy of a yes or no vote for Reagan—into tactics. . . .

Baker built his coalition around making all key votes a test of loyalty to the president, up or down. That was essential for pushing Reagan's ambitious budget cutting through Congress, for a budget is not just abstract figures—it is flesh-and-blood programs. A budget is a chart of national priorities, a menu of spending choices missiles vs. Medicare, Star Wars vs. student loans, aircraft carriers vs. Amtrak, farm-price supports and food stamps vs. F-18 jet fighters. In theory, everyone in Congress is for cutting the budget and the deficit, but in practice, all resist cutting programs that help their states or districts. That was the political habit that Baker wanted to override.

* * *

Rule number six: *Building a governing coalition hinges on a close working link between the president's top strategist and his party's congressional leaders.* The failures of Carter's aides, Hamilton Jordan and Frank Moore, demonstrated the cost of ignoring this link. In 1985 Reagan paid a high price for touchy relations between his new chief of staff, Don Regan, and Bob Dole, the new Senate majority leader. In his first term, Reagan had superb legislative liaisons led by Max Friedersdorf, a smooth diplomat from the Ford White House, and Ken Duberstein, an amiable, voluble political persuader, who worked the House. Reagan had a warm personal relationship with Howard Baker. But the crucial working alliance was between the two Bakers, Howard and Jim, who were constantly in touch.

"Jim Baker has a lot of great traits, but one is he can carry on a thirty-second conversation," Howard Baker said. "I place great value on the thirty-second conversation because my days were made up of hundreds of thirty-second conversations.

Both Jim and Howard Baker—no relation to each other—are mainstream Republicans, temperamentally disposed to compromise and to making the legislative system work. Both Bakers have that vital sense of what was politically doable and what was not. They loyally carried Reagan's water in public, but they argued with him in private, trying to save him from lost causes. Their pragmatic cast of mind made them natural allies and natural coalition makers. Neither was a true Reaganite; both had worked for Gerald Ford against Reagan in 1976 and had initially opposed Reagan in 1980. They had ties with other Republicans and could widen the circle of Reagan's support. Indeed, if it had been left to hard-core Reaganite ideologues such as Edwin Meese, William Clark, Lyn Nofziger, or Pat Buchanan to pass the first Reagan program, it probably would have been defeated. For ideological rigidity can derail even a partisan coalition, and both Bakers were masterful at bending at the margins and helping Reagan corral the final few votes needed for victory. . . .

The Senate provided Reagan with the cornerstone for his 1981 coalition, but the real challenge lay in the House, where Democrats outnumbered Republicans 243-192. How the Reaganites forged a House majority is a lesson in modern coalition building. To the steamroller tactic of reconciliation, the Reagan team added another tactic: the grass-roots-lobbying blitz. Rule number seven of the coalition game is: *Use the muscle of the president's nationwide political apparatus to swing votes into line for his legislative coalition.* The Reagan operation in 1981 was a textbook case of how to use campaign and lobbying techniques to produce a functioning coalition in Congress.

* * *

In the game of political persuasion, the Reagan White House took no chances. It played outside as well as inside politics, and it played hardball. Stockman lobbied his former allies in the Boll Weevil group. Reagan went public, stirring up popular support with nationally televised addresses. He sharpened the sense of economic crisis, focusing on the gloomy statistics of high inflation and economic stagnation. He bluntly reminded Congress on April 28 that it had been six months since his election and the people wanted action.

"The American people are slow to wrath but when their wrath is once kindled, it burns like a consuming flame," Reagan declared, quoting Theodore Roosevelt. "Well, perhaps that kind of wrath will be deserved," Reagan warned, if Congress resorted to "the old and comfortable way . . . to shave a little here and add a little there." His speech touched off an avalanche of mail to Congress. . . .

The Reagan team, working like a presidential campaign, generated direct mail, phone banks, radio and television ads, and sent out top speakers to put heat on targeted congressmen. They mobilized the Republican National Committee, Republican Congressional Campaign Committee, National Conservative Political Action Committee, Moral Majority, Fund for a Conservative Majority, and political action committees linked to the U.S. Chamber of Commerce, National Association of Manufacturers, Business Roundtable, American Medical Association, and scores of groups interested in cutting federal spending and taxes.

"The premise of the whole operation is that political reforms and the impact of media have made it so that a congressman's behavior on legislation can be affected more by pressure from within his own district than by lobbying here in Washington," Atwater told me during the operation. "The way we operate, within forty-eight hours any congressman will know he has had a major strike in his district. All of a sudden, Vice President Bush is in your district; Congressman Jack Kemp is in your district. Ten of your top contributors are calling you, the head of the local AMA, the head of the local realtors' group, local officials. Twenty letters come in. Within forty-eight hours, you're hit by paid media, free media, mail, phone calls, all asking you to support the president. . . .

Forming the coalition is only the first step; sustaining it long enough to lock up final legislative victory is much harder. In the American system, victory rarely ends the fight it marks the start of the next battle. This time, it was not Reagan's charm treatment or the grassroots blitz that rescued the Reagan coalition. It was old-fashioned, Lyndon Johnson-style barter politics: buying votes by doling out favors-what some call "running the soup kitchen." Rule number eight of the coalition game is: *Bend at the margins and wheedle votes where you can; don't get hung up on ideological purity.* Horse-trading is the way the battle is fought in the final clinches.

Reagan's battle was not over because entrenched committees of Congress resorted to intricate, arcane maneuvers to undo the effects of that first budget vote. The reconciliation measure passed required implementing by regular committees, and they had a field day with the fine print of the legislation, molding it their way. The White House was shocked to see conservative Republicans and Boll Weevils engaging in legislative chicanery along with liberal Democrats, all protecting their favorite programs. Many of the "cuts" enacted were empty numbers that reduced spending only in theory.

"Sabotage!" shouted David Stockman, himself no slouch at fudging budget numbers and tilting estimates when it suited him. In June 1981, he accused the committees of shady bookkeeping, false arithmetic, and phony cutbacks. Pro-Reagan Republicans and the Congressional Budget Office estimated that House committees cut $55 billion for the year 1984, but Stockman reckoned only $25 billion was valid.

In alarm, Stockman persuaded the president that he had to send another whole budget to Congress. "The committees have broken faith with the first budget resolution," Stockman told Reagan in mid-June. "It could jeopardize your entire economic program. We have to make a major fight to restore the provisions in your first budget. If you want to balance the budget in '84, you can't live with the cuts they've made."

Stockman secretly prepared a massive new reconciliation measure, a line-by-line substitute for the congressional bill. It was a high-handed tactic, because Congress—not the budget bureau—is supposed to draft money bills. It meant rejecting the congressional bills and making a fresh effort. Reagan went along with the plan, still counting on one up-or-down vote and the pull of his own popularity to preserve his coalition.

But it was now summer and the Reagan coalition had begun to fray. Moral appeals were not enough to restore it. The White House was short of votes. Gypsy Moths were threatening to bolt unless some modest programs favored in the urban East and Midwest were restored. New York's Bill Green wanted $50 million more for the National Endowment for the Arts, a higher cap on Medicaid for the poor, and guaranteed student loans provided to more families; Jim Leach of Iowa sought $100 million in family planning; Carl Pursell of Michigan wanted $50 million for nurses' training. Others wanted $100 million more for Amtrak and Conrail, another $400 million in energy subsidies for the poor, restoration of economic development grants, and so on. The White House paid their price to get their votes for the final budget package.

The Boll Weevils were demanding sweeteners, too. Georgia Democrats got state-owned cotton warehouses exempted from a new user fee. Some $400 million in cuts of veterans' programs were restored to satisfy Mississippi's Sonny Montgomery, a powerhouse for veterans. Louisiana's John Breaux was lured aboard with a promise to revive sugar import quotas to protect his home state.

"I went for the best deal," Breaux crassly admitted afterward. He maintained his vote had not been bought but he confessed—"I was rented."

The bargaining was like stock-market bidding, right to the wire. Ironically, to get votes, Stockman had to trade back to Congress things he had objected to in mid-June. The final budget was such a rush job that it reached the floor after the debate began, and it mistakenly listed the name and phone number of a congressional staffer—"Rita Seymour, 555-4844."—which someone had scribbled in the margin of a draft copy. Clearly, no one had proofread the retyped version. The critical test vote came on procedure, not substance. House Democratic leaders tried to outmaneuver the power of Reagan's single up-or-down vote. They figured Reagan's budget would be tougher to pass if it were broken into five packages, forcing Gypsy Moth Republicans and Boll Weevil Democrats to be counted on separate votes—and some of those votes were bound to be unpopular back home. Hoping to break up the Reagan coalition that way, Democratic leaders fashioned a procedural rule which divided the budget into five separate packages.

It was an ingenious tactic, but it backfired, because members wanted to avoid the wrath of constituents who were telling them: Cut the budget, but save our programs. One big vote spared House members that dilemma; it was politically easier to handle. (Rule number nine of the coalition game: *Make votes politically easy.*) Once the big package of cuts was fixed, members could not both cut the budget and save local programs; they had only one choice: yes or no. Since budget cutting was generally popular, they could justify swallowing some distasteful cuts. The Democratic tactic would expose members to cross-pressures to both cut and save programs; so it rankled many House members. As a result, the Gypsy Moths backed Reagan and just enough Boll Weevils defected to beat the Democratic procedural rule by the perilous margin of 217-210. A shift of four votes would have beaten Reagan and radically altered the outcome.

That procedural vote on June 25 was little understood by the public, but it demonstrated the power of technicalities: The vote on the "rule" (for handling the budget bill) framed the ultimate vote on the substance of the budget (one vote or five separate packages).

Defeat of the Democratic rule, moreover, solidified Reagan's coalition and shattered the Democratic leadership's control of the House. It cleared the way for Reagan, on the very next day, to win a similarly close victory on the biggest budget cuts ever enacted at one time.

THE PARADOX OF PRESIDENTIAL POWER

Godfrey Hodgson

Neither Genghis Khan, nor Alexander the Great, nor Napoleon, nor Louis XIV of France, had as much power as the President of the United States, whose acts or utterances might affect as many as one and one half billion people.

Harry S. Truman, in an interview with The New York Times, 1952

The principal power that the President has is to bring them in and try to persuade them to do what they ought to do without persuasion. That's what I spend most of the time doing. That's what the powers of the President amount to.

Harry S. Truman, in a speech on the national railroad strike, May, 1948.

The paradox of the presidency is simply stated—if hard to resolve. Never has any one office had so much power as the President of the United States possesses. Never has so powerful a leader been so impotent to do what he wants to do, what he is pledged to do, what he is expected to do, and what he knows he must do.

The disparity is not new. More than forty years ago Franklin Roosevelt heaved with a giant's strength against the bonds of the office and could not break them. The most even he could do was wriggle free a little some of the time. The tragedy of the presidency, he concluded, was the impotence of the President, and this was the man they accused of making himself into a dictator. All the strongest of his successors, Truman and Kennedy, Johnson and Nixon, have felt the same frustration and despair at the contrast between what people expect the President to be able to do and what he can actually achieve.

Over the years, the paradox—or apparent paradox—becomes more acute. The President still holds legitimate title to incomparable resources of power. Yet it is truer today than when Harry Truman left office that much of the time he is powerless to use that power.

His acts and utterances can still affect several billions of human beings. The economic resources, the technological creativity, the political influence, and the sheer military might of the United States are still superior to those of any rival power center. Yet the man who wields supreme authority over this unimaginably great complex of power still has to grab, as the political scientist Richard Neustadt once wrote of John F. Kennedy, "for just enough power to get by the next day's problems." Increasingly, it seems, his successors have been grabbing, and finding that their hands have closed on air; increasingly, they have simply failed to get through the next day's problems.

"The only power I've got is nuclear," Lyndon Johnson growled, "and I can't use that! He understood that the power Presidents do have, to alarming extent, is the power to do things that no one in his right mind would have them do: to declare martial law, to throw the world's currencies into chaos, to invade Cuba, blow up the Middle East oil fields, incinerate the Northern Hemisphere. The power that eludes them is the power to do the very things people expect them to do: to end inflation, to ensure law and order, to negotiate disarmament without endangering the United States, to end the energy crisis.

This frustrating contrast arises partly because the relative strength of the United States in the world has declined faster than Americans' perception of their strength. As a result, for all their arsenal of thunderbolts, Presidents find it harder and harder to induce foreigners to behave as Americans want them to behave. The President cannot prevent the rise in the price of oil, the fall of Saigon, the revolution in Iran, the invasion of Czechoslovakia or Afghanistan, or any of a dozen other unwelcome shifts in the political situation, here, there, or anywhere in Africa, Asia, or Latin America. He cannot persuade the Japanese to buy more American goods or the Europeans to sell fewer arms or nuclear power plants. Gone are the days when he could impose American standards or values even on friendly countries. He cannot be sure of persuading his European allies to do what he wants. And he must stand by while the Soviet Union implacably builds up its military strength and fishes in every troubled water from Afghanistan to Angola.

But his position in international affairs is almost enviable compared to his situation at home: so much so that a President in deadlock at home almost reflexively turns to what seem the easier problems of finding peace in the Middle East or redefining the West's relations with China At home, the President cannot seriously hope to persuade Congress to pass more than a wretched fragment of his legislative program, itself carefully tailored down from what he would have liked to see voted into law in a perfect world. He cannot hope to carry out more than a fraction of the program he campaigned and was elected on. Broad strategies of reform, liberal or conservative, are unthinkable. He will be lucky if he can cope with some of the most urgent items on the national agenda. He will do his best to manage the economy, though Congress can make fine tuning impossible and can rewrite legislation so as to give presidential initiatives the opposite effect to the one they were intended to have. He cannot end inflation. He cannot bring about a serious reduction in energy consumption or make more than a token start on the search for alternative energy sources. Still less can he hope to attack structural social or economic problems. Whether he is liberal or conservative, or even if—as seems increasingly inevitable—he is both at once, he is unlikely to be able to achieve his goals or to fulfill his promises. The more urgent a social or economic malady, the less reasonable has it become to imagine that the President will be able to reduce it, either with surgery or with medication, within his first term. . . .

It would be a mistake to expend too much concern on the paradox of presidential power in itself. Like most paradoxes, it can be made to vanish into thin air if its terms are analyzed with sufficient clarity. If the President has so much power, how can he be powerless? Is it not rather that his power is an illusion? Or that the power, alternatively, is real enough but does not really lie within the President's control? In part, the seeming paradox can be explained away by drawing a distinction between presidential powers and presidential power: the President may have vast powers in theory yet find them useless unless he can persuade others to execute them. In part, too, the paradox arises because people confuse the power of the United States with the power of the President, failing to realize that he has only limited possibilities of harnessing and commanding the nation's resources. . . .

I have spoken of "the President." I mean any President. Jimmy Carter has failed to make the presidency work. But he has fared no worse than Eisenhower or Kennedy or Johnson, far better than Nixon, better than Ford. There is no reason to suppose that any successor will fare any better than he has done. If we are to begin to understand why that is so, we ought to take a look now, not at the grand theory of the institution, but at a flesh-and-blood President; not at a moment of high and solemn drama, nor at a crisis when he was fighting for his political life with his back to the wall. Instead, let us look carefully at a President setting about a routine, though certainly not unimportant, piece of business at a time when things were going neither exceptionally well nor exceptionally badly for him. Let us try to analyze what his resources are for getting others to do what he wants them to do. The same realities have constrained all recent Presidents. Still, by way of example, let us take a close if slightly impressionistic look at Jimmy Carter in the White House, just before the midpoint of his first term, on the afternoon of Tuesday, September 26, 1978.

The East Room is the largest and most impressive room in the White House. It was formerly known as the "Public Audience room," and even if you happen to know that the John Adamses used it to hang up their washing, and that Franklin and Eleanor Roosevelt's boisterous children used it for roller skating, it still comes closer than any other room in the mansion to monarchical splendor. With something truly regal in the gracious sweep of his arm, George Washington bids the visitor welcome in the portrait by Gilbert Stuart which Dolley Madison personally rescued from the marauding Redcoats in 1814. A parquet floor, white Corinthian pilasters, gold damask curtains, and three brilliant chandeliers make it, as a nineteenth-century New England clergyman put it, "a seat worthy of the people's idol." Seven dead Presidents have lain in state here, including Lincoln and John Kennedy. On happier occasions, First Ladies have used it for their levees, receptions, concerts, and balls. And in recent times it has usually been from the East Room that Presidents have addressed the nation on television.

On this particular Tuesday afternoon, however, the East Room was being put to a more prosaic purpose: not pomp, but politics. Some three hundred guests, mostly middle-aged, predominantly male, and all unmistakably prosperous, were being shepherded to rows of elegant gilt chairs by military aides of both genders in crisply pressed white uniforms. In the pillared hall that leads into the East Room, three high officials who were scheduled to address the afternoon's meeting were chatting to pass the time until the meeting was due to begin. "Remember," said one of them, "about twenty percent of these people are against us!"

This not-wholly-reliable audience was made up, as it happened of hospital administrators. They had been dragooned to Washington from forty states at the suggestion of Anne Wexler, one of the President's political assistants. The purpose of this exercise of the presidential power to persuade was to try to convince a potentially influential group of opinion formers that the President was right and Congress wrong about the need for legislation to contain the rise of hospital bills. As a tactic, it bore a certain resemblance to the use of troop-carrying helicopters in what the military calls "vertical enfilade." Unable to make headway frontally against congressional resistance—in this as in many, many other matters—the President and his advisers were driven to try to leapfrog the congressional positions and take them in the rear.

The first speaker that afternoon was the Vice President, Walter F. Mondale. He went smoothly into a practiced routine of persuasion. Inflation was the nation's number one problem, he argued, and the inflation of hospital costs an important component cause of the general inflation rate. He appealed openly to the guests to go home and work on their congressmen. In effect, he was appealing over the heads of Congress to local opinion formers: to the director of the Baptist Medical Center of Little Rock, Arkansas, to the county commissioner of Summit County, Ohio, to the president of Blue Cross of Southern California, and all the others, in the hope of persuading them to go home and create a climate of opinion which congressmen, due to run for reelection only six weeks later, would not dare to ignore. After a few minutes of earnest admonition along these lines, the Vice President left to go to another meeting, trailing a small cloud of aides with him and shaking a surprising number of hands on his path to the door. "Nice to see *you*, sir," he was heard to say to one handshaker as he passed.

Mondale's place was taken by the President's top economic adviser, Charles L. Schultze. The cost of health care was rising at 15 percent each year, he began. "Think of the magic of exponential numbers!" Inflation was poisoning America. "You can only plan the future with dollars, and how do you plan the future with a yardstick that changes?" As an example, Schultze said that the increase in medical costs paid by an automobile manufacturer now added more to the price of a new car than the rise in the price of steel.

The third speaker was the under secretary of Health, Education, and Welfare, a plump, jovial Californian called Hale Champion. He came primed with flip charts and began attacking the counterarguments that would be made against the administration's case. The audience began to answer back. A lady from Florida said that controls were inflationary in themselves. Another woman, from Arizona, claimed that the Justice Department said that if the hospitals imposed voluntary restraints they could have antitrust problems. Champion was getting visibly annoyed and answered sharply that the Justice Department had said nothing of the kind.

The meeting did not seem to be going entirely according to plan.

A group of young men had gradually gathered outside the entrance to the East Room. White House staffers. I recognized Frank Moore, the President's top aide for congressional liaison, and then the President's closest aide, Hamilton Jordan himself, appeared. He was clowning a little, practicing putting shots in the air, and was surrounded by a respectful crowd of younger staffers.

Suddenly the chattering stopped.

A knot of men appeared at the opposite end of the corridor walking fast toward the crowd of White House staff. Several were Secret Service agents, identifiable by their dark suits and lapel pins. Some of them muttered self-importantly into walkie-talkies.

In the middle of them was a smallish, slim man with close-cropped gray hair, pale-blue eyes, and a nervous smile. He nodded absentmindedly to left and right as he hurried toward the rostrum.

A white-jacketed military aide, his hair shorn to the scalp, had just enough time to call out: "Ladies and gentlemen, the President of the United States!"

The atmosphere in the East Room changed subtly, as the atmosphere always changes when the President enters any room, even one filled with men and women he has known for years and sees every day.

A charge of emotional current passed.

The President spoke briefly, quietly, and to the point. He had mastered his brief, and he marshaled the arguments for holding down hospital costs as if there were nothing in the world dearer to his heart than that his hearers should go back to Little Rock, and Akron, and Los Angeles, and preach the gospel of cheaper health care.

His guests—even those who had voted for his opponent two years before and who, only a moment earlier, had been quite ready to heckle a high official of his administration—now listened respectfully, in silence, some even with a faint flush of excitement on their faces.

It was not that they were hearing from the President any arguments they had not already heard from the previous speakers. Most of them, certainly, were painfully familiar with all the arguments about hospital costs long before they were contacted by Anne Wexler's office and invited to the White House.

No: they were excited, almost deferential, because the man who was talking to them, who in a minute would find the time to stand in a receiving line in the state dining room, shake their hands, and murmur a perfunctory courtesy to each of them was the President.

What was taking place and in an infinitesimal way reproducing the essential reality of presidential power was a kind of trade.

This, really, was what they had flown to Washington for: to see the President in the knowledge that the encounter would be, as people say, "something to tell their grandchildren," a certain badge of social status, a small ratification of professional success. And in return the President expected them to go home and exert on his behalf their small quantum of influence on only one of the dozens of issues that he must be concerned with, to call their congressmen, or write a letter to the local paper, or at the very least to speak favorably in influential circles in their home city of what the President was trying to achieve. The President, in short, was seeking to exchange a small scintilla of the radiance of his office against the tiny parcel of influence each of his guests could bring him.

The President's fifteen-minute appearance at that particular meeting was somewhat casually billed on his schedule that day as a "drop-by briefing" on hospital cost containment, the last of nine official and many unofficial items on a schedule that kicked off with a briefing by the President's national security adviser, Zbigniew Brzezinski, at 7:15 A.M. There was nothing casual about it. The previous day a neatly typed, seventeen-page memorandum landed on the President's desk, initialed by Anne Wexler, by Frank Moore, and by his chief domestic policy adviser, Stuart Eizenstat. The memo spelled out to the President precisely why he was going to be at the meeting, who the other participants were and why they had been chosen, and what press arrangements had been made. Only a pool of White House correspondents would be at the meeting, but the President was warned that some reporters from hometown papers and health-trade-paper writers would stay for the whole meeting.

The President was provided with a complete list of all the participants and with a head count, four days old, on the position of all members of the U.S. Senate on the hospital costs issue, broken down into those who were "right," meaning in sympathy with the administration's position, "wrong," "leaning right," "leaning " wrong," and undecided. He was also given a two-page paper summarizing "talking points" his staff wanted him to bring out at the meeting. Nor did that exhaust the staff work that went into that single fifteen-minute appearance. Experts at the Council of Economic Advisers and the Department of Health, Education, and Welfare had briefed Schultze, Mondale, and Champion. The Vice President's staff had got in on the act. Three or four subunits in the White House, including Eizenstat's, Wexler's, and Moore's, had worked on the papers. And this, as we have seen, was only one of the President's multitude of concerns on that particular afternoon. . . .

Both the ceremonial prestige of the office and its institutional resources must be pressed into the service of what is an act of persuasion, not an act of imperative command. The President attempts to barter a part of his prestige and his authority in return for the sum of the microscopic quantities of indirect power which hospital administrators, for example, have to lend him. He is constrained to rely on personal persuasion, and indirect persuasion at that, because he has no other way of ensuring that the decisions he has taken are translated into political or executive action. If he wants to keep hospital costs down, he cannot order the hospital administrators to freeze charges, as he could as chief executive in many countries. Nor can he procure the passage of legislation to freeze those charges, as he could in many other countries where the chief executive is so by virtue of his control of the legislature. No great national bureaucracy can be relied on to carry his intentions to the remotest corners of the country. There is no great political party to generate political support for his plans. Painfully, precariously, and with infinite effort he must construct his own coalitions on each separate issue out of whatever sticks and string he finds to hand.

Above all, he must trade. A dozen times a day the President must routinely reinvest his stock of power and prestige—both the resources of the office on which he has a four-year lease and what he has accumulated by his own efforts. In return he hopes to win the support he will need to respond to other appeals for help. If he is successful, that will add to his reputation and lend him a further bonus of new power to stake. The ultimate rationale of all this merchant adventuring in the commodity of political credibility is the President's reelection: a renewed lease on the stock-in-trade and goodwill of the presidency for another four years' enterprise in the Washington marketplace.

* * *

The most elaborate cyclical analysis of the presidency was worked out by Stephen Hess in a book called *Organizing the Presidency*. Hess is a distinguished political scientist who has had the advantage of working in the White House, not merely under two different Presidents, Eisenhower and Nixon, but also at the two opposite ends of their terms: at the beginning of the Nixon administration and for the last two years of the second Eisenhower administration. He could therefore see clearly that while some of the differences between those two presidencies were to be explained in terms of the different political philosophies and temperaments of the two Presidents, or by the different assumptions and circumstances of the times, others seemed simply the product of the stage that had been reached in the life cycle of their two administrations. Hess believes that the point could be demonstrated by a year-by-year study of all presidencies, at least as far back as 1953. He has spelled out in some detail what might be called the natural history of a presidency.

All Presidents, when they enter the White House, are confronted by certain opportunities and by certain dangers by virtue of the mere fact that they are new. All Presidents and their staffs share an understandable arrogance. For at least two years their whole endeavors have been concentrated on one end, winning the presidency, and they have won it. They have succeeded where others have failed. Moreover, in the last months of the campaign, as their man emerged as a possible winner, they have been exposed to not a little flattery by the media and by those who hope to get favors from them. At the same time, all administrations tend to react directly against their predecessors. After all, one of the chief reasons why they are now in the White House, and their predecessors out, is because they knew how to campaign against their predecessors, their policies, their style, their conduct and all their works, in a way that evoked a favorable response from the electorate. So it is natural that they start off by trying to do the opposite of what the previous administration has done.

In spite of or perhaps because of this, every new President is granted a honeymoon. His first few months, Hess says, pass in a state of "euphoria." Congress is respectful. The media are willing to give him the benefit of the doubt. The new President becomes a national institution. He may even become a superstar.

Then, as his first year wears on, he has to do things: make appointments, take stands, propose legislation, react to crises at home and abroad. Every time he does something, he offends someone. A "coalition of minorities" begins to form against him. His administration, sometime in that first year, "has its first foreign crisis and its first domestic scandal." And the President's poll ratings start to drop. (The poll ratings of all recent Presidents have dropped at an average rate of six percentage points a year, with the sole exception of Eisenhower's, which rose during his first term at the rate of two and a half points a year.) "By the end of his first year," Hess went on, the President should have learned two important lessons: first, that the unexpected is likely to happen; second, that his plans are unlikely to work out as he had hoped. The Soviet Union launches Sputnik. A U-2 is shot down. There is an uprising in Hungary, a riot in Watts, a demonstration at Berkeley. . . . The President finds that much of his time is spent reacting to events over which he has no control or trying to correct the errors of others.

So Presidents start to "turn inward." They become resentful of the media and suspicious of their own cabinet. They begin to feel that if things are going to be done, they will have to do them themselves. They come to rely more and more on the White House staff, whose members are trusted, familiar old friends and who possess no rival power base that could enable them to resist the President's wishes.

By now, the midterm congressional elections are approaching. "The President tries to restore his luster at the polls. He always fails." (The only modern President to win seats for his party in both the Senate and the House was Franklin Roosevelt in 1934: an exception that proves the rule if ever there was one.)

In the third year, the President turns to foreign affairs. Perhaps as much as two-thirds of his time in that year is spent on foreign policy, Hess calculated. In part, he does so because he has to: there are foreign policy issues that cannot be avoided. But, as Hess put it, "He also turns to foreign policy because it is the area in which he has most authority to act and, until recently, the least public and congressional restraint on his actions." Besides, foreign policy offers the elusive reward of a statesman's place in the history books. In the third year, too, the exodus from government begins, as able and ambitious men, having enjoyed an experience of government, drift away to secure their futures. Divisions and dissensions in the administration become deeper and more envenomed.

In the fourth year, with equal abruptness, "the President's attention snaps back to domestic considerations." Now everything the administration does is conditioned by the President's desire to be reelected. He puts off ambitious but dangerous projects for reforms which he himself, only a few months earlier, had been urging his subordinates to press ahead with. He becomes more cautious, more concerned with bread-and-butter economic issues. He finds more and more excuses to make "nonpolitical" speeches around the country. By the summer of his fourth year he is blatantly, unashamedly running for office. . . .

That pattern has been one of frustration, disappointment, and failure. All Presidents enter the White House full of hope and honorable ambition. They have arrived there in large part because of their success in convincing the voters that they are capable of changing things. They want to improve the security and the standing of the United States in the world, to manage the economy and bring about greater prosperity, to "clean up the mess in Washington," to "get the country moving again," to "bring it together again," and to help it to "live up to its best ideals": in short, whatever the formula they have sold to the voters, they believe they can put right the wrongs left untouched by the ideological error or managerial incompetence of their predecessor. Conservative Presidents want to change things every bit as much as liberals, though of course they want to change different things. They find it equally hard to change anything.

* * *

The paradox of the presidency is that the office has at once too much power and too little. And so the crisis of the presidency over the past twenty years has been a crisis of effectiveness as well as a crisis of legitimacy.

CHAPTER 4

INTRODUCTION

An interesting irony of our political system is that the bureaucracy, an entity scarcely mentioned in the Constitution, now spends close to two trillion dollars annually and is comprised of better than four million military and civilian personnel. It takes little effort to locate bureaucracy "bashers" and the average American has little positive to say concerning the usefulness or the ability of the bureaucracy unless, of course, he/she needs something from the government. At that point, those "incompetent do-nothings" are expected to act quickly, purposefully and correctly. A monumental expectation, it seems to me, from a part of our government about which we speak so disdainfully.

So, what treats have I in store for you in this chapter? First, a piece from James Q. Wilson. He has written an excellent work which attempts to explain why the bureaucracy is the way it is. Some would probably call his work an apology for the bureaucracy, but I don't think so. While governmental bureaucracies share numerous characteristics with private sector bureaucracies, there are fundamental distinctions between them. And historically, efforts by the governmental bureaucracies to act like their private sector colleagues have normally resulted in complaints from the public, whining from the private sector and swift efforts by elected officials to override the bureaucracies' efforts. Look for the following in his article:

1. What are some similarities between public and private sector bureaucracies?

2. Name and explain the three key constraints faced by governmental bureaucracies.

3. How could one best evaluate the success or failure of a program or a bureaucratic unit?

Better than a century ago, then political scientist Woodrow Wilson said: *Administration lies outside the proper sphere of politics. Administrative questions are not political questions. Although politics sets the task for administration, it should not be suffered to manipulate its offices. The field of administration is a field of business. It is removed from the hurry and strife of politics*

While taken seriously at the time, it is not today. Instead, politicians, administrators, citizens and those who study politics and public administration wrestle with the relationship between elected officials and bureaucrats. What is the relationship between them in terms of policy making and how does the bureaucracy influence or perhaps even pre-determine the decisions made by elected officials. An interesting article by Ralph Hummel examines this relationship in some detail.

1. Why do Presidents sense that the bureaucracy pre-decides decisions by defining the problem?

2. In the minds of most people, does the bureaucracy properly perform its' functions most of the time?

3. How are bureaucratic structures superior to those of elected officials?

CONSTRAINTS

James Q. Wilson

By the time the office opens at 8:45 A.M., the line of people waiting to do business at the Registry of Motor Vehicles in Watertown, Massachusetts, often will be twenty-five deep. By midday, especially if it is near the end of the month, the line may extend clear around the building. Inside, motorists wait in slow-moving rows before poorly marked windows to get a driver's license or to register an automobile. When someone gets to the head of the line, he or she is often told by the clerk that it is the wrong line: "Get an application over there and then come back," or "This is only for people getting a new license; if you want to replace one you lost, you have to go to the next window." The customers grumble impatiently. The clerks act harried and sometimes speak brusquely, even rudely. What seems to be a simple transaction may take 45 minutes or even longer. By the time people are photographed for their driver's licenses, they are often scowling. The photographer valiantly tries to get people to smile, but only occasionally succeeds.

Not far away, people also wait in line at a McDonald's fast-food restaurant. There are several lines; each is short, each moves quickly. The menu is clearly displayed on attractive signs. The workers behind the counter are invariably polite. If someone's order cannot be filled immediately, he or she is asked to step aside for a moment while the food is prepared and then is brought back to the head of the line to receive the order. The atmosphere is friendly and good-natured. The room is immaculately clean. Many people have noticed the difference between getting a driver's license and ordering a Big Mac. Most will explain it by saying that bureaucracies are different from businesses. "Bureaucracies" behave as they do because they are run by unqualified "bureaucrats" and are enmeshed in "rules" and "red tape."

But business firms are also bureaucracies, and McDonald's is a bureaucracy that regulates virtually every detail of its employees' behavior by a complex and all-encompassing set of rules. Its operations manual is six hundred pages long and weighs four pounds. In it one learns that french fries are to be nine-thirty-seconds of an inch thick and that grill workers are to place hamburger patties on the grill from left to right, six to a row for six rows. They are then to flip the third row first, followed by the fourth, fifth, and sixth rows, and finally the first and second. The amount of sauce placed on each bun is precisely specified. Every window must be washed every day. Workers must get down on their hands and knees and pick up litter as soon as it appears. These and countless other rules designed to reduce the workers to interchangeable automata were inculcated in franchise managers at Hamburger University located in a $40 million facility. There are plenty of rules governing the Registry, but they are only a small fraction of the rules that govern every detail of every operation at McDonald's. Indeed, if the DMV manager tried to impose on his employees as demanding a set of rules as those that govern the McDonald's staff, they would probably rebel and he would lose his job.

It is just as hard to explain the differences between the two organizations by reference to the quality or compensation of their employees. The Registry workers are all adults, most with at least a high-school education; the McDonald's employees are mostly teenagers, many still in school. The Registry staff is well-paid compared to the McDonald's workers, most of whom receive only the minimum wage. When labor shortages developed in Massachusetts during the mid-1980s, many McDonald's stores began hiring older people (typically housewives) of the same sort who had long worked for the Registry. They behaved just like the teenagers they replaced.

Not only are the differences between the two organizations not to be explained by reference to "rules" or "red tape" or "incompetent workers," the differences call into question many of the most frequently mentioned complaints about how government agencies are supposed to behave. For example: "Government agencies are big spenders." The Watertown office of the Registry is in a modest building that can barely handle its clientele. The teletype machine used to check information submitted by people requesting a replacement license was antiquated and prone to errors. Three or four clerks often had to wait in line to use equipment described by the office manager as "personally signed by Thomas Edison." No computers or word processors were available to handle the preparation of licenses and registrations; any error made by a clerk while manually typing a form meant starting over again on another form.

Or: "Government agencies hire people regardless of whether they are really needed." Despite the fact that the citizens of Massachusetts probably have more contact with the Registry than with any other state agency, and despite the fact that these citizens complain more about Registry service than about that of any other bureau, the Watertown branch, like all Registry offices, was seriously understaffed. In 1981, the agency lost 400 workers—about 25 percent of its work force—despite the fact that its workload was rising.

Or: "Government agencies are imperialistic, always grasping for new functions." But there is no record of the Registry doing much grasping, even though one could imagine a case being made that the state government could usefully create at Registry offices "one-stop" multi-service centers where people could not only get drivers' licenses but also pay taxes and parking fines, obtain information, and transact other official business. The Registry seemed content to provide one service.

In short, many of the popular stereotypes about government agencies and their members are either questionable or incomplete. To explain why government agencies behave as they do, it is not enough to know that they are "bureaucracies"—that is, it is not enough to know that they are big, or complex, or have rules. What is crucial is that they are government bureaucracies. As the preceding chapters should make clear, not all government bureaucracies behave the same way or suffer from the same problems. There may even be registries of motor vehicles in other states that do a better job than the one in Massachusetts. But all government agencies have in common certain characteristics that tend to make their management far more difficult than managing a McDonald's. These common characteristics are the constraints of public agencies.

The key constraints are three in number. To a much greater extent than is true of private bureaucracies, government agencies (1) cannot lawfully retain and devote to the private benefit of their members the earnings of the organization, (2) cannot allocate the factors of production in accordance with the preferences of the organization's administrators, and (3) must serve goals not of the organization's own choosing. Control over revenues, productive factors, and agency goals is all vested to an important degree in entities external to the organization—legislatures, courts, politicians, and interest groups. Given this, agency managers must attend to the demands of these external entities. As a result, government management tends to be driven by the constraints on the organization, not the tasks of the organization. To say the same thing in other words, whereas business management focuses on the "bottom line" (that is, profits), government management focuses on the "top line" (that is, constraints). Because government managers are not as strongly motivated as private ones to define the tasks of their subordinates, these tasks are often shaped by the factors described in the preceding four chapters.

In the days leading up to September 30, the federal government is Cinderella, courted by legions of individuals and organizations eager to get grants and contracts from the unexpended funds still at the disposal of each agency. At midnight on September 30, the government's coach turns into a pumpkin. That is the moment—the end of the fiscal year—at which every agency, with a few exceptions, must return all unexpended funds to the Treasury Department. . . .

Nor can individual bureaucrats lawfully capture for their personal use any revenue surpluses. When a private firm has a good year, many of its officers and workers may receive bonuses. Even if no bonus is paid, these employees may buy stock in the firm so that they can profit from any growth in earnings (and, if they sell the stock in a timely manner, profit from a drop in earnings). Should a public bureaucrat be discovered trying to do what private bureaucrats routinely do, he or she would be charged with corruption. . . .

. . . These changes reflect our desire to eliminate moral hazards–namely, creating incentives for people to act wrongly. But why should this desire rule out more carefully designed compensation plans that would pay government managers for achieving officially approved goals and would allow efficient agencies to keep any unspent part of their budget for use next year?

Part of the answer is obvious. Often we do not know whether a manager or an agency has achieved the goals we want because either the goals are vague or inconsistent, or their attainment cannot be observed, or both. Bureau chiefs in the Department of State would have to go on welfare if their pay depended on their ability to demonstrate convincingly that they had attained their bureaus' objectives. . . .

The closest we can come to supplying a nonpolitical, nonarbitrary evaluation of an organization's performance is by its ability to earn from customers revenues in excess of costs. This is how business firms, private colleges, and most hospitals are evaluated. But government agencies cannot be evaluated by this market test because they either supply a service for which there are no willing customers (for example, prisons or the IRS) or are monopoly suppliers of a valued service (for example, the welfare department and the Registry of Motor Vehicles). Neither an organization with unwilling customers nor one with the exclusive right to serve such customers as exist can be evaluated by knowing how many customers they attract. When there is no external, nonpolitical evaluation of agency performance, there is no way to allow the agency to retain earnings that is not subject to agency manipulation.

If neither agencies nor their managers can appropriate surplus revenues for their own benefit, few agencies will try to produce surpluses by economizing on expenditures; instead, one would expect them to be spendthrifts. Within the limits of their appropriations and other applicable laws, they are. Grant-giving and contract-letting agencies in particular spend furiously every September. Economist William Niskanen, among others, has generalized this observation into a theory of bureaucratic behavior. He assumes that bureaus wish to maximize the size of their appropriations and that the legislature, though it does not want to spend any more than it has to, has no way of knowing how much it actually costs the bureaus to produce each additional unit of output (for example, dollars per additional letter delivered, bomb dropped, or crime prevented). As a result, each bureau will get a much bigger appropriation than it "needs"—that is, a bigger one than a well-informed legislature would supply. Thus, bureaucratic government means expensive government.

In chapter 13 we shall look more closely at these assumptions. For now it is enough to note the many and obvious exceptions to the Niskanen prediction. The Massachusetts Registry of Motor Vehicles does not have lavish offices, large staffs, nor expensive computers. In comparison to even a small insurance company, its facilities are spartan. The Social Security Administration occupies a large office-building complex, but the interior appointments are modest and the office spaces cramped. In almost every state, prisons are overcrowded. In Boston, the police occupy the same headquarters building in which they have worked since 1925; meanwhile, all about it there have risen new and luxurious office buildings to accommodate business firms. In the Pentagon, major generals sit in offices that the chief teller of a small bank would regard as claustrophobic. Having taught at both public and private universities, there is little doubt in my mind that the latter supply their faculty with nicer offices and more amenities than the former. . . .

If the bureaucrats are numerous, well-organized, and found in many districts (for example, letter carriers in the old Post Office Department or sanitation workers in New York City) they may have enough leverage to insure that their benefits increase faster than their workload. But even numerous and organized bureaucrats labor under a strategic disadvantage arising from the fact that legislators find it easier to constrain bureaucratic inputs than bureaucratic outputs. The reasons are partly conceptual, partly political. Conceptually, an office building or pay schedule is a tangible input, easily understood by all; "good health" or a "decent retirement" or an "educated child" are matters of opinion. Politically, legislators face more or less steady pressures to keep tax rates down while allowing program benefits to grow. The conceptual ambiguities combine neatly with the political realities: The rational course of action for a legislator is to appeal to taxpayers by ostentatiously constraining the budget for buildings, pay raises, and managerial benefits while appealing to program beneficiaries by loudly calling for more money to be spent on health, retirement, or education. (Witness the difficulty schoolteachers have in obtaining pay increases without threatening a strike, even at a time when expenditures on education are growing.) As a result, there are many lavish programs in this country administered by modestly paid bureaucrats working on out-of-date equipment in cramped offices. . . .

A business firm acquires capital by retaining earnings, borrowing money, or selling shares of ownership; a government agency (with some exceptions) acquires capital by persuading a legislature to appropriate it. A business firm hires, promotes, demotes, and fires personnel with considerable though not perfect freedom; a federal government agency is told by Congress how many persons it can hire and at what rate of pay, by the Office of Personnel Management (OPM) what rules it must follow in selecting and assigning personnel, by the Office of Management and Budget (OMB) how many persons of each rank it may employ, by the Merit Systems Protection Board (MSPB) what procedures it must follow in demoting or discharging personnel, and by the courts whether it has faithfully followed the rules of Congress, OPM, OMB, and MSPB. A business firm purchases goods and services by internally defined procedures (including those that allow it to buy from someone other than the lowest bidder if a more expensive vendor seems more reliable), or to skip the bidding procedure altogether in favor of direct negotiations; a government agency must purchase much of what it uses by formally advertising for bids, accepting the lowest, and keeping the vendor at arm's length. When a business firm develops a good working relationship with a contractor, it often uses that vendor repeatedly without looking for a new one; when a government agency has a satisfactory relationship with a contractor, ordinarily it cannot use the vendor again without putting a new project out for a fresh set of bids. When a business firm finds that certain offices or factories are no longer economical it will close or combine them; when a government agency wishes to shut down a local office or military base often it must get the permission of the legislature (even when formal permission is not necessary, informal consultation is). When a business firm draws up its annual budget each expenditure item can be reviewed as a discretionary amount (except for legally mandated payments of taxes to government and interest to banks and bondholders); when a government agency makes up its budget many of the detailed expenditure items are mandated by the legislature.

All these complexities of doing business in or with the government are well-known to citizens and firms. These complexities in hiring, purchasing, contracting, and budgeting often are said to be the result of the "bureaucracy's love of red tape." But few, if any, of the rules producing this complexity would have been generated by the bureaucracy if left to its own devices, and many are as cordially disliked by the bureaucrats as by their clients. These rules have been imposed on the agencies by external actors, chiefly the legislature. They are not bureaucratic rules but political ones. In principle the legislature could allow the Social Security Administration, the Defense Department, or the New York City public school system to follow the same rules as IBM, General Electric, or Harvard University. In practice they could not. The reason is politics, or more precisely, democratic politics.

The differences are made clear in Steven Kelman's comparison of how government agencies and private firms buy computers. The agency officials he interviewed were much less satisfied with the quality of the computers and support services they purchased than were their private counterparts. The reason is that private firms are free to do what every householder does in buying a dishwasher or an automobile—look at the past performance of the people with whom he or she previously has done business and buy a new product based on these judgments. Contrary to what many people suppose, most firms buying a computer do not write up detailed specifications and then ask for bids, giving the contract to the lowest bidder who meets the specifications. Instead, they hold conversations with a computer manufacturer with whom they, or other firms like them, have had experience. In these discussions they develop a sense of their needs and form a judgment as to the quality and reliability of the people with whom they may do business. When the purchase is finally made, only one firm may be asked to bid, and then on the basis of jointly developed (and sometimes rather general) guidelines.

No government purchasing agent can afford to do business this way. He or she would be accused (by unsuccessful bidders and their congressional allies) of collusion, favoritism, and sweetheart deals. Instead, agencies must either ask for sealed bids or for competitive written responses to detailed (very detailed) "requests for proposals" (RFPs). The agencies will not be allowed to take into account past performance or intangible managerial qualities. As a result, the agencies must deny themselves the use of the most important information someone can have—judgment shaped by personal knowledge and past experience. Thus, the government often buys the wrong computers from unreliable suppliers. But as we shall see in a moment, Congress—whatever it may claim—values "fairness" over effectiveness.

From the founding of the republic until 1971 the Post Office Department was a cabinet agency wholly subordinate to the president and Congress. As such it received its funds from annual appropriations, its personnel from presidential appointments and civil service examinations, and its physical plant from detailed political decisions about the appropriate location of post offices. Postal rates were set by Congress after hearings dominated by organized interests that mail in bulk (for example, directmail advertisers and magazine publishers) and influenced by an awareness of the harmful political effects of raising the rates for first-class letters mailed by individual citizens (most of whom voted). Congress responded to these pressures by keeping rates low (though never low enough to mollify the competing interests) and making up the difference between what the department earned from rates and paid in expenses by providing heavy subsidies drawn from general tax revenues (it was easier politically to hide larger appropriations that usually were not accompanied by a tax increase than higher rates that of course were translated immediately into prices customers had to pay). The wages of postal employees were set with an eye on the political power of the unions representing those employees: Congress rarely forgot that there were hundreds of organized letter carriers in every congressional district.

In 1971, the Post Office Department was transformed into the United States Postal Service (USPS), a semiautonomous government corporation. The USPS is headed by an eleven-member board of governors, nine appointed by the president and confirmed by the Senate; these nine then appoint a postmaster general and a deputy postmaster general. It derives its revenues entirely from the prices it charges and the money it borrows rather than from congressional appropriations (though subsidies still were paid to the USPS during a transition period). The postal rates are set not by Congress but by the USPS itself, guided by a legislative standard (the USPS must break even and each class of mail it handles must bear its proportionate share of the service's costs) and an independent advisory body (the Postal Rate Commission, which makes recommendations as to what the rates should be). No longer—in theory—are the prices charged for one class of mail (say, first-class letters) used to subsidize the rates charged for another class (say, second-class books and magazines). The USPS has its own personnel system, separate from that of the rest of the federal government, and bargains directly with its own unions.

Having loosened some of the constraints upon it, the Postal Service was able to do things that in the past it could do only with great difficulty if at all. John Tierney has described the changes. When it was still a regular government department, a small local post office could only be closed after a bitter fight with the member of Congress from the affected district. As a result, few were closed. After the reorganization, the number closed increased: Between 1976 and 1979, the USPS closed about twenty-four a year; between 1983 and 1986, it closed over two hundred a year. The service developed a formula by which to allocate costs to various classes of mail (and thus to allocate prices to various classes of users); despite interest-group opposition the Supreme Court has upheld the formula. When the old Post Office, in the interest of cutting costs, tried to end the custom of delivering mail to each recipient's front door and instead proposed to deliver mail (at least in new suburban communities) either to the curbside or to "cluster boxes," intense pressure on Congress forced the department to abandon the idea. By 1978 the USPS had acquired enough autonomy to implement the idea despite continued congressional grumblings. Because the USPS can raise its own capital by issuing bonds it has been able to forge ahead with the automation of mail-sorting procedures. It now has hundreds of sophisticated optical scanners and barcode readers that enable employees to sort mail much faster than before. By 1986 optical character readers were processing 90 million pieces of mail a day. Finally, despite political objections, the USPS was slowly expanding the use of the nine-digit zip code.

In short, acquiring greater autonomy increased the ability of the Postal Service to acquire, allocate, and control the factors of production. More broadly, the whole tone of postal management changed. It began to adopt corporate-style management practices, complete with elaborate "mission statements," glossy annual reports, a tightened organizational structure, and an effort to decentralize some decisions to local managers.

* * *

An agency's primary goal may be clear or vague, but its primacy usually is not in dispute. "Educate children," "prevent crime," "maintain relations with other nations"—ambiguous as these objectives may be, they nonetheless justify the existence of school systems, police forces, and the State Department.

But these primary goals are not the only ones an agency is expected to serve. In addition it must serve a large number of contextual goals—that is, descriptions of desired states of affairs other than the one the agency was brought into being to create. For example, a police department not only must try to prevent crime and catch criminals, it must protect the rights of the accused, safeguard the confidentiality of its records, and provide necessary health services to arrestees. These other goals define the context within which the primary goals can be sought.

The number and importance of contextual goals has risen dramatically in recent years. The Administrative Procedure Act (APA), passed in 1946, requires most federal agencies to observe certain standards of procedural fairness. They cannot adopt a new rule or policy without first giving written notice of their intention to do so (usually by publishing a "notice of proposed rulemaking" in the Federal Register) and soliciting comments from interested parties. If the agencies hold hearings, they must allow interested parties to appear and introduce evidence. In 1981, President Reagan required that the regulations an agency proposed to adopt also would have to be submitted to the Office of Information and Regulatory Affairs in the Office of Management and Budget. OMB had the power to block regulations if in its judgment the costs exceeded the benefits.

The Freedom of Information Act (FOIA), passed in 1966-67 and amended in 1986, gives citizens the right to inspect almost all government records with the exception of military, intelligence, trade secrets, and those files the disclosure of which reasonably could be expected to constitute an invasion of privacy or compromise a law-enforcement investigation. Even these exceptions are not absolute. For example, in response to an FOIA request the FBI must supply all of the requested documents after blacking out those specific words and sentences containing protected information, but a shrewd reader often can infer the deleted material from the context. To reduce even further the chances that an agency can manipulate the FOIA to its own advantage, the law requires the agency to prove that it need not release the information (rather than requiring the citizen to prove that it should release it). The Privacy Act, passed in 1974, created elaborate safeguards for insuring the confidentiality of the files the government keeps on individual citizens, such as Social Security, law enforcement, and personnel records. The open-meeting or "Government in the Sunshine" act, passed in 1976, requires that "every portion of every meeting of any agency shall be open to public observation" unless certain specified matters (such as military or trade secrets or private personnel records) are to be discussed. The National Environmental Policy Act (NEPA), passed in 1969, requires all federal agencies (and many others as well) to take into account the environmental consequences of their actions by preparing, among other things, an environmental impact statement before undertaking "any major Federal action significantly affecting the quality of the human environment. . . .

The existence of so many contextual goals and political constraints has several consequences for the management of public agencies. First, managers have a strong incentive to worry more about constraints than tasks, which means to worry more about processes than outcomes. Outcomes often are uncertain, delayed, and controversial; procedures are known, immediate, and defined by law or rule. It is hard to hold managers accountable for attaining a goal, easy to hold them accountable for conforming to the rules. Even when a bureau's primary goals are clear and progress toward them measurable, the managers of the bureau cannot be content with achieving them with the least use of resources; they also must worry about serving the contextual goals of the agency. These contextual goals are defended by powerful interests or by individuals and groups with access to important centers of power—the courts and congressional committees. The Army Corps of Engineers can describe exactly how a dam should be built and verify that it was built that way, but woe betide it if it goes ahead with the dam without extensive public consultation and close attention to environmental issues.

Second, the multiplicity of constraints on an agency enhances the power of potential intervenors in the agency. Every constraint or contextual goal is the written affirmation of the claim of some external constituency. Thus the agency has weak boundaries and a large, variegated "membership" consisting of all who have a stake in the maintenance of one or more constraints. In the United States, where courts have great authority and access to them is relatively easy, the multiplication of constraints enhances the power of the courts over bureaucratic processes. If an agency is bound by a procedural rule, such as the obligation to hold hearings, people affected by that agency's decisions can enforce the procedural rule by going to court. The rules have conferred rights; courts exist to enforce rights. If an interest (say, the clean-air interest) has acquired special legal status, then that claim to a special status can be enforced by appeal to the courts. Between 1963 and 1983, the number of appeals from the decisions of federal administrative agencies heard by U.S. courts of appeal nearly tripled.

Third, equity is more important than efficiency in the management of many government agencies. This follows from the first two consequences: if managers must follow the correct procedures and if courts exist to enforce those procedures, then a procedural rule often will be defended by claiming that it is essential to the fair or equitable treatment of agency members or clients. Equity issues always seem easier to judge than efficiency issues: We cannot easily say whether the pupils were educated, the streets made safer, or some diseases prevented; but we can say whether every pupil got the same textbook, every citizen got the same police response, and every patient got the same vaccine.

Some consequences of allowing equity issues to govern bureaucratic decisions can be seen in the differences between public and private agencies that handle juvenile delinquents. David Street, Robert Vinter, and Charles Perrow studied three institutions of each kind and found that public institutions had much greater difficulty in controlling their inmates than private ones. The reason was that the public institutions had to take any delinquent referred to them by the courts, whereas the private ones were free to select the kinds of delinquents they would accept. (They used this freedom to reject "difficult" cases: One excluded sex offenders and another violent ones.) The consequence of the differences in intake could be traced through every aspect of the management of the institutions. Given their heterogeneous, somewhat dangerous clientele, the public agencies emphasized custody and discipline and gave managerial power to staff members whose duty it was to maintain control. With their more homogeneous and tractable inmates, the private agencies emphasized therapy and rehabilitation and gave managerial power to members of the treatment staff. (The study is silent on whether the emphasis on rehabilitation actually produced any; judging from studies of other programs it is unlikely.)

Fourth, the existence of many contextual goals, like the existence of constraints on the use of resources, tends to make managers more risk averse. Police administrators rarely lose their jobs because the crime rate has gone up or win promotions because it has gone down. They can easily lose their jobs if somebody persuasively argues that the police department has abused a citizen, beaten a prisoner, or failed to answer a call for service. School administrators rarely lose their jobs when their pupils' reading scores go down or win promotions when scores go up. But they can lose their jobs or suffer other career-impeding consequences if students are punished, controversial textbooks assigned, or parents treated impolitely. Under these circumstances it is hardly surprising that police captains spend a lot of their time trying to make certain that their officers follow the rules and that school principals spend a lot of their time cultivating the goodwill of parents.

Fifth, standard operating procedures (SOPs) are developed in each 'agency to reduce the chance that an important contextual goal or constraint is not violated. All large bureaucracies have SOPs; public bureaucracies have many more because in addition to the managerial problems that arise out of size and complexity they must conform to the politically enforceable constraints asserted by external constituencies. As we shall see in later chapters, rules can multiply to the point where no action at all is possible if every action must conform to every rule. Nonetheless rules persist, both as a written commitment to respect the claims of constituencies and as a device to punish operators who upset those constituencies.

Sixth, public agencies will have more managers than private ones performing similar tasks. More constraints require more managers to observe and enforce them. Mark A. Emmert and Michael M. Crow compared forty-one governmental research and development (R&D) laboratories with forty-six private ones. The R&D labs were about the same size and age, but the ratio of administrators to total staff was much higher (almost twice as high) in the public than in the private ones. Government bureaucracies are more "bureaucratic" than industrial ones in large part because we—the people and our political representatives—insist that they be.

Finally, the more contextual goals and constraints that must be served the more discretionary authority in an agency is pushed upward to the top. In most organizations, front-line operators are in a better position to exercise judgment about operating problems than upper-level managers, who can know of a problem, if at all, only through delayed and much-condensed reports. It is easier to allow front-line operators to exercise discretion when only one clear goal is to be attained. The greater the number and complexity of those goals, the riskier it is to give authority to operators. Thus, public agencies, though often they acknowledge the principle of decentralization, more often act on the principle of centralization. If the administrator is going to get into trouble for what an operator does, the former will find ways of making the decision for the latter. . . .

The late Professor Wallace Sayre once said that public and private management is alike in all unimportant respects. . . .

. . . What distinguishes public from private organizations is neither their size nor their desire to "plan" (that is, control) their environments but rather the rules under which they acquire and use capital and labor. General Motors acquires capital by selling shares, issuing bonds, or retaining earnings; the Department of Defense acquires it from an annual appropriation by Congress. GM opens and closes plants, subject to certain government regulations, at its own discretion; DOD opens and closes military bases under the watchful guidance of Congress. GM pays its managers with salaries it sets and bonuses tied to its earnings; DOD pays its managers with salaries set by Congress and bonuses (if any) that have no connection with organizational performance. The number of workers in GM is determined by its level of production; the number in DOD by legislation and civil-service rules.

What all this means can be seen by returning to the Registry of Motor Vehicles and McDonald's. Suppose you were just appointed head of the Watertown office of the Registry and you wanted to improve service there so that it more nearly approximated the service at McDonald's. Better service might well require spending more money (on clerks, equipment, and buildings). Why should your political superiors give you that money? It is a cost to them if it requires either higher taxes or taking funds from another agency; offsetting these real and immediate costs are dubious and postponed benefits. If lines become shorter and clients become happier, no legislator will benefit. There may be fewer complaints, but complaints are episodic and have little effect on the career of any given legislator. By contrast, shorter lines and faster service at McDonald's means more customers can be served per hour and thus more money can be earned per hour. A McDonald's manager can estimate the marginal product of the last dollar he or she spends on improving service; the Registry manager can generate no tangible return on any expenditure he or she makes and thus cannot easily justify the expenditure.

Improving service at the Registry may require replacing slow or surly workers with quick and pleasant ones. But you, the manager, can neither hire nor fire them at will. You look enviously at the McDonald's manager who regularly and with little notice replaces poor workers with better ones. Alternatively, you may wish to mount an extensive training program (perhaps creating a Registration University to match McDonald's Hamburger University) that would imbue a culture of service in your employees. But unless the Registry were so large an agency that the legislature would neither notice nor care about funds spent for this purpose—and it is not that large—you would have a tough time convincing anybody that this was not a wasteful expenditure on a frill project.

If somehow your efforts succeed in making Registry clients happier, you can take vicarious pleasure in it; in the unlikely event a client seeks you out to thank you for those efforts, you can bask in a moment's worth of glory. Your colleague at McDonald's who manages to make customers happier may also derive some vicarious satisfaction from the improvement but in addition he or she will earn more money owing to an increase in sales.

In time it will dawn on you that if you improve service too much, clients will start coming to the Watertown office instead of going to the Boston office. As a result, the lines you succeeded in shortening will become longer again. If you wish to keep complaints down, you will have to spend even more on the Watertown office. But if it was hard to persuade the legislature to do that in the past, it is impossible now. Why should the taxpayer be asked to spend more on Watertown when the Boston office, fully staffed (naturally, no one was laid off when the clients disappeared), has no lines at all? From the legislature's point of view the correct level of expenditure is not that which makes one office better than another but that which produces an equal amount of discontent in all offices.

Finally, you remember that your clients have no choice: The Registry offers a monopoly service. It and only it supplies drivers' licenses. In the long run all that matters is that there are not "too many" complaints to the legislature about service. Unlike McDonald's, the Registry need not fear that its clients will take their business to Burger King or to Wendy's. Perhaps you should just relax. . . .

Bureaucracy as Polity

Ralph P. Hummel

Max Weber:

In a modern state, the actual ruler is necessarily and unavoidably the bureaucracy.

In a world of bureaucracy, administration replaces politics. As citizens accept bureaucratic values, they begin to judge the performance of politicians according to bureaucratic standards. Bureaucracies move into this field of opportunity. They begin successfully competing with political institutions. These now must measure up to rationalized standards in the shaping of issues and the making of policy. Inside bureaucracy itself, subordinates are told that politics has no place there; and everywhere they are discouraged from taking politics into the workplace. Yet they find politics whenever and wherever their managers make decisions. Politics seems to continue to exist within bureaucracy—except now citizens and the ordinary rank-and-file bureaucrat feel excluded from it. Bureaucratization conceals and denies the political experience.

At the same time, especially private bureaucracies are beginning to recognize the fact that their participation in a bureaucratic politics alone cannot solve problems of survival. Such problems emanate from those sources of "irrationality" that continue to exist in the increasingly rationalized world. Unrationalized international money markets and free trade cause troubles for American industry, accidentally giving a head start to the Japanese competition. Unrationalized citizens increasingly make new political demands on a system in which the bureaucrats thought they had figured out all the problems and were controlling all the answers. Here technology—rationalized science—seems to play a role: leading humanity into situations—such as the artificial prolongation of life or its artificial termination—for which there has been no previous human experience. As the fundamental questions of human life—What is it all about? What is the good life?—keep being reasserted, bureaucracies themselves initiate a third form of politics, neither traditionally political nor purely bureaucratic. . . . How can we make sense of these developments in the confrontation between politics and the bureaucratic experience?

* * *

PRESIDENTS

Even top politicians, the leaders of America, seem to notice that before they can get to an issue bureaucracy has already been there.

John F. Kennedy:

Sooner or later it seems that every problem mankind is faced with gets dumped into the lap of the president right here in the center of it all. But by the time it reaches here, the problem has been dissected, sanitized, and cast into a series of options—almost as though they were engraved in stone. What is missing is the heart behind them, what they mean in human terms.

President John F. Kennedy's complaints—that problems have been "dissected, sanitized, and cast into a series of options" long before reaching the White House—do not stand alone. If agencies and staff purportedly under the command of the chief executive are capable of pre-decision-making because of their superior knowledge and information about problems, they are also entirely capable of independent decision-making and of entering the political arena to get their own way. Listen to what another president, Franklin D. Roosevelt, is reported to have said in conversation with one of his top administrators:

> *When I woke up this morning, the first thing I saw was a headline in The New York Times to the effect that our Navy was going to spend two billion dollars on a shipbuilding program. Here I am, the Commander in Chief of the Navy, having to read about that for the first time in the press. Do you know what I said to that?*
> *No, Mr. President.*
> *I said, "Jesus Chr-rist!"*

Roosevelt is reported to have continued:

> *The Treasury . . . is so large and far-flung and ingrained in its practices that I find it is almost impossible to get the actions and results I want—even with Henry [Morgenthau] there. But the Treasury is not to be compared with the State Department. You should go through the experience of trying to get any changes in the thinking, policy and action of the career diplomats and then you'd know what a real problem was. But the Treasury and the State Department put together are nothing as compared with the na-a-vy.*

Thus a president of fifty years ago experienced in a very practical sense the error of Woodrow Wilson's statements of 1887:

> *Administration lies outside the proper sphere of politics. Administrative questions are not political questions. Although politics sets the task for administration, it should not be suffered to manipulate its offices. The field of administration is a field of business. It is removed from the hurry and strife of politics.*

Literary reports from practitioners—see, as a classic, C. P. Snow's *Corridors of Power*—established long ago that the permanent bureaucracy channels the currents that temporary political masters buck at their peril. Only recently has the dominance of bureaucracy over politics been recognized by American academic specialists. The bureaucratic experience of presidents is not unique. This is verified in a recent comparative study of bureaucracies here and elsewhere by B. Guy Peters. According to Peters, not only are agencies marked by "the ability of the permanent staff essentially to determine the agenda for their presumed political masters," but also:

> *Through the ability to control information, proposals for policy, and the knowledge concerning feasibility, the bureaucracy is certainly capable of influencing agency policy, if not determining it. It requires an unusual politician to be able to overcome this type of control within an agency.*

More sweepingly, Peter Woll comments in his study of the political role of bureaucracy in America:

> *The bureaucracy continues to run the government and often formulates its major policies, while the President and Congress play out the power game between them, and the courts stay in the background.*

While recent presidents (Jimmy Carter and Ronald Reagan) have attacked bureaucracy, through reorganization and budget cuts, their control seems not to have improved much. Whether from the liberal or the conservative perspective, there is every reason to believe that fiascoes such as Kennedy's Bay of Pigs decision and similar problems during the Iranian hostage crisis can be laid at the foot of the lopsided relations of power and influence between bureaucracy and the purported decision makers in the political realm.

In analyzing the disastrous invasion of Cuba at the Bay of Pigs, Arthur Schlesinger, Jr., a Kennedy adviser, pointed his finger at bureaucracy. As political scientist James David Barber reports, "The Bay of Pigs muckup, he [Schlesinger] suggested, had stemmed in large part from 'excessive concentration' on military and operational problems and wholly inadequate consideration of political issues." If by this Schlesinger meant an overemphasis on means and a neglect of considering ends and overall purpose, we are on familiar ground. It is the typical problem that arises in any attempt to solve human problems when bureaucracy gets involved. At one point during the Iranian hostage crisis, President Carter found that, to deal with "the apparent reluctance in the State Department to carry out my directives fully and with enthusiasm," he had to ask the Iranian desk officers and a few others to come to the White House:

> *I laid down the law to them as strongly as I knew how. I pointed out how difficult the Iranian question had become, and described my procedure for making decisions. [Ambassador to Iran William] Sullivan had not been the only one who had caused trouble . . . . I told them that if they could not support what I decided, their only alternative was to resign—and that if there was another outbreak of misinformation, distortions, or self-serving news leaks, I would direct the Secretary of State to discharge the officials responsible for that particular desk, even if some innocent people might be punished.*

While some might consider such an event a temporary breakdown in command control, there is every historical reason to believe that bureaucracies in America—especially the State Department—behave in political ways repeatedly and permanently. They base themselves on their own constituencies providing a power base separate from their political masters.

When there is an intellectually weak president, such as Ronald Reagan, the country can expect muffled wars between departments competing in a policy area, such as the State Department and the Defense Department. Such wars can usually be understood as contests over turf and power—each department head following the imperative of maximizing survival for his agency through constantly expanding its imperium—and the public be damned.

The experience of chief politicians seems to be that they feel surrounded by bureaucracy.

1. Presidents seem to sense that bureaucracy gets to problems before they do, *pre-deciding* decisions by *defining* the problem.

2. Presidents seem to feel that bureaucracy unduly *controls solutions,* manipulating them according to its own interests, which may not be the President intent or the public interest.

LEGISLATORS

Lawmakers sense a loss of integrity of the legitimate lawmaking bodies of the country, the legislatures, in the face of the private and public institutions the lawmakers are intended to control.

A speaker of the U.S. House of Representatives, Thomas (Tip) O'Neill (D-Mass.):

> *The House has always been a difficult body to lead; I do not believe, though, that even Henry Clay, despite the many problems he had with John Randolph of Roanoke who brought his hunting dogs on the floor of the House, ever had to deal with as many independent members as are found in the modern House of Representatives. The result has been a breakdown of party discipline and a refusal to follow party leadership, which leads in turn to congressional paralysis and an inability to act coherently as a legislative body.*

While the perception of a threat to the integrity of Congress is clear, the reference to members' growing "independence" needs explanation. This is forthcoming from another Congressman, Rep. Barber Conable (R-N.Y.), who put the apparent independence of Congressmen into context:

> *I'm scared. I'm scared. [So said Conable, the House expert on tax reform who later decided not to run again.] These new PACs [political action committees] not only buy incumbents, but affect legislation. It's the same crummy business as judges putting the arm on lawyers who appear before them to finance their next campaign.*

Conable was referring to growing control by modern institutions in the private sphere, especially corporations, over individual members of Congress through the use of political action committees (PACs).

Personal experiences are supported by measurement of their distribution. According to measurements of the percentage change in Congressional campaign contributions between 1974 and 1982, Congressmen's experience of the growing impact of PACs was backed by an actual 235 percent increase of PAC contributions compared with a 47 percent increase in contributions from individuals and candidates and a 176 percent increase from political parties. Senators were impacted by a 220 percent increase in PAC contributions versus a 68 percent *decrease* in party contributions and a 109 percent increase in contributions from individuals and candidates themselves.

* * *

POLITICAL SCIENTISTS

How do private organizations like corporations, public organizations like government bureaucracies, and politics fit together?

Economist and political scientist Charles Lindblom: "The large private organization fits oddly into democratic theory and vision. Indeed, it does not fit."

Yet somehow private organizations and politics are made to fit. How?

Political scientist Theodore J. Lowi explains that lawmaking is achieved through what he calls a "triangular trade in politics" among private groups, public bureaucracies, and congressional committees. But to make political deals, each participant has to have a power base. It is easy to see where the power base of private groups, especially corporations, is: in money. But only Congress can make laws; it divides up this legitimate authority among its committees. The money groups can do nothing politically legitimate without the authoritative lawmakers; the lawmakers will not get reelected without support from the money groups. Each needs the other. Where does bureaucracy come in?

Political scientist Peter Woll suggests two reasons for bureaucratic power: First, Congress has delegated authority to government bureaucracies. It is hard to take this power back. Second, those who run congressional committees, where the deals are made, have a harder time lining up constituencies for each of the many policy problems that pass through the committees. In contrast, each specific bureaucracy already has a supporting group or several lined up to back its demands. That is how the iron triangle comes together. Woll:

> *Administrative policies often have virtually automatic political support which will in turn have significant impact upon Congress, for the groups that support the bureaucracy are more frequently than not very powerful economically and politically.*

We may conclude that modern organizations—bureaucracies, both public and private—are the leading forces in contemporary politics because:

1. Bureaucracies with their centralized command structure are *structurally superior* to fragmented political institutions and the entities that make a democracy: individuals. Democratic institutions are simply more *disorganized,* and cannot get their act together; so are lone individuals.

2. Bureaucracies have their *own competitive cultural base* in citizens' belief in modern values. Rationalism, efficiency, and formal equality are seen as producing a life of seeming stability, a refuge against

the life of politics with its emotionally upsetting human passions and basic "irrationalism." Given the choice, citizens will often, in their attitudes and behavior, prefer stability to politics.

The result is that we often accept bureaucratic criticisms of politics such as the following.

BUREAUCRATS

Playing on modern human beings' search for stability and security, bureaucrats tend to attack politics.

A federal bureaucrat:

> *We draw up good legislation in the national interest with all the parts fitting into the whole properly, and what happens to it when it hits the [Capitol] Hill is like a Christian among the heathen. . . . So we spend lots of time figuring out how we can do something we want to do and think we should do, without taking a new piece of legislation over to Congress. . . .*

Apart from the use of engineering models in which all the parts neatly fit the whole, bureaucrats also tend to treat political issues as technical issues: matters for scientific research that will uncover the "facts" just waiting out there to be discovered.

Another federal bureaucrat:

> *The bureaucrat has a program to carry out that he believes in. The question of whether or not Congress has authorized it is not so important to him. He figures that if Congress really had the facts and knew what was right, it would agree with him.*

There is a tendency among bureaucrats to denigrate the official political process. Yet in it politicians get a sense for the needs and wants of their constituents by discussing such often barely formed needs and wants in public and shaping them into a problem. Used to dealing with the administration of pre-formed policies and programs, bureaucrats themselves become easy victims to those who are aware that the party who defines a problem also wins the power to shape the range and the quality of solutions. At other times, bureaucrats believe they can play this political game of shaping problems without reference to the public at all—a kind of nonpublic or apolitical politics.

Lawmakers themselves are seduced into accepting the bureaucratic approach viewing politics as technical issues to be decided according to technical (problem-solving) rather than political (problem-shaping) standards. For example, one political scientist studying the increased use of staff and reliance on experts by members of Congress observed: "Overburdened and somewhat intimidated by the material the 'experts' throw at them, they [Congressmen] are delighted when issues can be resolved in apparently noncontroversial, technocratic terms."

In trying to compete with the organizational superiority of public and private bureaucracies, some state legislatures have tried to rationalize their politics by bringing in the foremost tool of bureaucratic rationality: the computer. However, early studies have shown that an increase in legislative technology simply centralizes the power of decision-making at the top and center. Legislative leaders or the governors gain. But there is no evidence of any improvement in the *political* process of shaping reality-based problems founded on a sensitivity to the experiences of citizens.

As one political scientist, and former staff member of the Massachusetts legislature, observed: "A legislature can be entirely functional without being either efficient or productive."

* * *

In summary, just about everyone—presidents, aides, legislators, political scientists, and citizens—faces up to the growing experience that:

1. Bureaucracies are increasingly *politically active.*

2. Bureaucracies are more than simple conduits for the flow of authority originating in the political sphere and serving to implement legal policies and programs; they *generate their own power.*

Something paradoxical, unintended, and dangerous happens when bureaucracies use this self-generated power politically: the tool of politics tends to become the master of politics in the polity at large. Internal politization ultimately would seem to threaten to undermine even bureaucracy's own power base if bureaucrats lose faith in their bureaucratic values and adopt political ones. . . .

CHAPTER 5

INTRODUCTION

Clearly, massive changes have occurred in Congress. At the end of the 18th century, members of the House represented districts of no more than 30,000 people and the Senate was selected by the state legislatures. In our "new millennium", House members will likely represent districts of approximately 600,000 people and our senators are popularly elected. These two realities alone require today's Congress to be a very different institution that it was two centuries ago. As the latter three of the four articles in this chapter clearly illustrate, a lot more than that has changed in our Congress.

The first entry is, once again, a Federalist paper. Incredibly to the author(s) (history appears to be unclear concerning the authorship of this particular one), complaints emerged that the House of Representatives would be elitist and unconcerned about the people of the United States. Since the founding fathers had gone to great lengths to keep the other parts of the government out of the direct influence of the people, they had to be amazed that people would levy that charge against the ONE body of the national body that the people could directly elect! Nonetheless, since the charge was made, either Hamilton or Madison felt compelled to respond to it.

1. List the systemic reasons the author believed would insure that the representatives would not be "taken from that class which will have the least sympathy with the mass of the people".

2. What are the five other factors or reasons the author believed would keep representatives loyal to their constituents?

The remaining articles examine Congress from slightly different perspectives. Barbara Sinclair has written an excellent article noting changes in the way Congress functions legislatively. The rules and roles have changed in several areas in the past quarter century. The location of power shifts, the amount of power changes and the successful utilization of power is uneven. Some use it well; some don't.

Both of these pieces should be read and each asked the following questions:

1. What specific structural changes have occurred and how have they affected Congress?

2. How do the internal rules impact power struggles and decision making?

3. How has the moving of Congress from a white men's club to a more diverse institution affected the way Congress operates and how empowered are women and non whites?

THE FEDERALIST NO. 57: HAMILTON OR MADISON

Tuesday, February 19, 1788.

To the People of the State of New York:

The third charge against the House of Representatives is, that it will be taken from that class of citizens which will have least sympathy with the mass of the people, and be most likely to aim at an ambitious sacrifice of the many to the aggrandizement of the few.

Of all the objections which have been framed against the federal Constitution, this is perhaps the most extraordinary. Whilst the objection itself is levelled against a pretended oligarchy, the principle of it strikes at the very root of republican government.

The aim of every political constitution is, or ought to be, first to obtain for rulers men who possess most wisdom to discern, and most virtue to pursue, the common good of the society; and in the next place, to take the most effectual precautions for keeping them virtuous whilst they continue to hold their public trust. . . .

Who are to be the electors of the federal representatives? Not the rich, more than the poor; not the learned, more than the ignorant; not the haughty heirs of distinguished names, more than the humble sons of obscurity and unpropitious fortune. The electors are to be the great body of the people of the United States. They are to be the same who exercise the right in every State of electing the corresponding branch of the legislature of the State.

Who are to be the objects of popular choice? Every citizen whose merit may recommend him to the esteem and confidence of his country. No qualification of wealth, of birth, of religious faith, or of civil profession is permitted to fetter the judgement or disappoint the inclination of the people.

If we consider the situation of the men on whom the free suffrages of their fellow-citizens may confer the representative trust, we shall find it involving every security which can be devised or desired for their fidelity to their constituents.

In the first place, as they will have been distinguished by the preference of their fellow-citizens, we are to presume that in general they will be somewhat distinguished also by those qualities which entitle them to it, and which promise a sincere and scrupulous regard to the nature of their engagements.

In the second place, they will enter into the public service under circumstances which caimot fail to produce a temporary affection at least to their constituents. There is in every breast a sensibility to marks of honor, of favor, of esteem, and of confidence, which, apart from all considerations of interest, is some pledge for grateful and benevolent returns. Ingratitude is a common topic of declamation against human nature; and it must be confessed that instances of it are but too frequent and flagrant, both in public and in private life. But the universal and extreme indignation which it inspires is itself a proof of the energy and prevalence of the contrary sentiment.

In the third place, those ties which bind the representative to his constituents are strengthened by motives of a more selfish nature. His pride and vanity attach him to a form of government which favors his pretensions and gives him a share in its honors and distinctions. Whatever hopes or projects might be entertained by a few aspiring characters, it must generally happen that a great proportion of the men deriving their advancement from their influence with the people, would have more to hope from a preservation of the favor, than from innovations in the government subversive of the authority of the people.

All these securities, however, would be found very insufficient without the restraint of frequent elections. Hence, in the fourth place, the House of Representatives is so constituted as to support in the members an habitual recollection of their dependence on the people. Before the sentiments impressed on their minds by the mode of their elevation can be effaced by the exercise of power, they will be compelled to anticipate the moment when their power is to cease, when their exercise of it is to be reviewed, and when they must descend to the level from which they were raised; there forever to remain unless a faithful discharge of their trust shall have established their title to a renewal of it.

I will add, as a fifth circumstance in the situation of the House of Representatives, restraining them from oppressive measures, that they can make no law which will not have its full operation on themselves and their friends, as well as on the great mass of the society. This has always been deemed one of the strongest bonds by which human policy can connect the rulers and the people together. It creates between them that communion of interests and sympathy of sentiments, of which few governments have furnished examples; but without which every government degenerates into tyranny. If it be asked, what is to restrain the House of Representatives from making legal discriminations in favor of themselves and a particular class of the society? I answer: the genius of the whole system; the nature of just and constitutional laws; and above all, the vigilant and manly spirit which actuates the people of America, a spirit which nourishes freedom, and in return is nourished by it. If this spirit shall ever be so far debased as to tolerate a law not obligatory on the legislature, as well as on the people, the people will be prepared to tolerate anything but liberty.

Such will be the relation between the House of Representatives and their constituents. Duty, gratitude, interest, ambition itself, are the chords by which they will be bound to fidelity and sympathy with the great mass of the people. It is possible that these may all be insufficient to control the caprice and wickedness of man. But are they not all that government will admit, and that human prudence can devise? Are they not the genuine and the characteristic means by which republican government provides for the liberty and happiness of the people? Are they not the identical means on which every State government in the Union relies for the attainment of these important ends? . . .

PUBLIUS.

PARTY LEADERS AND THE NEW LEGISLATIVE PROCESS

Barbara Sinclair

As 1995 drew to a close, President Bill Clinton, Speaker of the House Newt Gingrich, and Senate Majority Leader Bob Dole sat face- to- face attempting to negotiate a comprehensive budget agreement, a task that entailed making a host of major changes in policy. That this mode of policy making did not strike Americans as particularly out of the ordinary indicates just how much the legislative process has changed in recent years. Although it received less media attention, the legislative process on the budget bill in the months before the summit talks was also far from what would have been considered normal only a few years ago. In both chambers a large number of committees had a hand in drafting the legislation, and the resulting bill was an enormous omnibus measure. In the House, floor procedure was tailored especially to the specific problems this bill raised, and in both chambers majority party leaders were intensely involved throughout the process.

As this example suggests, the how-a-bill-becomes-a-law diagram that is a staple of American government textbooks in reality describes the legislative process on fewer and fewer of the major measures Congress considers. Rather than being sent to one committee in each chamber, a measure may be considered by several committees, and some measures bypass committees altogether. In addition, after a bill has been reported, but before it reaches the floor, substantive changes are often worked out via informal processes. Omnibus measures of great scope are a regular part of the legislative scene, and formal executive-congressional summits to work out deals on legislation are no longer considered extraordinary. On the House floor, most major legislation is considered under complex and usually restrictive rules, often tailored to deal with problems specific to that bill. In the Senate, bills are regularly subject to large numbers of not necessarily germane floor amendments, and filibuster threats are an everyday fact of life, affecting all aspects of the legislative process and making cloture votes a routine part of the process. . . .

Although the evolution of a new, more varied legislative process was complex, several factors can be isolated as pivotal: internal reforms that changed the distribution of influence in both chambers in the 1970s and a political environment in the 1980s and early 1990s characterized by divided control, big deficits, and ideological hostility to the legislative goals of congressional Democrats.

During the 1970s both the Senate and House distributed internal influence more broadly. As the incentives to exploit fully the great powers Senate rules confer on the individual senator increased in the 1960s and 1970s, the restraint senators had exercised in the use of their prerogatives gave way, and they began to offer more floor amendments and use extended debate—filibusters—more often. As a result, the Senate floor became a more active decision- making arena, and filibusters, or the threat of them, became a routine part of the legislative process.

The change in the Senate's legislative process brought about by senators' greater individualism and activism put heavy demands on party leaders, especially on the majority leader, who is in charge of scheduling legislation for the floor. The majority leader is also expected to help party members pass the legislation they need and want. The change in process increased the majority leader's involvement, often casting him in the role of head negotiator. But the Senate gave the majority leader no new powers to carry out his job.

In the House, reformers redistributed influence through a number of rules changes mostly instituted between 1969 and 1975. Powers and resources were shifted from committee chairs not only down to subcommittee chairs and rank and file members but also up to the party leadership. Junior members gained resources, especially staff, that boosted their ability to participate in the legislative process. The Speaker, as leader of the majority party, was given the power to select the Democratic members of the Rules Committee, a greater say in the assignment of members to other committees, and new powers over the referral of bills.

By reducing the power of the committees and facilitating greater participation by the rank and file, the reforms made legislating more difficult for the majority Democrats. Republicans quickly became adept at using floor amendments to make political points, confronting Democrats with a stream of politically difficult votes. Compromises carefully crafted in committee were being picked apart on the floor, and floor sessions were stretching on interminably.

Democrats began to look to their party leaders, the only central leaders in the chamber, to counter these problems. The leaders responded by innovating in ways that led to alterations in the legislative process. The leadership became more involved with legislation before it reached the floor, at times negotiating post-committee adjustments to ease its passage. To respond to the barrage of amendments offered on the floor, the leadership developed special rules into devices for structuring floor decision making.

In the 1980s both the House and Senate were feeling the results of the changes in their internal distribution of influence. The highly individualistic Senate, in which each senator was accorded extraordinary latitude, was very good at agenda setting and publicizing problems, but poorly structured for legislative decision making. The House, which had expanded junior members' opportunities for participation, also had problems legislating, although its central leadership had begun to develop reasonably effective responses. . . .

The tough climate of the 1980s forced further innovation in the legislative process, especially in the House. Party leaders, as they tried to engineer passage of legislation that would satisfy their members, were more and more drawn into the substantive legislative process; in the House, leaders developed special rules into powerful and flexible tools for structuring floor decisions.

By the early 1990s the usefulness of many of the special processes for enacting legislation had become widely recognized, and congressional leaders continued to use them even though political circumstances changed. . . .

Omnibus legislation—bills with great substantive scope often involving directly or indirectly, many committees—is now a regular part of the congressional agenda. Such measures increased as a proportion of the congressional agenda of major legislation from zero in the 91st Congress (1969-1970) to 8 percent in the 94th (1975-1976) maII budget resolutions—to 20 percent in the 97th (1981-1982) and 100th (1987-1988). In the Congresses of the 1990s, omnibus measures made up about 11 percent of major measures.

Some omnibus measures are the result of the 1974 budget act. The act requires an annual budget resolution and, in the 1980s and 1990s, the budget resolution often called for a reconciliation bill. Beyond that, the decision to package legislation into an omnibus measure is discretionary, and it is principally the majority party leadership that decides. Measures may be packaged into an omnibus bill for several reasons: to pass unpalatable but necessary legislation; to force the president to accept legislative provisions that, were they sent to him in freestanding form, he would veto; or to raise the visibility of popular legislation and garner partisan credit. During the Reagan and Bush administrations, for example, House Democratic leaders packaged legislation on issues such as trade and drugs into high-profile omnibus measures to compete with the White House for media attention and public credit and to protect favored provisions from a veto. During the 103d Congress, congressional leaders did not need to pressure President Clinton into signing their legislation, but the usefulness of omnibus measures for enacting tough bills or for raising the visibility of popular measures led to their continued use. A number of modest provisions were packaged into a big anticrime bill, and omnibus budget measures were used to pass Clinton's economic program. . . .

In 1993 and 1995 central leaders used the budget process to try to enact comprehensive policy changes that in both years involved making some very difficult decisions. Clinton's economic program cut the deficit by $500 billion over five years and increased spending on high- priority programs; accomplishing that entailed tax increases, which are never popular, and a cut in spending for numerous lower-priority programs. The Republicans' 1995 program envisioned balancing the budget in seven years while also cutting taxes, which would require draconian cuts in domestic spending. It also included revamping major programs such as Medicare, Medicaid, and welfare. The budget process offered the only realistic hope for enacting either party's proposals. Wrapping the provisions into one omnibus bill cuts down the number of battles that need to be won—an important consideration in a system with a bias toward the status quo. Leaders can ask members to cast a handful of tough votes, but not dozens. With an omnibus bill, the stakes are so high, it is harder for members to vote against their party leaders. In 1993, for example, reluctant Democrats were warned that they would bring down the Clinton presidency if they contributed to the defeat of his economic program. In 1995 Newt Gingrich repeatedly warned his members that the Republican Party's ability to govern was at issue; that his own reputation and clout were at stake was clear to his members.

Divided government brought sharp differences in policy preferences between the president and the congressional majority. Combined with the painful decisions that huge budget deficits dictated, those differences have sometimes stalemated normal legislative processes. But the cost of failing to reach an agreement on budget issues was just too high, so when normal processes, even if supplemented by the more active role of majority party leaders, were incapable of producing legislation, the president and Congress had to find another way. The new device was the summit—relatively formal negotiations between congressional leaders and high-ranking administration officials representing the president or, as in 1995, the president himself. Between 1987 and 1990, four summits took place, and three concerned budget issues. Normal legislative processes foundered in the face of policy disagreements between the Democratic congressional majority and President Reagan in 1987 and between Congress and President Bush in 1989 and 1990, but the threat of severe automatic spending cuts dictated by the Gramm-Rudman Act, or the threat of an economic crisis, or both made a failure to reach agreement too costly. Aid to the Nicaraguan contras, another contentious issue, was the subject of the fourth summit.

When the congressional majority and the president are of the same party, normal processes, supplemented by informal consultation and negotiations, suffice to produce agreement on essential legislation such as budget bills. No summits were needed during the 103d Congress with the Democrats in control of both branches. Normal processes are more likely to fail when both policy and electoral goals are in conflict, as they tend to be when government is divided. The conflict between President Clinton and the conservative new Republican majority in the 104th Congress made agreement impossible through anything approaching normal processes. The Republicans attempted to use various legislative strategies to force Clinton to accept their priorities: they threatened to include "must pass" legislation, such as the measure to increase the debt limit, in the reconciliation bill, and they sent Clinton appropriations bills with provisions he had vowed to veto, and, when he did, they refused to pass continuing resolutions to keep the government funded. Clearly, a summit was the only hope of resolving the impasse.

This time, however, the differences between the president and the congressional majority were just too great. Although not reaching a comprehensive agreement was costly for both, the compromises such an agreement would have required entailed sacrificing policy principles and the interests of important constituencies for one or both parties and so were more costly than no agreement.

Traditionally, the legislative process would begin with the referral of a bill to a single committee, which would be largely responsible for its fate. In 1995 the Republicans' bill to abolish the Commerce Department was referred to eleven House committees. Although the number of committees was unusual, the fact that more than one committee was involved was not. In the contemporary House about one bill in five is referred to more than one committee. Major legislation is even more likely to be sent to several committees; between 1987 and 1995, about a third was.

Multiple referral of legislation was not possible before 1975, when the House passed a rule providing for it. The new rule came about for two reasons: the House's inability to realign outdated committee jurisdictions and reform minded members' desire to increase opportunities for broad participation in the legislative process. The rule was amended in 1977 to give the Speaker the power to set deadlines for committees to report legislation. As revised in 1995, the rule directs the Speaker to designate a lead committee with the most responsibility for the legislation; once that committee has reported, the other committees are required to report under fairly strict deadlines.

For the Speaker, the frequency with which major legislation is multiply referred presents opportunities, but also problems. One problem is that when legislation is referred to several committees, the number of people who must come to agreement is multiplied, complicating and slowing down the legislative process. Often, multiple referral forces the Speaker to be the jurisdictional and substantive mediator, a role that brings with it influence as well as headaches. On contentious legislation, the leaders of the several committees involved may not be able to work out their differences without help. If the party leaders have to get involved, they gain influence over the substance of the legislation. Furthermore, when several committees work on the same piece of legislation, the committee process is more open to influence by party leaders; no one committee can consider such a bill its private business. Multiple referral also gives the Speaker the opportunity to set time limits for the reporting out of legislation. During the first one hundred days of the 104th Congress, when the new Republican majority was attempting to bring all the items in the Contract with America to the floor, that power gave added weight to Speaker Gingrich's stringent informal deadlines.

Although legislation is routinely considered by more than one committee sometimes bills bypass committee consideration altogether. Skipping committee review was a rare occurrence before the 1980s; for example, in 1969 and 1970 and in 1975 and 1976, committees were bypassed on only 2 percent of the major legislation. By the late 1980s, however, almost 20 percent of major measures were never considered by a committee in the House. . . .

This method of passing legislation is a radical change from the way things used to be done. In the pre-reform House, autonomous committees crafted legislation behind closed doors and usually passed it unchanged on the floor with little help from the party leadership. As a matter of fact, party leadership intrusion into the legislative process on matters of substance was considered illegitimate. As House members became less willing to defer to committees and more willing to question committee bills on the floor, as multiple referral destroyed committees' monopoly over legislation in their area of jurisdiction, and as the political climate became harsher and the political stakes higher, committees became less capable of crafting legislation that could pass the chamber without help. In responding to their members' demands for assistance, majority party leaders were drawn more deeply into the substantive aspects of the legislative process and, in effect, changed how the process works. Now party leaders often involve themselves well before legislation is reported from committee.

Moreover, party leaders frequently take a role in working out substantive adjustments to legislation *after* it has been reported from committee. In the pre-reform 91st Congress, no major legislation was subject to such postcommittee adjustments; in the 94th, 4 percent was—all budget resolutions. In the early 1980s, the frequency jumped to almost one major measure in four and, in the late 1980s and early 1990s, averaged a little more than one in three. In 1995 almost half of major measures underwent some sort of postcommittee adjustment. . . .

The House considers most major legislation under a special rule that sets the conditions for floor debate. The variety in contemporary rules means that the legislative process differs quite substantially depending upon the choice of rule. Rules differ in many ways, but the most important is how amendments are to be treated. Rules can range from allowing no amendments, in which case the legislative battle is focused solely on the measure (or sometimes on the rule) and is clearly defined in time, to allowing all germane amendments, meaning that the amending process may stretch on for days and be unpredictable. Rules also can make otherwise nongermane amendments in order. Many rules allow some but not all germane amendments sometimes listing them, sometimes requiring they be printed in the *Congressional Record* before floor consideration begins, and sometimes allowing all germane amendments that can be offered in a given time.

In the contemporary House, major legislation is likely to be brought to the floor under a complex, restrictive rule. In the prereform era, only tax bills were considered under a closed rule that allowed no amendments. As late as the 95th Congress (1977-1978), 85 percent of the rules were open, meaning that all germane amendments were allowed. As legislation became more vulnerable to alteration on the floor, Democrats began demanding that their leadership use the control over the Rules Committee they had been given in the reform era to protect legislation and, where possible, to shield members from having to cast difficult votes. In response, the Democratic leadership began to use restrictive rules more frequently. Rules that restrict the offering of germane amendments accounted for two- thirds of the rules granted for initial consideration of legislation in the 102d Congress and for 70 percent in the 103d.

When only major measures are examined, the trend is even stronger. In the 1970s more than 80 percent of the rules for major legislation were simple open rules. In the early 1980s about 60 percent of major measures received simple open rules; the rest were considered under closed or, more frequently, some form of hybrid complex rule. By the late 1980s and continuing in the 1990s, 75 percent or more of major measures were considered under complex (or, rarely, closed) rules. From the early 1980s on, almost all the complex rules restrict amending activity. . . .

The rule for the reconciliation bill implementing Clinton's economic program in 1993 provides an example of how useful a strategically structured rule can be. That rule allowed a vote only on a comprehensive Republican substitute; amendments to delete various unpopular elements of the package—the BTU tax and the tax on high income recipients' Social Security payments—were not made in order. Passage was crucial for the young Clinton administration and for the Democratic Party, but the constraints imposed by the huge deficit and the need to reduce it made it difficult to put a package together and hold it together. The rule was intended to focus debate on the broad philosophical differences between the two parties' approaches to the problem of reducing the deficit and to protect Democrats from having to cast one tough vote after another. Many would have found it hard to explain to the folks back home why they had voted against amendments striking unpopular tax provisions, especially in response to thirty-second attack ads. If the Republicans were allowed to offer amendments, the Democrats would be forced to choose between casting a series of politically dangerous votes or letting a carefully constructed compromise—the passage of which, most believed, was crucial to the future of the country and the party--be picked apart on the floor.

When in the minority, Republicans had labeled restrictive rules dictatorial and illegitimate and had promised not to use them if they took control. In the 104th Congress, however, they were committed to passing an ambitious agenda in a short time. The usefulness of restrictive rules for promoting the party's legislative objectives overcame any Republican objections based on principle or the fear of seeming hypocritical. To be sure, the restrictions were sometimes of a different nature: Republicans often limited amending activity by restricting the time for consideration rather than specifying the number or kind of amendments that could be offered. Overall, the proportion of restrictive rules declined. In 1995 about half of all rules for the initial consideration of legislation were restrictive. However, when only major measures are considered, the picture is different; in 1995, 77 percent of rules for the consideration of major measures were restrictive.

In 1995 Republicans used a cleverly constructed restrictive rule to protect their rescission bill. It specified that anyone wishing to restore a spending cut in the bill had to offset the cost by cutting something else in the same section of the bill; in other words, no money could be transferred to social programs from defense spending or from disaster relief for California.

The contemporary legislative process in the Senate is shaped by senators' rampant individualism and their leaders' attempts to do their jobs within that context. Senators now routinely exploit the enormous prerogatives Senate rules give the individual to further their own agendas.

In an institutional setting where every member is able—and often willing-to impede the legislative process, leaders must accommodate individual members to legislate successfully. The increase in postcommittee adjustments to legislation in the Senate reflects this accommodation. Rare in the 1970s even on major legislation—only 2 percent of major measures underwent postcommittee adjustments in the 91st and 94th Congresses—the frequency jumped to about 20 percent in the 1980s and then to more than 33 percent in the early 1990s. In 1995 more than 60 percent of major legislation was subject to postcommittee adjustments. Although the negotiations that produce these modifications are sometimes undertaken by committee leaders or other interested senators, the party leaders often become involved.

Senate individualism is most evident on the floor. Senators can use their power to offer as many amendments as they choose to almost any bill, not only to further their policy preferences but also to bring up issues leaders might like to keep off the floor, to make political points, and to force their political opponents in the chamber to cast tough votes. Senators regularly use their amending prerogatives for all these purposes. Because, in most cases, amendments need not be germane, Barbara Boxer, D-Calif., was able to force onto the floor the issue of holding open hearings on the sexual harassment charges against Bob Packwood, R-Ore., even though Majority Leader Dole wanted to keep it off. Boxer offered it as an amendment to a defense authorization bill. For years, Jesse Helms, R- N.C., has been bringing up and forcing votes on amendments on hot button issues such as abortion, pornography, homosexuality, and school prayer. He often does not expect to win, but to provide ammunition for the electoral opponents of senators who disagree with him.

Senators' use of their amending prerogatives has resulted in many bills being subjected to a barrage of amendments on the floor. In the 1950s the proportion of legislation subject to high amending activity (ten or more amending roll calls) was tiny: for the 84th (1953-1954) and 86th (1959-1960) Congresses, it averaged 2.7 percent. In the 1960s and 1970s it rose to a mean of 8.2 percent per Congress, and in the 1980s it averaged 14.9 percent? In the 1980s and 1990s major legislation was considerably more likely to be subject to such amending marathons; on about 30 percent of major legislation, more than ten amendments were offered on the floor and pushed to a roll call vote. . . .

To lend some predictability to floor proceedings, the majority leader frequently negotiates unanimous consent agreements to govern the consideration of major legislation. Such an agreement limits floor time and may limit the amendments allowed; however, one senator's objection can kill a proposed unanimous consent agreement, so all senators' interests must be accommodated.

Senators' willingness to use their privilege of unlimited debate has had a major impact on the legislative process in the Senate. In the 1950s, filibusters occurred at a rate of about one per Congress; the rate rose to just under five per Congress in the 1960s and continued to rise at an accelerated pace in the 1970s and 1980s. The 103d Congress saw thirty filibusters. Major legislation often encounters some extended debate-related problem identifiable from the public record. In the late 1980s and early 1990s just under 30 percent did; in the first Congress of the Clinton presidency, almost 50 percent of major measures encountered such problems, and in 1995, 44 percent did. . . .

Given senators' willingness to exploit their right of extended debate, the majority leader, in scheduling legislation and often in crafting it, has little choice but to be responsive to small groups of members or even to individuals. On legislation of secondary importance, before a recess, or late in the session, one senator's objection will suffice to keep a bill off the floor. When a great deal of legislation is awaiting floor consideration, the majority leader cannot afford the time for a filibuster, so even an ambiguous threat to filibuster serves as a veto. This reality has become semi-institutionalized in the practice of holds. Any senator can inform the leader that he or she wishes to place a hold on a measure—a bill, a presidential nomination, or a treaty. Leaders assert that use of this device only guarantees that the senator will be informed before the measure is scheduled for floor consideration; however, if the hold represents a veiled threat to filibuster the measure and if other matters are more pressing, it often constitutes a de facto veto.

The mere threat to filibuster is often sufficient to extract concessions from the supporters of a measure. A number of the Contract with America items that sped through the House were held up in the Senate until their supporters made significant compromises—for example, a bill to impose a moratorium on all new regulations was transformed, under a filibuster threat, into a measure giving Congress forty-five days to review new regulations. In the 103d Congress a number of Clinton's priorities also ran into troubles in the Senate, not because they lacked the support of a majority but because the sixty votes to cut off debate could not be amassed. Supporters had to make concessions on national service legislation and the voter registration bill (motor voter), for example, to overcome a filibuster or a filibuster threat.

Sometimes a large minority defeats outright legislation supported by a majority. Clinton's stimulus package succumbed to this fate in 1993. Senate Majority Leader George Mitchell, D-Maine, attempted to invoke cloture a number of times, but, even though majorities supported cutting off debate, he was not able to put together the necessary sixty votes. In 1995 Senate Democrats forced Majority Leader Dole to abandon his own bill overhauling federal regulatory procedures; he mustered a majority on several cloture votes but fell short of the sixty needed. In the 103d Congress, of nineteen major measures that failed to become law, twelve were killed by the Senate alone; eight of those ran into filibuster- related problems. . . .

In the House, then, the new legislative process has on balance provided the majority party leadership with effective tools for facilitating the passage of legislation. Backed by a reasonably cohesive majority party, House leaders can engineer passage of legislation quickly and in a form consonant with the preferences of the members of the majority party. In the Senate, as in the House, the party leadership has become more central to the legislative process, but, unlike the Speaker, the Senate majority leader has gained few new tools for dealing with a more unruly membership. The need to accommodate most senators and to build supermajority coalitions to pass legislation in the Senate almost always means the process is slower and often results in more broadly based (or weakening) compromises. Sometimes, it results in no legislation at all. In the contemporary Congress, the legislative process in the two chambers is more distinct in form and in results than ever before.

CHAPTER 6

INTRODUCTION

The Judicial Branch of our government is intriguing, because a glimpse at the first three articles of the Constitution and the historical records that we do possess, indicate that the "Founding Fathers" did not spend an inordinate amount of time on this part of our system. There are, no doubt, many reasons for this brevity of time and paper which we will not explore here. Suffice it to say that the federal judicial system and the Supreme Court in particular has become much more than many, if not all, of the founders anticipated.

In this chapter, we will examine four readings. The first is a Federalist Paper (SURPRISE!!). Alexander Hamilton authored this writing which examines a variety of areas concerning the Supreme Court. The primary sections that I have left for you to peruse examines the independence of the Court and the necessity that the federal judges serve for life ("during good behavior"). Hamilton amply identifies elements in our system that render the judiciary the weakest of the three branches of our government. For this reason and others, Hamilton argues for lifetime appointments. Answer the following:

1. What are the specific reasons Hamilton believes the federal judiciary will be the weakest branch?

2. What are the factors which lead Hamilton to argue judges must serve for life?

The second entry comes from David O'Brien's *Storm Center*. The particular reading is part of a chapter which chronicles presidents' attempts to make the Supreme Court into the ideological image they prefer. Some presidents have had the fortune of appointing numerous Justices and others have been less fortunate. Even those presidents who have been successful in appointing the individuals they preferred to the Supreme Court have sometimes later found those choices to be somewhat different in their voting from what the president had anticipated. I have no particular questions that I want you to consider from this piece, but rather, get a flavor the issues and concerns in this arena.

The next reading is an excerpt from the famous Supreme Court case, *Marbury v. Madison*. This case is considered by some, including me, to be the most important case in the history of American jurisprudence. Exactly what power did the Supreme Court possess and, particularly, did it really possess the power to render acts of Congress unconstitutional? Some argued they did, others disagreed. In this case, the Court claimed the power and exercised it all at the same time. Questions to ponder:

1. What, specifically, were the questions to be answered in this case?

2. What, specifically, were the answers given by the Court?

3. How, legally, did the Court justify its' answers?

Finally, I include the famous (in some minds, infamous) case of *Roe v. Wade*. I have included this case for a variety of reasons. I think it is safe to say that it is the most controversial ruling of the Supreme Court since *Brown v. Board of Education* in 1954 and many, I'm sure, would argue that it was and is even more controversial than that. It is a ruling which most Americans think they know about, but few have ever read the ruling. It also is included because the excerpt allows you to see a sliver of the effort that many justices go through in researching and considering the Constitutional, legal, historical and practical issues of developing a ruling. Finally, I include a dissent opinion, so that you may see that dynamic as well. Yes, the excerpt is lengthy and yes, you'll have trouble reading it. Get over it.

THE FEDERALIST NO. 78: HAMILTON

To the People of the State of New York:

We proceed now to an examination of the judiciary department of the proposed government.

In unfolding the defects of the existing Confederation, the utility and necessity of a federal judicature have been clearly pointed out. It is the less necessary to recapitulate the considerations there urged, as the propriety of the institution in the abstract is not disputed; the only questions which have been raised being relative to the manner of constituting it, and to its extent. To these points, therefore, our observations shall be confined.

The manner of constituting it seems to embrace these several objects: 1st. The mode of appointing the judges. 2d. The tenure by which they are to hold their places. 3d. The partition of the judiciary authority between different courts, and their relations to each other.

First. As to the mode of appointing the judges; this is the same with that of appointing the officers of the Union in general, and has been so fully discussed in the two last numbers, that nothing can be said here which would not be useless repetition. Second. As to the tenure by which the judges are to hold their places; this chiefly concerns their duration in office; the provisions for their support; the precautions for their responsibility.

According to the plan of the convention, all judges who may be appointed by the United States are to hold their offices DURING GOOD BEHAVIOR; which is conformable to the most approved of the State constitutions and among the rest, to that of this State. Its propriety having been drawn into question by the adversaries of that plan, is no light symptom of the rage for objection, which disorders their imaginations and judgments. The standard of good behavior for the continuance in office of the judicial magistracy, is certainly one of the most valuable of the modem improvements in the practice of government. In a monarchy it is an excellent barrier to the despotism of the prince; in a republic it is a no less excellent barrier to the encroachments and oppressions of the representative body. And it is the best expedient which can be devised in any government, to secure a steady, upright, and impartial administration of the laws.

Whoever attentively considers the different departments of power must perceive, that, in a government in which they are separated from each other, the judiciary, from the nature of its functions, will always be the least dangerous to the political rights of the Constitution; because it will be least in a capacity to annoy or injure them. The Executive not only dispenses the honors, but holds the sword of the community. The legislature not only commands the purse, but prescribes the rules by which the duties and rights of every citizen are to be regulated. The judiciary, on the contrary, has no influence over either the sword or the purse; no direction either of the strength or of the wealth of the society; and can take no active resolution whatever. It may truly be said to have neither FORCE nor WILL, but merely judgment; and must ultimately depend upon the aid of the executive arm even for the efficacy of its judgments.

This simple view of the matter suggests several important consequences. It proves incontestably, that the judiciary is beyond comparison the weakest of the three departments of power; that it can never attack with success either of the other two; and that all possible care is requisite to enable it to defend itself against their attacks. It equally proves, that though individual oppression may now and then proceed "from the courts of justice, the general liberty of the people can never be endangered from that quarter; I mean so long as the judiciary remains truly distinct from both the legislature and the Executive. . . .

The complete independence of the courts of justice is peculiarly essential in a limited Constitution. By a limited Constitution, I understand one which contains certain specified exceptions to the legislative authority; such, for instance, as that it shall pass no bills of attainder, no ex-post-facto laws, and the like. Limitations of this kind can be preserved in practice no other way than through the medium of courts of justice, whose duty it must be to declare all acts contrary to the manifest tenor of the Constitution void. Without this, all the reservations of particular fights or privileges would amount to nothing.

Some perplexity respecting the fights of the courts to pronounce legislative acts void, because contrary to the Constitution, has arisen from an imagination that the doctrine would imply a superiority of the judiciary to the legislative power. It is urged that the authority which can declare the acts of another void, must necessarily be superior to the one whose acts may be declared void. As this doctrine is of great importance in all the American constitutions, a brief discussion of the ground on which it rests cannot be unacceptable.

There is no position which depends on clearer principles, than that every act of a delegated authority, contrary to the tenor of the commission under which it is exercised, is void. No legislative act, therefore, contrary to the Constitution, can be valid. To deny this, would be to affirm, that the deputy is greater than his principal; that the servant is above his master; that the representatives of the people are superior to the people themselves; that men acting by virtue of powers, may do not only what their powers do not authorize, but what they forbid.

If it be said that the legislative body are themselves the constitutional judges of their own powers, and that the construction they put upon them is conclusive upon the other departments, it may be answered, that this cannot be the natural presumption, where it is not to be collected from any particular provisions in the Constitution. It is not otherwise to be supposed, that the Constitution could intend to enable the representatives of the people to substitute their WILL to that of their constituents. It is far more rational to suppose, that the courts were designed to be an intermediate body between the people and the legislature, in order, among other things, to keep the latter within the limits assigned to their authority. The interpretation of the laws is the proper and peculiar province of the courts. A constitution is, in fact, and must be regarded by the judges, as a fundamental law. It therefore belongs to them to ascertain its meaning, as well as the meaning of any particular act proceeding from the legislative body. If there should happen to be an irreconcilable variance between the two, that which has the superior obligation and validity ought, of course, to be preferred; or, in other words, the Constitution ought to be preferred to the statute, the intention of the people to the intention of their agents.

Nor does this conclusion by any means suppose a superiority of the judicial to the legislative power. It only supposes that the power of the people is superior to both; and that where the will of the legislature, declared in its statutes, stands in opposition to that of the people, declared in the Constitution, the judges ought to be governed by the latter rather than the former. They ought to regulate their decisions by the fundamental laws, rather than by those which are not fundamental. . . .

If, then, the courts of justice are to be considered as the bulwarks of a limited Constitution against legislative encroachments, this consideration will afford a strong argument for the permanent tenure of judicial offices, since nothing will contribute so much as this to that independent spirit in the judges which must be essential to the faithful performance of so arduous a duty.

This independence of the judges is equally requisite to guard the Constitution and the rights of individuals from the effects of those ill humors, which the arts of designing men, or the influence of particular conjunctures, sometimes disseminate among the people themselves, and which, though they speedily give place to better information, and more deliberate reflection, have a tendency, in the meantime, to occasion dangerous innovations in the government, and serious oppressions of the minor party in the community. Though I trust the friends of the proposed Constitution will never concur with its enemies, in questioning that fundamental principle of republican government, which admits the right of the people to alter or abolish the established Constitution, whenever they find it inconsistent with their happiness, yet it is not to be inferred from this principle, that the representatives of the people, whenever a momentary inclination happens to lay hold of a majority of their constituents, incompatible with the provisions in the existing Constitution, would, on that account, be justifiable in a violation of those provisions; . . .

But it is not with a view to infractions of the Constitution only, that the independence of the judges may be an essential safeguard against the effects of occasional ill humors in the society. These sometimes extend no farther than to the injury of the private rights of particular classes of citizens, by unjust and partial laws. Here also the firmness of the judicial magistracy is of vast importance in mitigating the severity and confining the operation of such laws. It not only serves to moderate the immediate mischiefs of those which may have been passed, but it operates as a check upon the legislative body in passing them; who, perceiving that obstacles to the success of iniquitous intention are to be expected from the scruples of the courts, are in a manner compelled, by the very motives of the injustice they meditate, to qualify their attempts. This is a circumstance calculated to have more influence upon the character of our governments, than but few may be aware of. The benefits of the integrity and moderation of the judiciary have already been felt in more States than one; and though they may have displeased those whose sinister expectations they may have disappointed, they must have commanded the esteem and applause of all the virtuous and disinterested. Considerate men, of every description, ought to prize whatever will tend to beget or fortify that temper in the courts: as no man can be sure that he may not be to-morrow the victim of a spirit of injustice, by which he may be a gainer to-day. And every man must now feel, that the inevitable tendency of such a spirit is to sap the foundations of public and private confidence, and to introduce in its stead universal distrust and distress.

That inflexible and uniform adherence to the rights of the Constitution, and of individuals, which we perceive to be indispensable in the courts of justice, can certainly not be expected from judges who hold their offices by a temporary commission. Periodical appointments, however regulated, or by whomsoever made, would, in some way or other, be fatal to their necessary independence. If the power of making them was committed either to the Executive or legislature, there would be danger of an improper complaisance to the branch which possessed it; if to both, there would be an unwillingness to hazard the displeasure of either; if to the people, or to persons chosen by them for the special purpose, there would be too great a disposition to consult popularity, to justify a reliance that nothing would be consulted but the Constitution and the laws.

There is yet a further and a weightier reason for the permanency of the judicial offices, which is deducible from the nature of the qualifications they require. It has been frequently remarked, with great propriety, that a voluminous code of laws is one of the inconveniences necessarily connected with the advantages of a free government. To avoid an arbitrary discretion in the courts, it is indispensable that they should be bound down by strict rules and precedents, which serve to define and point out their duty in every particular case that comes before them; and it will readily be conceived from the variety of controversies which grow out of the folly and wickedness of mankind, that the records of those precedents must unavoidably swell to a very considerable bulk, and must demand long and laborious study to acquire a competent knowledge of them. Hence it is, that there can be but few men in the society who will have sufficient skill in the laws to qualify them for the stations of judges. And making the proper deductions for the ordinary depravity of human nature, the number must be still smaller of those who unite the requisite integrity with the requisite knowledge. These considerations apprise us, that the government can have no great option between fit character; and that a temporary duration in office, which would naturally discourage such characters from quitting a lucrative line of practice to accept a seat on the bench, would have a tendency to throw the administration of justice into hands less able, and less well qualified, to conduct it with utility and dignity. In the present circumstances of this country, and in those in which it is likely to be for a long time to come, the disadvantages on this score would be greater than they may at first sight appear; but it must be confessed, that they are far inferior to those which present themselves under the other aspects of the subject.

Upon the whole, there can be no room to doubt that the convention acted wisely in copying from the models of those constitutions which have established GOOD BEHAVIOR as the tenure of their judicial offices, in point of duration; and that so far from being blamable on this account, their plan would have been inexcusably defective, if it had wanted this important feature of good government. The experience of Great Britain affords an illustrious comment on the excellence of the institution.

PUBLIUS.

STORM CENTER—"PACKING THE COURT"

David O'Brien

The presidential impulse to pack the Court with politically compatible justices is irresistible. The "tendency to choose a known, rather than all unknown, evil," as Stone put it, "can never be eliminated from the practical administration of government." Yet Court packing depends on the politics of the possible oil presidential prestige and political expediency. The politics of packing the Court is well illustrated by the appointments of Roosevelt, Truman, Eisenhower, Nixon, Reagan, and Bush.

With the exception of George Washington, no President has had more opportunities to pack the Court than Franklin Roosevelt. He made eight appointments and elevated Justice Stone to the chief justiceship. Although Nixon and Reagan later achieved remarkable success in remolding the Court in their images, Roosevelt succeeded more than any other President in packing the Court. Moreover, perhaps no other President before Nixon and Reagan had as great a contempt for the Court. Nixon vehemently opposed the "liberal jurisprudence" of the Warren Court, and Reagan attacked many of the social-policy rulings of the more conservative Burger Court, specifically its decisions permitting abortion, allowing affirmative action, and upholding the Fourth Amendment's exclusionary rule. Nixon and Reagan named only those who they believed shared their "strict constructionist" judicial philosophies and agreed with their conservative social-policy positions. By contrast, Roosevelt attacked the conservative economic politics of the Court in the 1930s for thwarting the country's recovery from the Great Depression.

During FDR's first term, the Court invalidated most of the early New Deal program. Yet the President had no opportunity to fill a seat on the bench. After his landslide reelection in 1936, Roosevelt proposed judicial reforms allowing him to expand the size of the Court to fifteen by appointing a new member for every justice over seventy years of age. In the spring of 1937, when the Senate Judiciary Committee was debating his "Court-packing plan," the Court abruptly upheld major pieces of New Deal legislation. The Court had been badly divided five to four in striking down progressive New Deal legislation. George Sutherland, James McReynolds, Pierce Butler, and Willis Van Devanter—the "Four Horsemen" voted together against economic legislation, while Stone and Cardozo followed Brandeis in supporting progressive economic legislation. Hughes and Roberts were the "swing votes," the latter, more conservative justice casting the crucial fifth vote to strike down FDR's programs. Roberts then changed his mind. In March he abandoned the Four Horsemen in *West Coast Hotel Co. v. Parfish* (1937) to uphold Washington State's minimum-wage law. Two weeks later, in *National Labor Relations Board v. Jones & Laughlin Steel Corporation* (1937), he again switched sides to affirm a major piece of New Deal legislation, the National Labor Relations Act. The Court's "switch in time that saved nine" was widely speculated to have been due to FDR's Court-packing plan. But even though the rulings did not come down until the spring, Roberts had switched his vote at conference in December 1936, two months before FDR announced his plan. The reversal of the Court's position nonetheless contributed to the Senate Judiciary Committee's rejection of FDR's proposal in May. Then Van Devanter one of the President's staunchest opponents—told the President that he would resign at the end of the term. FDR had the first of eight appointments in the next six years to infuse his own political philosophy into the Court. Although his plan to enlarge the size of the Court failed, FDR eventually succeeded in packing the Court.

When FDR made his first appointment, he was angry at the Senate for defeating his plan to enlarge the Court and angry at the Court for destroying his program for recovery. For the appointment, FDR chose Senator Hugo Black, who "had led the unsuccessful fight for the Court-packing plan." Roosevelt, recalled Robert Jackson, wanted to "humiliate [the Senate and the Court] at a single stroke by naming Black." Only in extraordinary circumstances would the Senate refuse to confirm one of its own. "The Senate would have to swallow hard and approve," Jackson observed. "The Court would be humiliated by having to accept one of its most bitter and unfair critics and one completely alien to the judicial tradition.

At Black's confirmation hearings, rumors circulated that he had been a member of the Ku Klux Klan in the mid-1920s, when the Klan membership reached its peak of over four million and virtually assured the election of Democrats in the in Deep South. When evidence of Black's prior Klan membership materialized after his confirmation, the revelation confirmed for many that the appointment had been an act of revenge. Roosevelt claimed "that he had not known of any Klan link when he appointed Black to the Court." Black went on national radio to explain briefly, though not to apologize for, his membership in the Klan from 1922 to 1925. Although he denied having any knowledge of the KKK association, Roosevelt must have known. Black, moreover, left a note in his private papers to "correct for posterity any idea about Pres. Roosevelt's having been fooled about my membership in the Klan." He recollected:

> President Roosevelt, when I went up to lunch with him, told me that there was no reason for my worrying about having been a member of the Ku Klux Klan. He said that some of the best friends and supporters he had in the State of Georgia were strong members of the organization. He never in any way, by word or attitude, indicated any doubt about my having been in the Klan nor did he indicate any criticism of me for having been a member of that organization. The rumors and statements to the contrary are wrong.

Roosevelt's subsequent appointments all turned on support for the New Deal. When the conservative westerner George Sutherland retired in 1938, the President momentarily considered nominating another senator—either South Carolina's James Byrnes, later appointed in 1941, or Indiana's Sherman Minton, who was forced to await Truman's selection in 1949. But he worried about taking too many supporters from the Senate. Attorney General Homer Cummings urged the elevation of Solicitor General Stanley Reed. Reed was from Kentucky, and the President initially remarked, "Well, McReynolds is from Kentucky, and Stanley will have to wait until McReynolds is no longer with us." Cummings countered that McReynolds was "closely identified with New York City" because of his earlier law practice and that Reed's record justified his nomination. Roosevelt agreed: "Tell Stanley to make himself so disagreeable to McReynolds that the latter will retire right away.

Reed joined the Court in 1938, but McReynolds did not retire until 1941, and the pressure for an appointee from the West steadily grew. In 1938 Cardozo died. The vacancy would be hard to fill, for "Cardozo was not only a great Justice, but a great character, a great person and a great soul . . . held in reverence by multitudes of people and," Cummings observed, "whoever followed him, no matter how good a man he might be would suffer by comparison." Roosevelt had long contemplated appointing Frankfurter to Brandeis's seat. Anticipating "a terrible time getting Frankfurter confirmed," he had earlier unsuccessfully urged Frankfurter to become solicitor general. "I want you on the Supreme Court, Felix," Roosevelt told him, "but I can't appoint you out of the Harvard Law School. What will people say? 'He's a Red. He's a professor. He's had no judicial experience.' But I could appoint you to the Court from the Solicitor General's office." When Cardozo died, Roosevelt at first told Frankfurter, "I've got to appoint a fellow west of the Mississippi—I promised the party leaders he'd be a Westerner the next time." A number of westerners were considered, but FDR found lesser-known candidates unacceptable. Frankfurter was appointed, despite criticism that it would put two Jews and an excessive number of justices from the Atlantic seaboard on the Court.

Geography did not dissuade Roosevelt from then filling Brandeis's seat in 1939 with his Securities and Exchange Commission Chairman, William O. Douglas. At first, Senator Lewis Schwellenbach was considered, but opposition emerged from the other senator from the state of Washington. Frank Murphy had replaced Cummings as attorney general and urged the President to disregard pressure for the selection of a westerner. "Members of the Supreme Court are not called upon nor expected to represent any single interest or group, area or class of persons," Murphy insisted. "They speak for the country as a whole. Considerations of residential area or class, interest, creed or racial extraction, ought therefore be subordinate if not entirely disregarded. Brandeis had recommended Douglas. Born in Minnesota and raised in Yakima, Washington, Douglas claimed Connecticut as his legal residence because he had taught at Yale Law School before joining the SEC. There was accordingly opposition to naming another nonwesterner, but powerful Senate leader's like Idaho's William Borah endorsed the nomination. Douglas later recalled, "When Roosevelt named me he didn't name me from the State of Washington, but he stuck to the record, and named me from Connecticut."

When the midwesterner Pierce Butler died in 1939, there was even greater pressure on Roosevelt to appoint a westerner and a Catholic. Butler was a Catholic, and Catholics were a crucial part of the New Deal coalition. Roosevelt settled on Attorney General Murphy—a Catholic, an affable "Irish mystic," and a former governor of Michigan. Murphy's midwestern Catholic background, however, was only a politically useful rationalization. No less important, morale within the Department of Justice was abysmally low. Murphy was not intellectually equipped to handle the position of attorney general. White House Press Secretary Stephen Early, among others, viewed him "as a complete washout." His appointment was another example of the President's lack of concern for the Court. Roosevelt was not unaware of Murphy's faults. Assistant Attorney General Robert Jackson told him, "Mr. President, I don't think that Mr. Murphy's temperament is that of a judge." His elevation to the Court was nevertheless politically opportune. The President explained to Jackson, "It's the only way I can appoint you Attorney General."

Roosevelt promised later to make Jackson chief justice if he accepted the attorney generalship. Jackson reluctantly agreed. In 1941, McReynolds retired and Chief Justice Hughes informed the President that he would step down at the end of the term. FDR had the opportunity to fill two more seats and to appoint Jackson. Hughes suggested that the chief justiceship go to Stone. He had long aspired to the position and been disappointed because his friend President Hoover passed him over when appointing Hughes. Frankfurter preferred Jackson but agreed that Stone was "senior and qualified professionally to be C.J." He also told FDR that the elevation of Stone, a Republican, would inspire confidence in him "as a national and not a partisan President. In July, Senator Byrnes was named to McReynolds's seat, Stone elevated to the post of chief justice, and Jackson nominated associate justice. When trying to mollify Jackson, the President noted that Stone was within a couple of years of retirement and explained, "I will have another chance at appointment of a Chief Justice, at which time you'd already be over there [in the Court] and would be familiar with the job." At the moment, the arrangement appeared politically advantageous: "one Republican for Chief Justice and two Democrats will not be too partisan." Roosevelt, however, made his last appointment little over a year later. Byrnes was persuaded to leave the Court to become director of the Office of Economic Stabilization, and Rutledge got his seat on the Court.

Roosevelt's appointments illustrate the importance of presidential prestige. FDR was able to overcome pressures imposed on Presidents for political, geographic, and religious representation on the Court. He turned a conservative Court into a liberal one and changed the direction of the Court's policy-making. As a legacy of FDR's liberalism, Black and Douglas remained on the Court until the 1970s and helped forge the Warren Court's decisions on school desegregation, reapportionment, and criminal procedure. . .

MARBURY V. MADISON

(WILLIAM MARBURY v. JAMES MADISON,
SECRETARY OF STATE OF THE UNITED STATES.)

SUPREME COURT OF THE UNITED STATES

OPINION BY MARSHALL

OPINION:
    Afterwards, on the 24th of February the following opinion of the court was delivered by the chief justice.

Opinion of the court.
    . . . In the order in which the court has viewed this subject, the following questions have been considered and decided.
    1st. Has the applicant a right to the commission he demands?
    2dly. If he has a right, and that right has been violated, do the laws of his country afford him a remedy?
    3dly. If they do afford him a remedy, is it a mandamus issuing from this court?
    The first object of enquiry is,
    1st. Has the applicant a right to the commission he demands?
    His right originates in an act of congress passed in February, 1801, concerning the district of Columbia.
    After dividing the district into two counties, the 11th section of this law, enacts, "that there shall be appointed in and for each of the said counties, such number of discreet persons to be justices of the peace as the president of the United States shall, from time to time, think expedient, to continue in office for five years."
    It appears, from the affidavits, that in compliance with this law, a commission for William Marbury as a justice of peace for the county of Washington, was signed by John Adams, then president of the United States; after which the seal of the United States was affixed to it; but the commission has never reached the person for whom it was made out.
    In order to determine whether he is entitled to this commission, it becomes necessary to enquire whether he has been appointed to the office. For if he has been appointed, the law continues him in office for five years, and he is entitled to the possession of those evidences of office, which, being completed, became his property.
    The 2d section of the 2d article of the constitution, declares, that "the president shall nominate, and, by and with the advice and consent of the senate, shall appoint ambassadors, other public ministers and consuls, and all other officers of the United States, whose appointments are not otherwise provided for."
    The third section declares, that "he shall commission all the officers of the United States."
    An act of congress directs the secretary of state to keep the seal of the United States, "to make out and record, and affix the said seal to all civil commissions to officers of the United States, to be appointed by the President, by and with the consent of the senate, or by the President alone; provided that the said seal shall not be affixed to any commission before the same shall have been signed by the President of the United States."
    These are the clauses of the constitution and laws of the United States, which affect this part of the case. . . .
    This is an appointment by the President, by and with the advice and consent of the senate, and is evidenced by no act but the commission itself. In such a case therefore the commission and the appointment seem inseparable; it being almost impossible to show an appointment otherwise than by proving the

existence of a commission; still the commission is not necessarily the appointment; though conclusive evidence of it.

But at what state does it amount to this conclusive evidence?

The answer to this question seems an obvious one. The appointment being the sole act of the President, must be completely evidenced, when it is shown that he has done every thing to be performed by him.

Should the commission, instead of being evidence of an appointment, even be considered as constituting the appointment itself; still it would be made when the last act to be done by the President was performed, or, at furthest, when the commission was complete.

The last act to be done by the President, is the signature of the commission. He has then acted on the advice and consent of the senate to his own nomination. The time for deliberations has then passed. He has decided. His judgment, on the advice and consent of the senate concurring with his nomination, has been made, and the officer is appointed. This appointment is evidenced by an open, unequivocal act; and being the last act required from the person making it, necessarily excludes the idea of its being, so far as respects the appointment, an inchoate and incomplete transaction.

* * *

It is therefore decidedly the opinion of the court, that when a commission has been signed by the President, the appointment is made; and that the commission is complete, when the seal of the United States has been affixed to it by the secretary of state. . . .

Mr. Marbury, then, since his commission was signed by the President, and sealed by the secretary of state, was appointed; and as the law creating the office, gave the officer a right to hold for five years, independent of the executive, the appointment was not revocable; but vested in the officer legal rights, which are protected by the laws of his country.

To withhold his commission, therefore, is an act deemed by the court not warranted by law, but violative of a vested legal right.

This brings us to the second enquiry; which is,

2dly. If he has a right, and that right has been violated, do the laws of his country afford him a remedy?

* * *

It is then the opinion of the court,

1st. That by signing the commission of Mr. Marbury, the president of the United States appointed him a justice of peace, for the county of Washington in the district of Columbia; and that the seal of the United States, affixed thereto by the secretary of state, is conclusive testimony of the verity of the signature, and of the completion of the appointment; and that the appointment conferred on him a legal right to the office for the space of five years.

2dly. That, having this legal title to the office, he has a consequent right to the commission; a refusal to deliver which, is a plain violation of that right, for which the laws of his country afford him a remedy.

It remains to be enquired whether,

3dly. He is entitled to the remedy for which he applies. This depends on,

1st. The nature of the writ applied for, and,

2dly. The power of this court.

1st. The nature of the writ.

Blackstone, in the 3d volume of his commentaries, page 110, defines a mandamus to be, "a command issued in the King's name from the court of King's Bench, and directed to any person, corporation, or inferior court of judicature within the King's dominions, requiring them to do some particular thing therein specified, which appertains to their office and duty, and which the court of King's Bench has previously determined, or at least supposed, to be consonant to right and justice."

Lord Mansfield, in 3d Burrows 1266, in the case of the King v. Baker, et al. states with much precision and explicitness the cases in which this writ may be used.

"Whenever," says that very able judge, "there is a right to execute an office, perform a service, or exercise a franchise (more specifically if it be in a matter of public concern, or attended with profit) and a person is kept out of the possession, or dispossessed of such right, and has no other specific legal remedy, this court ought to assist by mandamus, upon reasons of justice, as the writ expresses, and upon reasons of public policy, to preserve peace, order and good government." In the same case he says, "this writ ought to be used upon all occasions where the law has established no specific remedy, and where in justice and good government there ought to be one."

In addition to the authorities now particularly cited, many others were relied on at the bar, which show how far the practice has conformed to the general doctrines that have been just quoted.

This writ, if awarded, would be directed to an officer of government, and its mandate to him would be, to use the words of Blackstone, "to do a particular thing therein specified, which appertains to his office and duty and which the court has previously determined, or at least supposes, to be consonant to right and justice." Or, in the words of Lord Mansfield, the applicant, in this case, has a right to execute an office of public concern, and is kept out of possession of that right.

These circumstances certainly concur in this case.

* * *

It is not by the office of the person to whom the writ is directed, but the nature of the thing to be done that the propriety or impropriety of issuing a mandamus, is to be determined. Where the head of a department acts in a case, in which executive discretion is to be exercised; in which he is the mere organ of executive will; it is again repeated, that any application to a court to control, in any respect, his conduct, would be rejected without hesitation.

But where he is directed by law to do a certain act affecting the absolute rights of individuals, in the performance of which he is not placed under the particular direction of the President, and the performance of which, the President cannot lawfully forbid, and therefore is never presumed to have forbidden; as for example, to record a commission, or a patent for land, which has received all the legal solemnities; or to give a copy of such record; in such cases, it is not perceived on what ground the courts of the country are further excused from the duty of giving judgment, that right be done to an injured individual, than if the same services were to be performed by a person not the head of a department.

* * *

It is true that the mandamus, now moved for, is not for the performance of an act expressly enjoined by statute.

It is to deliver a commission; on which subject the acts of Congress are silent. This difference is not considered as affecting the case. It has already been stated that the applicant has, to that commission, a vested legal right, of which the executive cannot deprive him. He has been appointed to an office, from which he is not removable at the will of the executive; and being so appointed, he has a right to the commission which the secretary has received from the president for his use. The act of congress does not indeed order the secretary of state to send it to him, but it is placed in his hands for the person entitled to it; and cannot be more lawfully withheld by him, than by any other person.

It was at first doubted whether the action of detinue was not a specified legal remedy for the commission which has been withheld from Mr. Marbury; in which case a mandamus would be improper. But this doubt has yielded to the consideration that the judgment in detinue is for the thing itself, or its value. The value of a public office not to be sold, is incapable of being ascertained; and the applicant has a right to the office itself, or to nothing. He will obtain the office by obtaining the commission, or a copy of it from the record.

This, then, is a plain case for a mandamus, either to deliver the commission, or a copy of it from the record; and it only remains to be enquired,

Whether it can issue from this court.

The act to establish the judicial courts of the United States authorizes the supreme court "to issue writs of mandamus, in cases warranted by the principles and usages of law, to any courts appointed, or persons holding office, under the authority of the United States."

The secretary of state, being a person holding an office under the authority of the United States, is precisely within the letter of the description; and if this court is not authorized to issue a writ of mandamus to such an officer, it must be because the law is unconstitutional, and therefore absolutely incapable of conferring the authority, and assigning the duties which its words purport to confer and assign.

The constitution vests the whole judicial power of the United States in one supreme court, and such inferior courts as congress shall, from time to time, ordain and establish. This power is expressly extended to all cases arising under the laws of the United States; and consequently, in some form, may be exercised over the present case; because the right claimed is given by a law of the United States.

In the distribution of this power it is declared that "the supreme court shall have original jurisdiction in all cases affecting ambassadors, other public ministers and consuls, and those in which a state shall be a party. In all other cases, the supreme court shall have appellate jurisdiction."

It has been insisted, at the bar, that as the original grant of jurisdiction, to the supreme and inferior courts, is general, and the clause, assigning original jurisdiction to the supreme court, contains no negative or restrictive words; the power remains to the legislature, to assign original jurisdiction to that court in other cases than those specified in the article which has been recited; provided those cases belong to the judicial power of the United States.

If it had been intended to leave it to the discretion of the legislature to apportion the judicial power between the supreme and inferior courts according to the will of that body, it would certainly have been useless to have proceeded further than to have defined the judicial powers, and the tribunals in which it should be vested. The subsequent part of the section is mere surplusage, is entirely without meaning, if such is to be the construction. If congress remains at liberty to give this court appellate jurisdiction, where the constitution has declared their jurisdiction shall be original; and original jurisdiction where the constitution has declared it shall be appellate; the distribution of jurisdiction, made in the constitution, is form without substance. . . .

When an instrument organizing fundamentally a judicial system, divides it into one supreme, and so many inferior courts as the legislature may ordain and establish; then enumerates its powers, and proceeds so far to distribute them, as to define the jurisdiction of the supreme court by declaring the cases in which it shall take original jurisdiction, and that in others it shall take appellate jurisdiction; the plain import of the words seems to be, that in one class of cases its jurisdiction is original, and not appellate; in the other it is appellate, and not original. If any other construction would render the clause inoperative, that is an additional reason for rejecting such other construction, and for adhering to their obvious meaning.

To enable this court then to issue a mandamus, it must be shown to be an exercise of appellate jurisdiction, or to be necessary to enable them to exercise appellate jurisdiction. . . .

It is the essential criterion of appellate jurisdiction, that it revises and corrects the proceedings in a cause already instituted, and does not create that cause. Although, therefore, a mandamus may be directed to courts, yet to issue such a writ to an officer for the delivery of a paper, is in effect the same as to sustain an original action for that paper, and therefore seems not to belong to appellate, but to original jurisdiction. Neither is it necessary in such a case as this, to enable the court to exercise its appellate jurisdiction.

The authority, therefore, given to the supreme court, by the act establishing the judicial courts of the United States, to issue writs of mandamus to public officers, appears not to be warranted by the constitution; and it becomes necessary to enquire whether a jurisdiction, so conferred, can be exercised.

The question, whether an act, repugnant to the constitution, can become the law of the land, is a question deeply interesting to the United States; but, happily, not of an intricacy proportioned to its interest. It seems only necessary to recognize certain principles, supposed to have been long and well established, to decide it.

That the people have an original right to establish, for their future government, such principles as, in their opinion, shall most conduce to their own happiness, is the basis, on which the whole American fabric has been erected. The exercise of this original right is a very great exertion; nor can it, nor ought it to be frequently repeated. The principles, therefore, so established, are deemed fundamental. And as the authority, from which they proceed, is supreme, and can seldom act, they are designed to be permanent.

This original and supreme will organizes the government, and assigns, to different departments, their respective powers. It may either stop here; or establish certain limits not to be transcended by those departments.

The government of the United States is of the latter description. The powers of the legislature are defined, and limited; and that those limits may not be mistaken, or forgotten, the constitution is written. To what purpose are powers limited, and to what purpose is that limitation committed to writing, if these limits may, at any time, be passed by those intended to be restrained? The distinction, between a government with limited and unlimited powers, is abolished, if those limits do not confine the persons on whom they are imposed, and if acts prohibited and acts allowed, are of equal obligation. It is a proposition too plain to be contested, that the constitution controls any legislative act repugnant to it; or, that the legislature may alter the constitution by an ordinary act.

Between these alternatives there is no middle ground. The constitution is either a superior, paramount law, unchangeable by ordinary means, or it is on a level with ordinary legislative acts, and like other acts, is alterable when the legislature shall please to alter it.

If the former part of the alternative be true, then a legislative act contrary to the constitution is not law: if the latter part be true, then written constitutions are absurd attempts, on the part of the people, to limit a power, in its own nature illimitable.

Certainly all those who have framed written constitutions contemplate them as forming the fundamental and paramount law of the nation, and consequently the theory of every such government must be, that an act of the legislature, repugnant to the constitution, is void. . . .

It is emphatically the province and duty of the judicial department to say what the law is. Those who apply the rule to particular cases, must of necessity expound and interpret that rule. If two laws conflict with each other, the courts must decide on the operation of each.

So if a law be in opposition to the constitution; if both the law and the constitution apply to a particular case, so that the court must either decide that case conformably to the law,   disregarding the constitution; or conformably to the constitution, disregarding the law; the court must determine which of these conflicting rules governs the case. This is of the very essence of judicial duty.

* * *

The oath of office, too, imposed by the legislature, is completely demonstrative of the legislative opinion on the subject. It is in these words, "I do solemnly swear that I will administer justice without respect to persons, and do equal right to the poor and to the rich; and that I will faithfully and impartially discharge all the duties incumbent on me as according to the best of my abilities and understanding, agreeably to the constitution, and laws of the United States."

Why does a judge swear to discharge his duties agreeably to the constitution of the United States, if that constitution forms no rule for his government? if it is closed upon him, and cannot be inspected by him?

If such be the real state of things, this is worse than solemn mockery. To prescribe, or to take this oath, becomes equally a crime.

It is also not entirely unworthy of observation, that in declaring what shall be the supreme law of the land, the constitution itself is first mentioned; and not the laws of the United States generally, but those only which shall be made in pursuance of the constitution, have that rank.

Thus, the particular phraseology of the constitution of the United States confirms and strengthens the principle, supposed to be essential to all written constitutions, that a law repugnant to the constitution is void; and that courts, as well as other departments, are bound by that instrument.

The rule must be discharged.

ROE V. WADE

(ROE ET AL. v. WADE, DISTRICT ATTORNEY OF DALLAS COUNTY)

SUPREME COURT OF THE UNITED STATES

December 13, 1971, Argued/January 22, 1973, Decided

OPINION BY BLACKMUN

OPINION:

This Texas federal appeal and its Georgia companion, *Doe v. Bolton*, present constitutional challenges to state criminal abortion legislation. The Texas statutes under attack here are typical of those that have been in effect in many States for approximately a century. . . .

We forthwith acknowledge our awareness of the sensitive and emotional nature of the abortion controversy, of the vigorous opposing views, even among physicians, and of the deep and seemingly absolute convictions that the subject inspires. One's philosophy, one's experiences, one's exposure to the raw edges of human existence, one's religious training, one's attitudes toward life and family and their values, and the moral standards one establishes and seeks to observe, are all likely to influence and to color one's thinking and conclusions about abortion.

In addition, population growth, pollution, poverty, and racial overtones tend to complicate and not to simplify the problem.

Our task, of course, is to resolve the issue by constitutional measurement, free of emotion and of predilection. We seek earnestly to do this, and, because we do, we have inquired into, and in this opinion place some emphasis upon, medical and medical-legal history and what that history reveals about man's attitudes toward the abortion procedure over the centuries. We bear in mind, too, "Mr. Justice Holmes' admonition in his now-vindicated dissent in *Lochner v. New York*, 198 U.S. 45, 76 (1905):

"[The Constitution] is made for people of fundamentally differing views, and the accident of our finding certain opinions natural and familiar or novel and even shocking ought not to conclude our judgment upon the question whether statutes embodying them conflict with the Constitution of the United States."

The Texas statutes that concern us here are Arts. 1191-1194 and 1196 of the State's Penal Code. These make it a crime to "procure an abortion," as therein defined, or to attempt one, except with respect to "an abortion procured or attempted by medical advice for the purpose of saving the life of the mother." Similar statutes are in existence in a majority of the States. . . .

Jane Roe, a single woman who was residing in Dallas County, Texas, instituted this federal action in March 1970 against the District Attorney of the county. She sought a declaratory judgment that the Texas criminal abortion statutes were unconstitutional on their face, and an injunction restraining the defendant from enforcing the statutes.

Roe alleged that she was unmarried and pregnant; that she wished to terminate her pregnancy by an abortion "performed by a competent, licensed physician, under safe, clinical conditions"; that she was unable to get a "legal" abortion in Texas because her life did not appear to be threatened by the continuation of her pregnancy; and that she could not afford to travel to another jurisdiction in order to secure a legal abortion under safe conditions. She claimed that the Texas statutes were unconstitutionally vague and that they abridged her right of personal privacy, protected by the First, Fourth, Fifth, Ninth, and Fourteenth Amendments. By an amendment to her complaint Roe purported to sue "on behalf of herself and all other women" similarly situated. . . .

Viewing Roe's case as of the time of its filing and thereafter until as late as May, there can be little dispute that it then presented a case or controversy and that, wholly apart from the class aspects, she, as a pregnant single woman thwarted by the Texas criminal abortion laws, had standing to challenge those statutes. . . .

The appellee notes, however, that the record does not disclose that Roe was pregnant at the time of the District Court hearing on May 22, 1970, or on the following June 17 when the court's opinion and judgment were filed. And he suggests that Roe's case must now be moot because she and all other members of her class are no longer subject to any 1970 pregnancy.

The usual rule in federal cases is that an actual controversy must exist at stages of appellate or certiorari review, and not simply at the date the action is initiated. But when, as here, pregnancy is a significant fact in the litigation, the normal 266-day human gestation period is so short that the pregnancy will come to term before the usual appellate process is complete. If that termination makes a case moot, pregnancy litigation seldom will survive much beyond the trial stage, and appellate review will be effectively denied. Our law should not be that rigid. Pregnancy often comes more than once to the same woman, and in the general population, if man is to survive, it will always be with us. Pregnancy provides a classic justification for a conclusion of nonmootness. It truly could be "capable of repetition, yet evading review."

We, therefore, agree with the District Court that Jane Roe had standing to undertake this litigation, that she presented a justiciable controversy, and that the termination of her 1970 pregnancy has not rendered her case moot. . . .

The principal thrust of appellant's attack on the Texas statutes is that they improperly invade a right, said to be possessed by the pregnant woman, to choose to terminate her pregnancy. Appellant would discover this right in the concept of personal "liberty" embodied in the Fourteenth Amendment's Due Process Clause; or in personal, marital, familial, and sexual privacy said to be protected by the Bill of Rights or its penumbras; or among those rights reserved to the people by the Ninth Amendment. Before addressing this claim, we feel it desirable briefly to survey, in several aspects, the history of abortion, for such insight as that history may afford us, and then to examine the state purposes and interests behind the criminal abortion laws.

It perhaps is not generally appreciated that the restrictive criminal abortion laws in effect in a majority of States today are of relatively recent vintage. Those laws, generally proscribing abortion or its attempt at any time during pregnancy except when necessary to preserve the pregnant woman's life, are not of ancient or even of common-law origin. Instead, they derive from statutory changes effected, for the most part, in the latter half of the 19th century.

The Common Law

It is undisputed that at common law, abortion performed before "quickening" — the first recognizable movement of the fetus in utero, appearing usually from the 16th to the 18th week of pregnancy— was not an indictable offense. The absence of a common-law crime for pre-quickening abortion appears to have developed from a confluence of earlier philosophical, theological, and civil and canon law concepts of when life begins. These disciplines variously approached the question in terms of the point at which the embryo or fetus became "formed" or recognizably human, or in terms of when a "person" came into being, that is, infused with a "soul" or "animated." A loose consensus evolved in early English law that these events occurred at some point between conception and live. . . . . The significance of quickening was echoed by later common-law scholars and found its way into the received common law in this country.

Whether abortion of a quick fetus was a felony at common law, or even a lesser crime, is still disputed. . . . A recent review of the common-law precedents . . . makes it now appear doubtful that abortion was ever firmly established as a common-law crime even with respect to the destruction of a quick fetus.

The American Law

In this country, the law in effect in all but a few States until mid-19th century was the pre-existing English common law. Connecticut, the first State to enact abortion legislation, adopted in 1821 that part of Lord Ellenborough's Act that related to a woman "quick with child." The death penalty was not imposed. Abortion before quickening was made a crime in that State only in 1860. In 1828, New York enacted legislation that, in two respects, was to serve as a model for early anti-abortion statutes. First, while barring destruction of an unquickened fetus as well as a quick fetus, it made the former only a misdemeanor, but the latter second-degree manslaughter. Second, it incorporated a concept of therapeutic abortion by providing that an abortion was excused if it "shall have been necessary to preserve the life of such mother, or shall have been advised by two physicians to be necessary for such purpose." By 1840, when Texas had received the common law, only eight American States had statutes dealing with abortion. It was not until after the War Between the States that legislation began generally to replace the common law. Most of these initial statutes dealt severely with abortion after quickening but were lenient with it before quickening. Most punished attempts equally with completed abortions. While many statutes included the exception for an abortion thought by one or more physicians to be necessary to save the mother's life, that provision soon disappeared and the typical law required that the procedure actually be necessary for that purpose.

Gradually, in the middle and late 19th century the quickening distinction disappeared from the statutory law of most States and the degree of the offense and the penalties were increased. By the end of the 1950's, a large majority of the jurisdictions banned abortion, however and whenever performed, unless done to save or preserve the life of the mother. The exceptions, Alabama and the District of Columbia, permitted abortion to preserve the mother's health. Three States permitted abortions that were not "unlawfully" performed or that were not "without lawful justification," leaving interpretation of those standards to the courts. In the past several years, however, a trend toward liberalization of abortion statutes has resulted in adoption, by about one-third of the States, of less stringent laws . . .

It is thus apparent that at common law, at the time of the adoption of our Constitution, and throughout the major portion of the 19th century, abortion was viewed with less disfavor than under most American statutes currently in effect. Phrasing it another way, a woman enjoyed a substantially broader right to terminate a pregnancy than she does in most States today. At least with respect to the early stage of pregnancy, and very possibly without such a limitation, the opportunity to make this choice was present in this country well into the 19th century. Even later, the law continued for some time to treat less punitively an abortion procured in early pregnancy.

The Position of the American Medical Association

The anti-abortion mood prevalent in this country in the late 19th century was shared by the medical profession. Indeed, the attitude of the profession may have played a significant role in the enactment of stringent criminal abortion legislation during that period.

An AMA Committee on Criminal Abortion was appointed in May 1857. It presented its report, to the Twelfth Annual Meeting. That report observed that the Committee had been appointed to investigate criminal abortion "with a view to its general suppression." It deplored abortion and its frequency and it listed three causes of "this general demoralization":

"The first of these causes is a wide-spread popular ignorance of the true character of the crime — a belief, even among mothers themselves, that the "foetus is not alive till after the period of quickening.",

"The second of the agents alluded to is the fact that the profession themselves are frequently supposed careless of foetal life. . . .",

"The third reason of the frightful extent of this crime is found in the grave defects of our laws, both common and statute, as regards the independent and actual existence of the child before birth, as a living being. These errors, which are sufficient in most instances to prevent conviction, are based, and only based, upon mistaken and exploded medical dogmas. With strange inconsistency, the law fully acknowledges the foetus in utero and its inherent rights, for civil purposes; while personally and as criminally affected, it fails to recognize it, and to its life as yet denies all protection." The Committee then offered, and the Association adopted, resolutions protesting "against such unwarrantable destruction of human life," calling upon state legislatures to revise their abortion laws, and requesting the cooperation of state medical societies "in pressing the subject."

In 1871 a long and vivid report was submitted by the Committee on Criminal Abortion. It ended with the observation, "We had to deal with human life. In a matter of less importance we could entertain no compromise. An honest judge on the bench would call things by their proper names. We could do no less." It proffered resolutions, adopted by the Association, recommending, among other things, that it "be unlawful and unprofessional for any physician to induce abortion or premature labor, without the concurrent opinion of at least one respectable consulting physician, and then always with a view to the safety of the child — if that be possible," and calling "the attention of the clergy of all denominations to the perverted views of morality entertained by a large class of females — aye, and men also, on this important question."

Except for periodic condemnation of the criminal abortionist, no further formal AMA action took place until 1967. In that year, the Committee on Human reproduction urged the adoption of a stated policy of opposition to induced abortion, except when there is "documented medical evidence" of a threat to the health or life of the mother, or that the child "may be born with incapacitating physical deformity or mental deficiency," or that a pregnancy "resulting from legally established statutory or forcible rape or incest may constitute a threat to the mental or physical health of the patient," two other physicians "chosen because of their recognized professional competence have examined the patient and have concurred in writing, "and the procedure "is performed in a hospital accredited by the Joint Commission on Accreditation of Hospitals.". . .

In 1970, after the introduction of a variety of proposed resolutions, and of a report from its Board of Trustees, a reference committee noted "polarization of the medical profession on this controversial issue"; division among those who had testified; a difference of opinion among AMA councils and committees; "the remarkable shift in testimony" in six months, felt to be influenced "by the rapid changes in state laws and by the judicial decisions which tend to make abortion more freely available;" and a feeling "that this trend will continue." On June 25, 1970, the House of Delegates adopted preambles and most of the resolutions proposed by the reference committee. The preambles emphasized "the best interests of the patient," "sound clinical judgment," and "informed patient consent," in contrast to "mere acquiescence to the patient's demand." The resolutions asserted that abortion is a medical procedure that should be performed by a licensed physician in an accredited hospital only after consultation with two other physicians and in conformity with state law, and that no party to the procedure should be required to violate personally held moral principles. The AMA Judicial Council rendered a complementary opinion. . . .

Three reasons have been advanced to explain historically the enactment of criminal abortion laws in the 19th century and to justify their continued existence.

It has been argued occasionally that these laws were the product of a Victorian social concern to discourage illicit sexual conduct. Texas, however, does not advance this justification in the present case, and it appears that no court or commentator has taken the argument seriously . . .

A second reason is concerned with abortion as a medical procedure. When most criminal abortion laws were first enacted, the procedure was a hazardous one for the woman. This was particularly true prior to the development of antisepsis. Antiseptic techniques, of course, were based on discoveries by Lister, Pasteur, and others first announced in 1867, but were not generally accepted and employed until about the turn of the century. Abortion mortality was high. Even after 1900, and perhaps until as late as the development of antibiotics in the 1940's, standard modem techniques such as dilation and curettage were not nearly so safe as they are today. Thus, it has been argued that a State's real concern in enacting a criminal abortion law was to protect the pregnant woman, that is, to restrain her from submitting to a procedure that placed her life in serious jeopardy.

Modern medical techniques have altered this situation. . . .

The third reason is the State's interest—some phrase it in terms of duty—in protecting prenatal life. Some of the argument for this justification rests on the theory that a new human life is present from the moment of conception. The State's interest and general obligation to protect life then extends, it is argued, to prenatal life. Only when the life of the pregnant mother herself is at stake, balanced against the life she carries within her, should the interest of the embryo or fetus not prevail. Logically, of course, a legitimate state interest in this area need not stand or fall on acceptance of the belief that life begins at conception or at some other point prior to live birth. In assessing the State's interest, recognition may be given to the less rigid claim that as long as at least potential life is involved, the State may assert interests beyond the protection of the pregnant woman alone. Parties challenging state abortion laws have sharply disputed in some courts the contention that a purpose of these laws, when enacted, was to protect prenatal life. Pointing to the absence of legislative history to support the contention, they claim that most state laws were designed solely to protect the woman.

Parties challenging state abortion laws have sharply disputed in some courts the contention that a purpose of these laws, when enacted, was to protect prenatal life. Pointing to the absence of legislative history to support the contention, they claim that most state laws were designed solely to protect the woman.

Because medical advances have lessened this concern, at least with respect to abortion in early pregnancy, they argue that with respect to such abortions the laws can no longer be justified by any state interest. There is some scholarly support for this view of original purpose. The few state courts called upon to interpret their laws in the late 19th and early 20th centuries did focus on the State's interest in protecting the woman's health rather than in preserving the embryo and fetus. Proponents of this view point out that in many States, including Texas, by statute or judicial interpretation, the pregnant woman herself could not be prosecuted for self-abortion or for cooperating in an abortion performed upon her by another. They claim that adoption of the "quickening" distinction through received common law and state statutes tacitly recognizes the greater health hazards inherent in late abortion and impliedly repudiates the theory that life begins at conception.

It is with these interests, and the weight to be attached to them, that this case is concerned.

The Constitution does not explicitly mention any right of privacy. In a line of decisions, however, going back perhaps as far as *Union Pacific R. Co. v. Botsford*, the Court has recognized that a right of personal privacy, or a guarantee of certain areas or zones of privacy, does exist under the Constitution. In varying contexts, the Court or individual Justices have, indeed, found at least the roots of that right in the First Amendment; in the Fourth and Fifth Amendments; in the penumbras of the Bill of Rights; in the Ninth Amendment; or in the concept of liberty guaranteed by the first section of the Fourteenth Amendment. These decisions make it clear that only personal rights that can be deemed "fundamental" or "implicit in the concept of ordered liberty," are included in this guarantee of personal privacy. They also make it clear that the right has some extension to activities relating to marriage; procreation; contraception; family relationships; and child rearing and education. This right of privacy, whether it be founded in the Fourteenth Amendment's concept of personal liberty and restrictions upon state action, as we feel it is, or, as the District Court determined, in the Ninth Amendment's reservation of rights to the people, is broad enough to encompass a woman's decision whether or not to terminate her pregnancy. The detriment that the State would impose upon the pregnant woman by denying this choice altogether is apparent. Specific and direct harm medically diagnosable even in early pregnancy may be involved. Maternity, or additional offspring, may force upon the woman a distressful life and future. Psychological harm may be imminent. Mental and physical health may be taxed by child care. There is also the distress, for all concerned, associated with the unwanted child, and there is the problem of bringing a child into a family already unable, psychologically and otherwise, to care for it. In other cases, as in this one, the additional difficulties and continuing stigma of unwed motherhood may be involved. All these are factors the woman and her responsible physician necessarily will consider in consultation.

On the basis of elements such as these, appellant and some *amici* argue that the woman's right is absolute and that she is entitled to terminate her pregnancy at whatever time, in whatever way, and for whatever reason she alone chooses. With this we do not agree. Appellant's arguments that Texas either has no valid interest at all in regulating the abortion decision, or no interest strong enough to support any limitation upon the woman's sole determination, are unpersuasive. The Court's decisions recognizing a right of privacy also acknowledge that some state regulation in areas protected by that right is appropriate. As noted above, a State may properly assert important interests in safeguarding health, in maintaining medical standards, and in protecting potential life. At some point in pregnancy, these respective interests become sufficiently compelling to sustain regulation of the factors that govern the abortion decision. The privacy right involved, therefore, cannot be said to be absolute. In fact, it is not clear to us that the claim asserted by some *amici* that one has an unlimited right to do with one's body as one pleases bears a close relationship to the right of privacy previously articulated in the Court's decisions. The Court has refused to recognize an unlimited right of this kind in the past.

We, therefore, conclude that the right of personal privacy includes the abortion decision, but that this right is not unqualified and must be considered against important state interests in regulation.

The appellee and certain amici argue that the fetus is a "person" within the language and meaning of the Fourteenth Amendment. In support of this, they outline at length and in detail the well-known facts of fetal development. If this suggestion of personhood is established, the appellant's case, of course, collapses, for the fetus' right to life would then be guaranteed specifically by the Amendment. The appellant conceded as much on reargument. On the other hand, the appellee conceded on reargument that no case could be cited that holds that a fetus is a person within the meaning of the Fourteenth Amendment.

The Constitution does not define "person" in so many words. Section 1 of the Fourteenth Amendment contains three references to "person." The first, in defining "citizens," speaks of "persons born or naturalized in the United States." The word also appears both in the Due Process Clause and in the Equal Protection Clause. "Person" is used in other places in the Constitution: in the listing of qualifications for Representatives and Senators, in the Apportionment Clause, in the Migration and Importation provision, in the Emolument Clause, in the Electors provisions, in the provision outlining qualifications for the office of President, in the Extradition provisions, and the superseded Fugitive Slave Clause 3; and in the Fifth, Twelfth, and Twenty-second Amendments, as well as in the Fourteenth Amendment. But in nearly all these instances, the use of the word is such that it has application only postnatally. None indicates, with any assurance, that it has any possible pre-natal application.

All this, together with our observation, supra, that throughout the major portion of the 19th century prevailing legal abortion practices were far freer than they are today, persuades us that the word "person," as used in the Fourteenth Amendment, does not include the unborn. This is in accord with the results reached in those few cases where the issue has been squarely presented. Indeed, our decision in *United States v. Vuitch*, inferentially is to the same effect, for we there would not have indulged in statutory interpretation favorable to abortion in specified circumstances if the necessary consequence was the termination of life entitled to Fourteenth Amendment protection.

Texas urges that, apart from the Fourteenth Amendment, life begins at conception and is present throughout pregnancy, and that, therefore, the State has a compelling interest in protecting that life from and after conception. We need not resolve the difficult question of when life begins. When those trained in the respective disciplines of medicine, philosophy, and theology are unable to arrive at any consensus, the judiciary, at this point in the development of man's knowledge, is not in a position to speculate as to the answer.

It should be sufficient to note briefly the wide divergence of thinking on this most sensitive and difficult question. There has always been strong support for the view that life does not begin until live birth. This was the belief of the Stoics. It appears to be the predominant, though not the unanimous, attitude of the Jewish faith. It may be taken to represent also the position of a large segment of the Protestant community, insofar as that can be ascertained; organized groups that have taken a formal position on the abortion issue have generally regarded abortion as a matter for the conscience of the individual and her family. As we have noted, the common law found greater significance in quickening. Physicians and their scientific colleagues have regarded that event with less interest and have tended to focus either upon conception, upon live birth, or upon the interim point at which the fetus becomes "viable," that is, potentially able to live outside the mother's womb, albeit with artificial aid. Viability is usually placed at about seven months (28 weeks) but may occur earlier, even at 24 weeks. . . .

In areas other than criminal abortion, the law has been reluctant to endorse any theory that life, as we recognize it, begins before live birth or to accord legal rights to the unborn except in narrowly defined situations and except when the rights are contingent upon live birth. . . . In short, the unborn have never been recognized in the law as persons in the whole sense.

In view of all this, we do not agree that, by adopting one theory of life, Texas may override the rights of the pregnant woman that are at stake. We repeat, however, that the State does have an important and legitimate interest in preserving and protecting the health of the pregnant woman, whether she be a resident of the State or a nonresident who seeks medical consultation and treatment there, and that it has still another important and legitimate interest in protecting the potentiality of human life. These interests are separate and distinct. Each grows in substantiality as the woman approaches term and, at a point during pregnancy, each becomes "compelling."

With respect to the State's important and legitimate interest in the health of the mother, the "compelling" point, in the light of present medical knowledge, is at approximately the end of the first trimester. This is so because of the now-established medical fact, . . . that until the end of the first trimester mortality in abortion may be less than mortality in normal childbirth. It follows that, from and after this point, a State may regulate the abortion procedure to the extent that the regulation reasonably relates to the preservation and protection of maternal health. Examples of permissible state regulation in this area are requirements as to the qualifications of the person who is to perform the abortion; as to the licensure of that person; as to the facility in which the procedure is to be performed, that is, whether it must be a hospital or may be a clinic or some other place of less-than-hospital status; as to the licensing of the facility; and the like. This means, on the other hand, that, for the period of pregnancy prior to this "compelling" point, the attending physician, in consultation with his patient, is free to determine, without regulation by the State, that, in his medical judgment, the patient's pregnancy should be terminated. If that decision is reached, the judgment may be effectuated by an abortion free of interference by the State.

With respect to the State's important and legitimate interest in potential life, the "compelling" point is at viability. This is so because the fetus then presumably has the capability of meaningful life outside the mother's womb. State regulation protective of fetal life after viability thus has both logical and biological justifications. If the State is interested in protecting fetal life after viability, it may go so far as to proscribe abortion during that period, except when it is necessary to preserve the life or health of the mother. Measured against these standards, Art. 1196 of the Texas Penal Code, in restricting legal abortions to those "procured or attempted by medical advice for the purpose of saving the life of the mother," sweeps too broadly. The statute makes no distinction between abortions performed early in pregnancy and those performed later, and it limits to a single reason, "saving" the mother's life, the legal justification for the procedure. The statute, therefore, cannot survive the "constitutional attack made upon it here.

"To summarize and to repeat:",

1. A state criminal abortion statute of the current Texas type, that excepts from criminality only a life-saving procedure on behalf of the mother, without regard to pregnancy stage and without recognition of the other interests involved, is violative of the Due Process Clause of the Fourteenth Amendment.

   (a) For the stage prior to approximately the end of the first trimester, the abortion decision and its effectuation must be left to the medical judgment of the pregnant woman's attending physician.

   (b) For the stage subsequent to approximately the end of the first trimester, the State, in promoting its interest in the health of the mother, may, if it chooses, regulate the abortion procedure in ways that are reasonably related to maternal health.

   (c) For the stage subsequent to viability, the State in promoting its interest in the potentiality of human life may, if it chooses, regulate, and even proscribe, abortion except where it is necessary, in appropriate medical judgment, for the preservation of the life or health of the mother. . . .

This holding, we feel, is consistent with the relative weights of the respective interests involved, with the lessons and examples of medical and legal history, with the lenity of the common law, and with the demands of the profound problems of the present day. The decision leaves the State free to place increasing restrictions on abortion as the period of pregnancy lengthens, so long as those restrictions are tailored to the recognized state interests. The decision vindicates the right of the physician to administer medical treatment according to his professional judgment up to the points where important state interests provide compelling justifications for intervention. Up to those points, the abortion decision in all its aspects is inherently, and primarily, a medical decision, and basic responsibility for it must rest with the physician. If an individual practitioner abuses the privilege of exercising proper medical judgment, the usual remedies, judicial and intra-professional, are available.

It is so ordered.

"DISSENT BY: REHNQUIST",

"DISSENT: MR. JUSTICE REHNQUIST, dissenting.",

The Court's opinion brings to the decision of this troubling question both extensive historical fact and a wealth of legal scholarship. While the opinion thus commands my respect, I find myself nonetheless in fundamental disagreement with those parts of it that invalidate the Texas statute in question, and therefore dissent.

The Court's opinion decides that a State may impose virtually no restriction on the performance of abortions during the first trimester of pregnancy. Our previous decisions indicate that a necessary predicate for such an opinion is a plaintiff who was in her first trimester of pregnancy at some time during the pendency of her lawsuit. While a party may vindicate his own constitutional rights, he may not seek vindication for the rights of others. The Court's statement of facts in this case makes clear, however, that the record in no way indicates the presence of such a plaintiff. We know only that plaintiff Roe at the time of filing her complaint was a pregnant woman; for aught that appears in this record, she may have been in her last trimester of pregnancy as of the date the complaint was filed.

Nothing in the Court's opinion indicates that Texas might not constitutionally apply its proscription of abortion as written to a woman in that stage of pregnancy. Nonetheless, the Court uses her complaint against the Texas statute as a fulcrum for deciding that States may impose virtually no restrictions on medical abortions performed during the first trimester of pregnancy. In deciding such a hypothetical lawsuit, the Court departs from the longstanding admonition that it should never "formulate a rule of constitutional law broader than is required by the precise facts to which it is to be applied.

Even if there were a plaintiff in this case capable of litigating the issue which the Court decides, I would reach a conclusion opposite to that reached by the Court. I have difficulty in concluding, as the Court does, that the right of "privacy" is involved in this case. Texas, by the statute here challenged, bars the performance of a medical abortion by a licensed physician on a plaintiff such as Roe. A transaction resulting in an operation such as this is not "private" in the ordinary usage of that word. Nor is the "privacy" that the Court finds here even a distant relative of the freedom from searches and seizures protected by the Fourth Amendment to the Constitution, which the Court has referred to as embodying a right to privacy.

If the Court means by the term "privacy" no more than that the claim of a person to be free from unwanted state regulation of consensual transactions may be a form of "liberty" protected by the Fourteenth Amendment, there is no doubt that similar claims have been upheld in our earlier decisions on the basis of that liberty. I agree with the statement of MR. JUSTICE STEWART in his concurring opinion that the "liberty," against deprivation of which without due process the Fourteenth Amendment protects, embraces more than the rights found in the Bill of Rights. But that liberty is not guaranteed absolutely against deprivation, only against deprivation without due process of law. The test traditionally applied in the area of social and economic legislation is whether or not a law such as that challenged has a rational relation to a valid state objective. The Due Process Clause of the Fourteenth Amendment undoubtedly does place a limit, albeit a broad one, on legislative power to enact laws such as this. If the Texas statute were to prohibit an abortion even where the mother's life is in jeopardy, I have little doubt that such a statute would lack a rational relation to a valid state objective under the test stated in Williamson, supra. But the Court's sweeping invalidation of any restrictions on abortion during the first trimester is impossible to justify under that standard, and the conscious weighing of competing factors that the Court's opinion apparently substitutes for the established test is far more appropriate to a legislative judgment than to a judicial one.

The Court eschews the history of the Fourteenth Amendment in its reliance on the "compelling state interest" test. But the Court adds a new wrinkle to this test by transposing it from the legal considerations associated with the Equal Protection Clause of the Fourteenth Amendment to this case arising under the Due Process Clause of the Fourteenth Amendment. Unless I misapprehend the consequences of this transplanting of the "compelling state interest test," the Court's opinion will accomplish the seemingly impossible feat of leaving this area of the law more confused than it found it.

While the Court's opinion quotes from the dissent of Mr. Justice Holmes in *Lochner v. New York*, the result it reaches is more closely attuned to the majority opinion of Mr. Justice Peckham in that case. As in Lochner and similar cases applying substantive due process standards to economic and social welfare legislation, the adoption of the compelling state interest standard will inevitably require this Court to examine the legislative policies and pass on the wisdom of these policies in the very process of deciding whether a particular state interest put forward may or may not be "compelling." The decision here to break pregnancy into three distinct terms and to outline the permissible restrictions the State may impose in each one, for example, partakes more of judicial legislation than it does of a determination of the intent of the drafters of the Fourteenth Amendment.

The fact that a majority of the States reflecting, after all, the majority sentiment in those States, have had restrictions on abortions for at least a century is a strong indication, it seems to me, that the asserted right to an abortion is not "so rooted in the traditions and conscience of our people as to be ranked as fundamental." Even today, when society's views on abortion are changing, the very existence of the debate is evidence that the "right" to an abortion is not so universally accepted as the appellant would have us believe.

To reach its result, the Court necessarily has had to find within the scope of the Fourteenth Amendment a right that was apparently completely unknown to the drafters of the Amendment. As early as 1821, the first state law dealing directly with abortion was enacted by the Connecticut Legislature. By the time of the adoption of the Fourteenth Amendment in 1868, there were at least 36 laws enacted by state or territorial legislatures limiting abortion. While many States have amended or updated their laws, 21 of the laws on the books in 1868 remain in effect today. Indeed, the Texas statute struck down today was, as the majority notes, first enacted in 1857 and "has remained substantially "unchanged to the present time."

There apparently was no question concerning the validity of this provision or of any of the other state statutes when the Fourteenth Amendment was adopted. The only conclusion possible from this history is that the drafters did not intend to have the Fourteenth Amendment withdraw from the States the power to legislate with respect to this matter.

Even if one were to agree that the case that the Court decides were here, and that the enunciation of the substantive constitutional law in the Court's opinion were proper, the actual disposition of the case by the Court is still difficult to justify. The Texas statute is struck down in toto, even though the Court apparently concedes that at later periods of pregnancy Texas might impose these selfsame statutory limitations on abortion. My understanding of past practice is that a statute found to be invalid as applied to a particular plaintiff, but not unconstitutional as a whole, is not simply "struck down" but is, instead, declared unconstitutional as applied to the fact situation before the Court.

For all of the foregoing reasons, I respectfully dissent.

CHAPTER 7

INTRODUCTION

This chapter is the most revised from the first to the second edition. In the first edition, I had separate chapters for political parties and interest groups. However, as has been accepted by the authors of most American Government textbooks, these two entities have such an influence on the American political system that the combination makes sense. So, I have also chosen to combine them and have also added a new article.

Concerning political parties, what are political parties and why do we have them? No less an authority than George Washington, in his farewell address as President of the United States, warned against the development of political parties! Why did we not heed his advice? What are their functions? Why only two major parties? Are today's political parties the same as those of fifty years ago? These are at least some of the issues addressed by the first four entries in this chapter.

Have interest groups enhanced or corrupted our political system? Have they allowed those previously unheard or unempowered to be full or partial participants? Have they opened doors of access or are they just another entry point for those who have always been able to use the system? Debates range considerably concerning interest groups and the tone of conversation frequently becomes hostile. Whether it is because they have diminished the role of political parties or because they have brought "unwholesome" amounts of money into the political arena or because they offer the false promise of power to the powerless, few people who closely observe the political system are blase about interest groups.

The first article, written by V. O. Key addresses a variety of issues concerning political parties. The most important questions for you to be able to answer are:

1. How and why did early political parties develop?

2. What are the purposes of political parties?

3. What are the factors that have influenced or perpetuated the existence of a two party system in the United States?

Douglas Amy wrote the second piece which is interesting to me because of its' perspective. Many scholars write fascinating articles concerning the existence of a two party system, why it exists, etc. (see the Key article). Amy addresses what would need to be done to move us away from a two party system and why this would be beneficial. The questions for this reading are rather obvious and straightforward:

1. What changes would need to be made to move us away from a two party system?

2. What would be the advantages, according to Amy, of having a multi-party system?

I don't know if Morris Fiorina had brothers and/or sisters or if he had friends who did. In either case, Fiorina seems to be bothered by that which bothers many Americans–the failure of our leaders to take as much responsibility for their mistakes as they are for their glowing triumphs. Now, their failure to do so should cause us no shock, but we all probably tire of watching "news" programs where representatives of the parties argue like small children over who broke the window! They wear nicer clothes and use longer words, but the outcome is the same. "I Didn't Do It!!!" Fiorina decries this loss of responsibility. He and I might disagree over how much responsibility the parties used to take for their mistakes, but we certainly agree over their total failure to do so today. Answer the following:

1. What are the benefits of strong political parties?

2. Name/describe the consequences of the collective responsibility decline listed in the article.

3. Food for thought: How much blame should we, as American citizens shoulder for the problems highlighted by Fiorina?

W. John Moore argues that a principal danger of interest groups is their drive to polarize the political debate. There are few news stories which extol the virtues of compromise or political effectiveness. What highlights the papers, periodicals and networks are the shouting matches between extremists and, to be honest, that's what draws the ratings and the contributions. Many political observers have also noted the exodus of political moderates from our system. They tire, according to reports, of the extremism and unwillingness to tone down the rhetoric log enough to hear the other side. From the material in Moore's article (and your own head), think about the following:

1. Are peoples' interests truly represented by the extremes?

2. What are the characteristics of our current system and society that reward extremism?

The Birnbaum selection presents to you a world that most of us never see the world of big money politics. Consider these questions:

1. As you read this excerpt, think about the influence of money in our political system.

2. How can one best use those resources to impact the system?

3. How can causes without those resources similarly impact the world of political decision-making?

NATURE AND FUNCTION OF PARTY

V. O. Key

. . . The proclamation of the right of men to have a hand in their own governing did not create institutions by which they might exercise that right. Nor did the machinery of popular government come into existence overnight. By a tortuous process party systems came into being to implement democratic ideas. As democratic ideas corroded the old foundations of authority, members of the old governing elite reached out to legitimize their positions under the new notions by appealing for popular support. That appeal compelled deference to popular views, but it also required the development of organization to communicate with and to manage the electorate. Thus, members of a parliamentary body, who earlier occupied their seats as an incident to the ownership of property or as a perquisite of class position, had to defer to the people—or to those who had the suffrage—and to create electoral organizations to rally voters to their support. In a sense, government, left suspended in mid-air by the erosion of the old justifications for its authority, had to build new foundations in the new environment of a democratic ideology. In short, it had to have machinery to win votes. While the exact events of institutional development rarely fit precisely any such neat pattern, such a theory of the genesis of political parties is suggestive of their basic function.

A variant of this broad explanation refines the theory to find the birth of political parties in virtual revolution. As democratic ideas spread, those dissatisfied with the old order rallied the masses, or at least many of those who had had no hand in government, against the established holders of authority. In effect, the outs played demagogue, lined up the unwashed in their support, and, at the elections, by superiority of numbers and organization they bested those dominant in government. Those who suffered such indignities were compelled in self-defense to defer to the people, no matter how distasteful it was, and to form organizations to solicit electoral support.

Early events in the development of American parties accord to some extent with these general patterns. Until after the adoption of the Constitution the gentry by and large ruled. They held office, not so much from their skill in swaying the multitude, but as a matter of generally recognized right associated with their status. The essence of the political system appears in the early processes of nomination. Members of the dominant political classes became nominees by individual announcement of their availability; or a friend of the candidate put him in nomination by an address published in the press. Leading personages, at least in the areas where aristocratic influence prevailed most strongly, needed no party organization to nominate them or to campaign for them; gentlemen ordinarily regarded electioneering as bad form.

The Jeffersonian Republicans, who sought to oust the old order, developed party organization both to nominate candidates and to enlist voter support. A step was taken on the way to party organization in the formation of the Democratic societies, which flourished in 1793 and 1794. They provided channels for the expression of hostility toward the Federalists, friendship toward France, and antipathy toward "monarchical aristocratical" principles. Some of them did a bit of electioneering for candidates. The controversy they aroused indicated a significant transformation of attitude that had to occur before party government could exist. The notion that assaults on the government by the outs should be expected and could be tolerated had scarcely become established. In his message of 1794, Washington spoke of the commotions "fomented by combinations of men" who were "careless of consequences" and disregarded "the unerring truth that those who rouse cannot always appease a civil convulsion." The differentiation between criticism by the outs and the threat of revolution had not become understood by the ins—and perhaps not by the outs either.

The Democratic societies died out and the Jeffersonians took basic steps in the formation of a party system as they contrived a new political organization to throw the Federalists out of office. In Pennsylvania, New Jersey, New York, and Delaware they developed the delegate convention to nominate candidates upon whom their strength might be concerted. The convention—in sharp contrast with the individual modes of nomination congenial to the gentry—provided a means for centering popular strength on candidates. Moreover, the convention permitted a combination of strength over large areas. Delegates from precincts gathered at the county seats, and those from the counties met at the state capital. To assemble delegates at the county seat—given the means of travel of the day—was an operation quite as great as gathering a state convention today. The political activists who shared in the nominating process in turn worked in their own territories to round up the vote for their candidates.

This new organization of political activity marked a profound change in the political system. Earlier, gentlemen of status offered themselves to the voters as candidates. The new system produced candidates whose nomination proceeded, in appearance at least, from the voters. It also provided an organizational apparatus reaching out into the electorate to rouse the voters. Often, as the system developed, the number of voters increased remarkably as political workers stirred the electorate to action. A party mechanism purporting to represent the generality drove the unorganized Federalists from power. . . .

In a broad sense party organization to nominate candidates, to rally electoral support, and to link officialdom to voters evolved as a means of consolidating the outs to capture control of the government. The technique amounted to a functional equivalent of revolution. When, in his Farewell Message, Washington warned against the spirit of party he was expressing the fears of the upper orders against those who would rouse the rabble. He was also speaking for an era that had not yet seen the possibility of routinely conducting government in an environment of continuous partisan attack by a minority seeking to gain power.

After his review of these events Henry Jones Ford concluded that Jefferson's "great unconscious achievement" was "to open constitutional channels of political agitation." Into his Republican party flowed all the discontents that might otherwise have found expression in revolutionary strife or insurrection. By the channeling and the organization of these forces into a political party, change "became possible without destruction." . . .

The party system gradually achieved what we now regard as its characteristic form, a process that occurred more rapidly in some states than in others. A major second phase in its growth was the establishment of organization among the opponents of the Republicans, the group that had first capitalized upon the possibilities of organized effort. As party practices took root, party conflict became institutionalized: that is, generally expected and accepted patterns of organization, of behavior, and of action developed. By the groping and halting processes by which human organization evolves, new habitual ways of governing came into being. Those new methods implemented the ideas of popular government; they provided a means for obtaining popular consent in keeping with democratic ideologies. But party did more. Party operations provided a substitute for revolt and insurrection and a new means for determining succession to authority. As the party process took form, the workability of organized nonviolent conflict for control of government became established. Organized criticism and concerted efforts to replace those in power came to be regarded as routine. Once authority becomes subject to such challenges, and once sequences of elections occur, party government is extending its roots. The institutionalization of party warfare marked a major innovation—or invention—in the art of government. Rituals, ceremonies, and rules of the game developed to guide the conduct of domestic hostilities which in an earlier day might have been fought out at the barricades.

A salient characteristic of the American party system is its dual form. During most of our history power has alternated between two major parties. While minor parties have arisen from time to time and exerted influence on governmental policy, the two major parties have been the only serious contenders for the Presidency. On occasion a major party has disintegrated, but in due course the biparty division has reasserted itself. For relatively long periods, single parties have dominated the national scene, yet even during these eras the opposition has retained the loyalty of a substantial proportion of the electorate. Most voters consistently place their faith in one or the other of two parties; and neither party has been able to wipe out the other's following.

Since many of the peculiarities of American politics are associated with the duality of the party system, the significant features of that system need to be set out concretely. An identification of its main operating characteristics will supplement the insights gained about the role of party in the governing process from our excursion into the genesis of party. To speak of a party *system* is to imply a patterned relationship among elements of a larger whole. A pattern or system of relationships exists between, for example, two football teams. Each team has a role to play in the game, a role that changes from time to time. Within each team a subsystem of relationships ties together the roles of each player. Or, if one prefers mechanical figures, the components of an internal combustion engine combine and perform in specified relation to each other to produce the total engine, or system.

Similarly, a party system consists of interrelated components, each of which has an assigned role. The American party system consists of two major elements, each of which performs in specified ways or follows customary behavior patterns in the total system. To remove or alter the role of one element would destroy the system or create a new one. If one ignores for the moment the internal complexities of parties, the broad features of the system as a whole are simple. The major parties compete for electoral favor by presenting alternate slates of candidates and differing programs of projected action. It is a basic characteristic of the system that each party campaigns with hope of victory, if not in this election perhaps at the next.

In their relations to the electorate, another element of the system, the parties confront the voters with an either-or choice. Commonly the electoral decision either continues a party in power or replaces the executive and a legislative majority by the slate of the outs. The system, thus, differs fundamentally from a multiparty system which ordinarily presents the electorate with no such clear-cut choice; an election may be followed by only a mild modification of the majority coalition. The dual arrangement assigns to its parties a radically different role from that played by parties of a multiparty system. The voters may throw the old crowd out of power and install a completely new management even if they do not set an entirely new policy orientation. The differences in the roles that their respective systems assign to them make a party of a multiparty system by no means the equivalent of a party of a two-party system. A party that may expect to gain complete control of the government must act far differently from one that may expect, at most, to become a component of a parliamentary coalition.

To be distinguished from the roles of parties in electoral competition are the functions of party in the operation of government. The candidates of the victorious party assume public office. As public officers they may become more than partisans: they are cast in public rather than party roles. Yet the party role remains, for the government is operated under the expectation that the party may be held accountable at the next election for its stewardship. To the minority falls the role of criticism, of opposition, and of preparation for the day when it may become the government itself. These functions belong mainly to the minority members in the representative body, but they may also be shared by the party organization outside the government. The minority role constitutes a critical element of the system. The minority may assail governmental ineptitude, serve as a point for the coalescence of discontent, propose alternative governmental policies, and influence the behavior of the majority as well as lay plans to throw it out of power. . . .

Foreign observers manifest the utmost bewilderment as they contemplate the American two-party system, and native scholars are not overwhelmingly persuasive in their explanations of it. The pervasive effects on American political life of the dual form make the quest for the causes of this arrangement a favorite topic of speculation. Given the diversity of interests in American society one might expect numerous parties to be formed to represent groups with conflicting aims and objectives. Yet that does not occur. In the less sophisticated explanations of why, the system is attributed to a single "cause." A more tenable assumption would be that several factors drive toward dualism on the American scene.

Human institutions have an impressive capacity to perpetuate themselves or at least to preserve their form. The circumstances that happened to mold the American party system into a dual form at its inception must bear a degree of responsibility for its present existence. They included the confrontation of the country with a great issue that could divide it only into the ayes and the nays: the debate over the adoption of the Constitution. As party life began to emerge under the Constitution, again the issues split the country into two camps.

The initial lines of cleavage built also on a dualism of interest in a nation with a far less intricate economic and social structure than that of today. Arthur Macmahon concludes that, in addition to other influences, the two-party division was "induced by the existence of two major complexes of interest in the country." A cleavage between agriculture and the interests of the mercantile and financial community antedated even the adoption of the Constitution. This conflict, with a growing industry allying itself with trade and finance, was fundamental in the debate on the adoption of the Constitution and remained an issue in national politics afterward. The great issues changed from time to time but each party managed to renew itself as it found new followers to replace those it lost. The Civil War, thus, brought a realignment in national politics, yet it re-enforced the dual division. For decades southern Democrats recalled the heroes of the Confederacy and the Republicans waved the "bloody shirt" to rally their followers. As memories of the war faded new alignments gradually took shape within the matrix of the pre-existing structure, with each party hierarchy struggling to maintain its position in the system.

A recurring question in political analysis is whether formal institutional structure and procedure influence the nature of party groupings. Though it is doubtful that formal governmental structures cause dualism, certain features of American institutions are congenial to two-partyism and certainly over the short run obstruct the growth of splinter parties.

Some commentators, in seeking the influences that lead to two-partyism, attribute great weight to the practice of choosing representatives from single-member districts by a plurality vote in contrast with systems of proportional representation which are based on multimember districts. In a single-member district only two parties can contend for electoral victory with any hope of success; a third party is doomed to perpetual defeat unless it can manage to absorb the following of one of the major parties and thereby become one of them. Parties do not thrive on the certainty of defeat. That prospect tends to drive adherents of minor parties to one or the other of the two major parties. The single-member district thus re-enforces the bipartisan pattern. Each of the contending groups in such a district must formulate its appeals with an eye to attracting a majority of the electors to its banner.

An essential element of the theory is its plurality-election feature. If, so the hypothesis goes, a plurality—be it only 25 per cent of the total vote is sufficient for victory in a single-member district, the leaders of a group consisting of, say, 15 per cent of the electorate, will join with other such groups before the voting to maximize their chance of being on the winning side. They assume that if they do not form such coalitions, others will. Moreover, concessions will be made to attract the support of smaller groups. If a majority, instead of a plurality, is required to elect, a second election to choose between the two high candidates in the first polling becomes necessary. Such a situation may encourage several parties to enter candidates at the first election, each on the chance that its candidate may be one of the two leaders. Of course, under systems of proportional representation the incentive to form two coalitions, each approaching a majority, is destroyed by the opportunity to elect candidates in proportion to popular strength whatever the number of parties.

The validity of the single-member-district theory has not been adequately tested against the evidence. Obviously, in those states of the United States in which third parties have developed fairly durable strength, the institutional situation has stimulated moves toward coalitions and mergers with one or another of the major parties. Yet the single-member-district and plurality election can at most encourage a dual division—or discourage a multiparty division—only within each representative district. Other influences must account for the federation of the district units of the principal party groups into two competing national organizations.

The popular election of the Chief Executive is commonly said to exert a centripetal influence upon party organization and to encourage a dualism. The supposed effect of the mode of choice of the President resembles that of the single-member constituency. The winner takes all. The Presidency, unlike a multiparty cabinet, cannot be parceled out among minuscule parties. The circumstances stimulate coalition within the electorate before the election rather than within the parliament after the popular vote. Since no more than two parties can for long compete effectively for the Presidency, two contending groups tend to develop, each built on its constituent units in each of the 50 states. The President is, in effect, chosen by the voters in 50 single-member constituencies which designate their electors by a plurality vote. The necessity of uniting to have a chance of sharing in a victory in a presidential campaign pulls the state party organizations together. . . .

Explanations of the factors determinative of so complex a social structure as a party system must remain unsatisfactory. The safest explanation is that several factors conspired toward the development of the American dual party pattern. These included the accidents of history that produced dual divisions on great issues at critical points in our history, the consequences of our institutional forms, the clustering of popular opinions around a point of central consensus rather than their bipolarization, and perhaps others. The assignment of weights to each of these is an enterprise too uncertain to be hazarded.

BREAKING THE TWO-PARTY MONOPOLY

Douglas Amy

In July 1989, the convention of the National Organization for Women was meeting in Cincinnati, Ohio. Delegates were expressing a high degree of political frustration, both about recent U.S. Supreme Court decisions threatening the right to abortions and the failure of the 1988 Democratic presidential candidate, Michael Dukakis, to make women's issues a prominent part of his campaign.

The discontent produced an unexpected political development. Urged on by the rank and file, NOW officials issued a "Declaration of Political Independence," which stated that NOW would no longer automatically support Democratic party candidates. The declaration went on to say that NOW "recognizes the failure of both major political parties to address women's needs," and that NOW would "form an exploratory commission to investigate the formation of a new party dedicated to equality for women and an expanded Bill of Rights for the Twenty-first century." After a series of nationwide hearings in 1990 and 1991, that commission decided to support the formation of a new party. In the summer of 1992 the party was christened the 21st Century party and pledged to promote equality and justice, peace, and a healthy environment.

Some political observers see this direct challenge to the two-party system as somewhat quixotic. But the sense of disenchantment with the two-party system that led to the emergence of this new party is well understood. Many Americans are dissatisfied with our party system, and they express it in many ways. Persistent low voter turnout is, in part, a measure of voter disillusionment with the choices offered by the major parties. Americans also have a low level of identification with the major parties. Since the 1950s fewer and fewer people identify with either political party, and for those who do, the intensity of their identification is declining. In the 1980s only about 25 percent of Americans said they strongly identified with the Republican or Democratic party. In contrast, the number of people declaring as political independents has been rising, growing from 22 percent in 1950 to 35 percent in the 1980s. In the 1992 presidential election millions of voters endorsed the independent candidacy of H. Ross Perot, despite his admission early on in the campaign that he had few thought-out positions on major issues. His rise in the polls was clearly a measure of the depth and breadth of the public disenchantment with the candidates offered by the two major parties.

In addition, interest in founding so-called third parties continues to grow. The last few years have seen not only the emergence of the 21st Century party but also the conservative U.S. Taxpayers party and the leftist New party. Also, in the summer of 1992 former presidential candidate John Anderson and Connecticut Governor Lowell Weicker met to discuss starting a new independent centrist party. Others exploring the third-party option include labor activists, consumer activists, and environmentalists. These efforts to break out of the bonds of our two-party system have a great deal of sympathy in the general public. In the summer of 1992 two major polls found that about 60 percent of Americans supported the establishment of a new political party to compete with the Republicans and Democrats. Significantly, most new party supporters were not on the political fringes; most were moderates. The decline in public enthusiasm for the two-party system has also been echoed by a series of books by political commentators and political scientists, whose pessimism is reflected in such titles as *The Party's Over, American Parties in Decline, and Parties in Crisis*.

Much of the disenchantment with the two-party system is expressed in a familiar litany of complaints: the major parties are out of touch with the people, they are so similar on many issues that they offer little choice, both parties are dominated by monied interests, neither party is a source of new or innovative policy ideas, and so on. All are valid complaints. However, what often goes largely unrecognized is that all these problems are linked directly or indirectly to how our single-member plurality voting rules affect the nature of our party system. Adoption of proportional representation in the United States would alleviate, if not cure, all of them. . . .

Americans have suffered under our two-party system for so long that we tend to view its problems and limitations as unfortunate but inevitable. In reality, of course, many of these problems are inevitable only under single-member plurality voting rules. The adoption of proportional representation in the United States would go a long way toward addressing many of these shortcomings. PR would allow for the development of a multiparty system with a variety of genuine political alternatives. Minor parties would no longer be unfairly penalized, and they would be able to elect representatives in numbers that reflect their political strength in the electorate. In short, PR would be an antitrust law for the party system. It would discourage party monopolies and oligopolies and allow for free competition among parties. It would create a level playing field on which all parties could vie fairly for public support.

A more hospitable political environment for minor parties under PR would probably result in the expansion of the party system in the United States. Voter support for minor parties would increase as voters realize that voting for minor-party candidates no longer means wasting their votes. Talented politicians would be more attracted to these parties. They could run for office on those tickets without fearing that they are throwing their careers away. Donations to these parties would probably increase as the contributors realize that these investments could actually produce some electoral dividends.

It is important to recognize that the adoption of PR in the United States would not *force* us to have a multiparty system; it simply would *allow* such a system to develop, if it reflected the wishes of the American voter. As political scientists often observe, many factors other than electoral systems help determine the number of parties in a political system—such as the number and depth of political cleavages in a society. Thus if American voters choose to support only the two major parties, PR would produce a two-party system, as has happened in Austria. In this sense, PR does not mandate any particular kind of party system; it simply does not inhibit the development of a multiparty system the way plurality rules do. With proportional representation what the public wants in a party system, it gets.

This principle was evident in the experiments with PR in U.S. cities. The effect of PR on party systems varied from city to city, depending on local political conditions and public preferences. In some cities that adopted PR, such as Cincinnati, essentially two parties still contested local elections, though PR produced a much more accurate representation of those parties in the city council. In cities with more heterogeneous political populations, like New York, a vigorous multiparty system emerged. Before the adoption of proportional representation, New York City was dominated by the Democratic machine, which elected virtually the entire city council. The onset of PR broke the political monopoly of the Democrats, and what was a one-party system became a multiparty system. The PR city council in 1947 reflected the wide variety of political persuasions among the New York city electorate and consisted of twelve Democrats, five Republicans, two Liberals, two Communists, and two American Laborite. . . .

Development of an authentic multiparty system would have a number of significant advantages for American voters. First they would have a larger number of genuine political options. And with a wider variety of choice, voters would be more likely to find a party with which they could truly identify. Instead of having to choose the lesser of two evils, they could choose a candidate and party that more accurately reflect their political philosophies and policy preferences. To be able to vote for a candidate in whom they truly believe would undoubtedly be a new and refreshing experience for many American voters. Ultimately, of course, the main advantage of a multiparty system is felt in our legislatures. For the first time our city councils and state and federal legislatures would become truly representative institutions. They would more accurately reflect the variety of political views present in the American electorate, and an authentic political pluralism would finally become a reality in the United States.

The emergence of a healthy multiparty system also would open up political debate in election campaigns, the media, and our legislative bodies. Presumably, the news media would have to cover not just the two major parties but also the candidates from all the parties with a realistic chance of winning some seats. With a variety of truly different views being espoused, candidate debates would become much livelier and informative affairs. Moreover, television viewers would find that such programs as "Nightline," "The MacNeil-Lehrer Newshour," and "Crossfire" would have a wider variety of elected officials as guests a refreshing alternative to the usual Republican and Democratic figures who now are interviewed night after night on these programs.

A multiparty system could also raise the quality of political debate within our legislatures. In a democracy, legislatures are not only decision-making bodies; they are deliberative institutions that serve as forums for political discussion and debate. A multiparty legislature would encourage a truly pluralistic debate over the issues and would ensure a forum for the views of even minority political groups. One major tenet of proportional representation is that even though minor parties may not win enough seats to affect the outcome of a legislative vote, they deserve to be represented and to have a voice in the proceedings. . . .

Under PR, minor parties in the legislature keep the major parties honest and ensure that new political ideas and new political voices are heard in a timely fashion. One of the most frequent complaints about the two parties is that they are slow to respond to new issues and new political perspectives. Indeed, their dominance of the legislative and media forums often makes it difficult for those new voices to be heard and to gain some legitimacy. In the United States, third parties have often served as alternative forums for new ideas and policies. Parties like the Socialists, Progressives, Populists, and Farmer-Laborites often publicized and promoted new policy ideas that were being ignored by the major parties. Many of the social, economic, and political reforms that we now take for granted such as free public education, abolition of slavery, regulation of railroads and business monopolies, progressive income taxes, child labor laws, women's suffrage, direct election of senators, Social Security, and unemployment insurance—were first proposed and championed by minor parties. Many of these issues were quite controversial when the smaller parties first embraced them, and it is not surprising that the major parties shied away from them, viewing them as too divisive for the large electoral coalitions they sought to build. Minor parties helped to develop popular interest and support for reform in these areas. Along with other pressure groups, these parties played an important role in forcing many of these issues out into the open and ensured that they received a place on the political agenda of the nation. . . .

PR and a multiparty system could also help to address another persistent problem in our party system the tendency for monied interests to dominate both parties. As political campaigns have become more expensive, effective electoral participation has been increasingly limited to those who have substantial amounts of money. As a result, both parties have turned to wealthy organizations for funds—particularly political action committees (PACs) and most particularly corporate and trade PACs. Even the Democratic party, which traditionally has been thought of as less indebted to the wealthy and the business community, is relying increasingly on those interests for financial support. Indeed, part of the reason that the Democratic party moved toward the right in the 1980s was so that it could cultivate these money sources and thus be better able to compete with the large campaign chests amassed by the Republican party.

With both major parties politically tied to the haves of society, the have-nots the poor, racial minorities, the working class often have o party speaking to their problems or promoting their interests. And without a party base these groups stand little chance of gaining political power through the electoral process. As Benjamin Ginsberg explains:

> In the absence of party organization, the likelihood that groups lacking substantial economic or institutional resources can acquire some measure of power is considerably diminished. . . . Electoral politics essentially becomes a contest in which only those who command very substantial private resources or have access to governmental resources can hope to successfully compete. This type of politics holds out little hope for the acquisition of even a measure of power by subordinate social and economic groups.

For this reason subordinate groups have often turned to minor parties to try to gain some degree of political power. Many third-party efforts in the United States have been grassroots efforts, organized by those on the bottom of the economic ladder. The Populist party, the Socialist party, LaFollette's Progressive party, and similar efforts all had a substantial part of their political base in the lower classes. Even third parties on the right, such as George Wallace's American Independent party, often were rooted in conservative middle- and working-class whites who felt that the major parties were dominated by elites who had little interest in their problems.

But with the handicaps imposed by the plurality system, few of these parties have had a chance to gain any significant political power. This could change under proportional representation. In a PR system, such have-not parties would be viable alternatives to the major parties. Even though they might begin with only a small amount of public support, they could nevertheless have a fair chance of electing at least some representatives to speak for their interests in government. Also, such have-not parties could serve as centers for fund-raising and political organizing. One union activist, Tony Mazzocchi, argues that a new Labor party could be a base for organizing a movement of working people: "People will pay dues to it. It will have its own newspapers and other means of communication. It will be an educational and analytical forum."

Minor political parties could also serve to concentrate the political strength of what are now disparate political groups, each pursuing their own issue agendas. Such a party might resemble the Rainbow Coalition of the late 1980s, which sought to bring together racial minorities, the poor, feminists, gays and lesbians, left liberals, and others. A minor party uniting these groups would still not be able to rival the financial and institutional resources of the major parties, but it could serve as an organizational base for mobilizing and aggregating their power and gain them a more powerful voice in government.

PR could work to blunt the political power of monied interests in another, somewhat unexpected way. Much special interest influence in our legislatures is a function of lobbying efforts. And like elections, lobbying success is strongly influenced by money. The special interests with the most money have a distinct advantage in the lobbying process. They can give more and larger campaign contributions, which can often buy sympathetic ears from legislators. Wealthy lobbies can hire the most talented lobbyists with the best political connections-and they can hire more of them. They can also afford to generate larger amounts of policy research and analysis, a valuable currency in many lobbying efforts. In short, lobbying is a money game, and those with more money tend to do better at it. Translating financial resources into political influence is a matter of serious concern to many political observers. The growing role of political action committees and special interest lobbyists in the legislative process is often seen as at best unfair and at worst as undermining the democratic nature of our political process.

PR could undermine the lobbying power of wealthy interests by encouraging stronger, more disciplined, and more ideological political parties, as are found in most other democracies. Such parties tend to discourage effective lobbying by special interests in several different ways. First, most campaign funds for candidates come from these parties, thus helping to sever any direct financial links between special interests and legislative officials. In contrast, most members of Congress receive the bulk of their campaign funds directly from individuals and political action committees. PACs expect something for their money if not a vote for their bill, at least ready access to a legislator to pitch their case. Party funding of campaigns tends to make legislators less directly indebted to special interests for their political survival.

Disciplined parties also lessen the impact of lobbying by reducing the opportunities for legislators to be persuaded to change their votes. In most European party systems, legislators must vote with their parties on important parliamentary votes or be subject to disciplinary action, including expulsion from the party. Americans, with their individualistic bent, often see this requirement as an unreasonable restriction on individual legislators' discretion or their ability to respond to their particular constituents. But strong party discipline can greatly reduce the opportunities for special interests to wield influence over individual legislators. If, for example, a Republican senator must vote with the party, it does little good for a highly paid lobbyist—no matter how persuasive—to try to convince the senator to vote with the Democrats this time. . . .

However, while the potential for PR to help blunt the influence of powerful lobbies is intriguing, it is important not to exaggerate it. PR will not eliminate the corrupting influence of special interest money in our elections and legislatures. The problem is much too complex and deep-seated to be solved by such simple procedural reforms. Even if we were to see the emergence of more disciplined and ideological parties, the influence of money would continue to be felt. Special interest money simply would go to the parties, rather than to individual candidates. And expensive lobbying efforts would probably switch their focus more to the administrative branch—as is the case in the British political system. Nevertheless, any changes in the nature of political parties that could undermine even partially the unfair influence of special interest money in our political system would be a welcome development, and PR clearly may have something to contribute in that regard.

Voting is one of our most fundamental acts of political choice. But a crucial difference exists between simply having a choice and having a real or a meaningful choice. For any choice to be real, we must have some control over the options we are given. Otherwise our choice may be only a fraud or an illusion. If we were told that we were free to choose between being hit in the face and kicked in the stomach, we would probably protest that this is hardly freedom and really no choice at all. Many Americans find themselves in just that situation with our two-party system. Plurality rules artificially limit our choices to two similar parties, and for many voters this does not seem like a real choice at all. In contrast, proportional representation elections would ensure that voters have as wide a variety of distinct political choices as they desire. The adoption of PR in the United States would finally allow the American voter—not our plurality election rules—to decide which political parties and political views deserve to be represented in our legislatures. Putting this power of choice back in the hands of the American voters would help make our election system much more fair and democratic.

THE DECLINE OF COLLECTIVE RESPONSIBILITY
IN AMERICAN POLITICS

Morris P. Fiorina

Though the Founding Fathers believed in the necessity of establishing a genuinely national government, they took great pains to design one that could not lightly do things to its citizens; what government might do for its citizens was to be limited to the functions of what we know now as the "watchman state." Thus the Founders composed the constitutional litany familiar to every schoolchild: they created a federal system, they distributed and blended powers within and across the federal levels, and they encouraged the occupants of the various positions to check and balance each other by structuring incentives so that one officeholder's ambitions would be likely to conflict with others'. The resulting system of institutional arrangements predictably hampers efforts to undertake major initiatives and favors maintenance of the status quo.

Given the historical record faced by the Founders, their emphasis on constraining government is understandable. But we face a later historical record, one that shows two hundred years of increasing demands for government to act positively. Moreover, developments unforeseen by the Founders increasingly raise the likelihood that the uncoordinated actions of individuals and groups will inflict serious damage on the nation as a whole. The by-products of the industrial and technological revolutions impose physical risks not only on us, but on future generations as well. Resource shortages and international cartels raise the spectre of economic ruin. And the simple proliferation of special interests with their intense, particularistic demands threatens to render us politically incapable of taking actions that might either advance the state of society or prevent foreseeable deteriorations in that state. None of this is to suggest that we should forget about what government can do to us—the contemporary concern with the proper scope and methods of government intervention in the social and economic omen is long overdue. But the modern age demands as well that we worry about our ability to make government work for us. The problem is that we are gradually losing that ability, and a principal reason for this loss is the steady erosion of responsibility in American politics.

What do I mean by this important quality, responsibility? To say that some person or group is responsible for a state of affairs is to assert that he or they have the ability to take legitimate actions that have a major impact on that state of affairs. More colloquially, when someone is responsible, we know whom to blame. Human beings have asymmetric attitudes toward responsibility, as captured by the saying "Success has a thousand fathers, but failure is an orphan." This general observation applies very much to politicians, not surprisingly, and this creates a problem for democratic theory, because clear location or responsibility is vitally important to the operation of democratic governments. Without responsibility, citizens can only guess at who deserves their support; the act of voting loses much of its meaning. Moreover, the expectation of being held responsible provides representatives with a personal incentive to govern in their constituents' interest. As ordinary citizens we do not know the proper rate of growth of the money supply, the appropriate level of the federal deficit, the advantages of the MX over alternative missile systems, and so forth. We elect people to make those decisions. But only if those elected know they will be held accountable for the results of their decisions (or nondecisions, as the case may be), do they have a personal incentive to govern in our interest.

Unfortunately, the importance of responsibility in a democracy is matched by the difficulty of attaining it. In an autocracy, individual responsibility suffices; the location of power in a single individual locates responsibility in that individual as well. But individual responsibility is insufficient whenever more than one person shares governmental authority. We can hold a particular congressman individually responsible for a personal transgression such as bribe-taking. We can even hold a president individually

Reprinted by permission of *Daedalus, Journal of the American Academy of Arts and Sciences*, from the issue entitled, "The End of Consensus?", Summer 1980, Vol. 109, No. 3.

responsible for military moves where he presents Congress and the citizenry with a fait accompli. But on most national issues individual responsibility is difficult to assess. If one were to go to Washington, randomly accost a Democratic congressman, and berate him about a 20-percent rate of inflation, imagine the response. More than likely it would run, "Don't blame me. If 'they' had done what I've advocated for x years, things would be fine today." And if one were to walk over to the White House and similarly confront President Carter, he would respond as he already has, by blaming Arabs, free-spending congressmen, special interests, and, of course, us.

American institutional structure makes this kind of game-playing all too easy. In order to overcome it we must lay the credit or blame for national conditions on all those who had any hand in bringing them about: some form of collective responsibility is essential.

The only way collective responsibility has ever existed, and can exist given our institutions, is through the agency of the political party; in American politics, responsibility requires cohesive parties. This is an old claim to be sure, but its age does not detract from its present relevance. In fact, the continuing decline in public esteem for the parties and continuing efforts to "reform" them out of the political process suggest that old arguments for party responsibility have not been made often enough or, at least, convincingly enough, so I will make these arguments once again in this essay.

A strong political party can generate collective responsibility by creating incentive for leaders, followers, and popular supporters to think and act in collective terms. First, by providing party leaders with the capability (e.g., control of institutional patronage, nominations, and so on) to discipline party members, genuine leadership becomes possible. Legislative output is less likely to be a least common denominator–a residue of myriad conflicting proposals—and more likely to consist of a program actually intended to solve a problem or move the nation in a particular direction. Second, the subordination of individual officeholders to the party lessens their ability to separate themselves from party actions. Like it or not, their performance becomes identified with the performance of the collectivity to which they belong. Third, with individual candidate variation greatly reduced, voters have less incentive to support individuals and more incentive to support or oppose the party as a whole. And fourth, the circle closes as party-line voting in the electorate provides party leaders with the incentive to propose policies that will earn the support of a national majority, and party backbenchers with the personal incentive to cooperate with leaders in the attempt to compile a good record for the party as a whole.

In the American context, strong parties have traditionally clarified politics in two ways. First, they allow citizens to assess responsibility easily, at least when the government is unified, which it more often was in earlier eras when party meant more than it does today. Citizens need only evaluate the social, economic, and international conditions they observe and make a simple decision for or against change. They do not need to decide whether the energy, inflation, urban, and defense policies advocated by their congressman would be superior to those advocated by Carter—were any of them to be enacted!

The second way in which strong parties clarify American politics follows from the first. When citizens assess responsibility on the party as a whole, party members have personal incentives to see the party evaluated favorably. They have little to gain from gutting their president's program one day and attacking him for lack of leadership the next, since they share in the president's fate when voters do not differentiate within the party. Put simply, party responsibility provides party members with a personal stake in their collective performance.

Admittedly, party responsibility is a blunt instrument. The objection immediately arises that party responsibility condemns junior Democratic representatives to suffer electorally for an inflation they could do little to affect. An unhappy situation, true, but unless we accept it, Congress as a whole escapes electoral retribution for an inflation they could have done something to affect. Responsibility requires acceptance of both conditions. The choice is between a blunt instrument or none at all. . . .

In earlier times, when citizens voted for the party, not the person, parties had incentives to nominate good candidates, because poor ones could have harmful fallout on the ticket as a whole. In particular, the existence of presidential coattails (positive and negative) provided an inducement to avoid the nomination of narrowly based candidates, no matter how committed their supporters. And, once in office, the existence of party voting in the electorate provided party members with the incentive to compile a good party record. In particular, the tendency of national midterm elections to serve as referenda on the performance of the president provided a clear inducement for congressmen to do what they could to see that their president was perceived as a solid performer. By stimulating electoral phenomena such as coattail effects and mid-term referenda, party transformed some degree of personal ambition into concern with collective performance.

In the contemporary period, however, even the preceding tendencies toward collective responsibility have largely dissipated. . . .

* * * *

Some Consequences of the Decline of Collective Responsibility

The weakening of party has contributed directly to the severity of several of the important problems the nation faces. For some of these, such as the government's inability to deal with inflation and energy, the connections are obvious. But for other problems, such as the growing importance of single-issue politics and the growing alienation of the American citizenry, the connections are more subtle.

Immobilism

As the electoral interdependence of the party in government declines, its ability to act also declines. If responsibility can be shifted to another level or to another officeholder, there is less incentive to stick one's neck out in an attempt to solve a given problem. Leadership becomes more difficult, the ever-present bias toward the short-term solution becomes more pronounced, and the possibility of solving any given problem lessens.

Consider the two critical problems facing the country today, energy and inflation. Major energy problems were forecast years ago, the 1973 embargo underlined the dangers, and yet what passes for our national energy policy is still only a weak set of jerry-built compromises achieved at the expense of years of political infighting. The related inflation problem has festered for more than a decade, and our current president is on his fourth anti-inflation plan, a set of proposals widely regarded as yet another instance of too little, too late. The failures of policy-making in these areas are easy to identify and explain. A potential problem is identified, and actions that might head it off are proposed "for discussion." But the problem lies in the future, while the solutions impose costs in the present. So politicians dismiss the solutions as unfeasible and act as though the problem will go away. When it doesn't, popular concern increases. The president, in particular, feels compelled to act—he will be held responsible, both at election time and in the judgment of history. But congressmen expect to bear much less responsibility; moreover, the representatives face an election in less than two years, whereas the president can wait at least four (longer for the lame duck) for the results of his policy to become evident. Congressmen, logically enough, rebel. They denounce every proposed initiative as unfair, which simply means that it imposes "costs on their constituents, whereas they prefer the costs to fall on everyone else's constituents. At first, no policy will be adopted; later, as pressure builds, Congress adopts a weak and ineffectual policy for symbolic purposes. Then, as the problem continues to worsen, congressmen join with the press and the public and attack the president for failures of leadership.

The preceding scenario is simplified, to be sure, but largely accurate, and in my opinion, rather disgusting. What makes it possible is the electoral fragmentation produced by the decline of party. Members of Congress are aware that national problems arising from inaction will have little political impact on them, and that the president's failures in dealing with those problems will have similarly little impact. Responsibility for inflation and energy problems? Don't look at congressmen.

In 1958 the Fourth Republic of France collapsed after years of Immobilism. The features of congressional policy-making just discussed were carried to their logical extremes in that Parliamentary regime. According to contemporary observers, the basic principle of the French Deputy was to avoid responsibility. To achieve that goal the deputies followed subsidiary rules, the most important of which was delay. Action would take place only when crisis removed any possible alternative to action (and most of the alternative actions as well). A slogan of the time was "Those who crawl do not fall."

No one seriously believes that the American constitutional order is in danger of collapse (and certainly we have no de Gaulle waiting in the wings). But political inability to take actions that entail short-run costs ordinarily will result in much higher costs in the long run—we cannot continually depend on the technological fix. So the present American Immobilism cannot be dismissed lightly. The sad thing is that the American people appear to understand the depth of our present problems and, at least in principle, appear prepared to sacrifice in furtherance of the long-run good. But they will not have an opportunity to choose between two or more such long-term plans. Although both parties promise tough, equitable policies, in the present state of our politics, neither can deliver.

Single-Issue Politics

In recent years both political analysts and politicians have decried the increased importance of single-issue groups in American politics. Some in fact would claim that the present Immobilism in our politics owes more to the rise of single-issue groups than to the decline of party. A little thought, however, should reveal that the two trends are connected. Is single-issue politics a recent phenomenon? The contention is doubtful; such groups have always been active participants in American politics. The gun lobby already was a classic example at the time of President Kennedy's assassination. And however impressive the antiabortionists appear today, remember the temperance movement, which succeeded in getting its constitutional amendment. American history contains numerous forerunners of today's groups, from anti-Masons to abolitionists to the Klan—singularity of purpose is by no means a modern phenomenon. Why, then, do we hear all the contemporary hoopla about single-issue groups? Probably because politicians fear them now more than before and thus allow them to play a larger role in our politics. Why should this be so? Simply because the parties are too weak to protect their members and thus to contain single-issue politics.

In earlier times single-issue groups were under greater pressures to reach accommodations with the parties. After all, the parties nominated candidates, financed candidates, worked for candidates, and, perhaps most important, party voting protected candidates. When a contemporary single-issue group threatens to "get" an officeholder, the threat must be taken seriously. The group can go into his district, recruit a primary or general election challenger, or both, and bankroll that candidate. Even if the sentiment espoused by the group is not the majority sentiment of the district, few officeholders relish the thought of a strong, well-financed opponent. Things were different when strong parties existed. Party leaders controlled the nomination process and would fight to maintain that control. An outside challenge would merely serve to galvanize the party into action to protect its prerogatives. Only if a single-issue group represented the dominant sentiment in a given area could it count on controlling the party organization itself, and thereby electoral politics in that area.

Not only did the party organization have greater ability to resist single-issue pressures at the electoral level, but the party in government had greater ability to control the agenda, and thereby contain single-issue pressures at the policy-making level. Today we seem condemned to go through an annual agony over federal abortion funding. There is little doubt that politicians on both sides would prefer to reach some reasonable compromise at the committee level and settle the issue. But in today's decentralized Congress there is no way to put the lid on. In contrast, historians tell us that in the late nineteenth century a large portion of the Republican constituency was far less interested in the tariff and other questions of national economic development than in whether German immigrants should be permitted to teach their native language in their local schools, and whether Catholics and "liturgical Protestants" should be permitted to consume alcohol. Interestingly, however, the national agenda of the period is devoid of such issues. And when they do show up on the state level, the exceptions prove the rule; they produce party splits and striking defeats for the party that allowed them to surface.

One can cite more recent examples as well. Prior to 1970 popular commentators frequently criticized the autocratic antimajoritarian behavior of congressional committee chairmen in general, and of the entire Rules Committee in particular. It is certainly true that the seniority leadership killed many bills the rank and file might have passed if left to their own devices. But congressional scholars were always aware as well that the seniority leadership buried many bills that the rank and file wanted buried but lacked the political courage to bury themselves. In 1961, for example, the House Rules Committee was roundly condemned for killing a major federal aid to education bill over the question of extension of that aid to parochial schools. Contemporary accounts, however, suggest that congressmen regarded the action of the Rules Committee as a public service. Of course, control of the agenda is a double-edged sword (a point we return to below), but today commentators on single-issue groups clearly are concerned with too little control rather than too much.

In sum, a strong party that is held accountable for the government of a nation-state has both the ability and the incentive to contain particularistic pressures. It controls nominations, elections, and the agenda, and it collectively realizes that small minorities are small minorities no matter how intense they are: But as the parties decline they lose control over nominations and campaigns, they lose the loyalty of the voters, and they lose control of the agenda. Party officeholders cease to be held collectively accountable for party performance, but they become individually exposed to the political pressure of myriad interest groups. The decline of party permits interest groups to wield greater influence, their success encourages the formation of still more interest groups, politics becomes increasingly fragmented, and collective responsibility becomes still more elusive.

Popular Alienation from Government

For at least a decade political analysts have pondered the significance of survey data indicative of a steady increase in the alienation of the American public from the political process. Table 28 (editor's note: Table not included) presents some representative data: two-thirds of the American public feel the government is run for the benefit of big interests rather than for the people as a whole, three-quarters believe that government officials waste a lot of tax money and half flatly agree with the statement that government officials are basically incompetent. The American public is in a nasty mood, a cynical, distrusting, and resentful mood. The question is, Why?

Specific events and personalities clearly have some effect: we see pronounced "Watergate effects" between 1972 and 1976. But the trends clearly began much earlier. Indeed, the first political science studies analyzing the trends were based on data no later than 1972. At the other extreme it also appears that the American data are only the strongest manifestation of a pattern evident in many democracies, perhaps for reasons common to all countries in the present era, perhaps not. I do think it probable however, that the trends thus far discussed bear some relation to the popular mood in the United States.

If the same national problems not only persist but worsen while ever-greater amounts of revenue are directed at them, why shouldn't the typical citizen conclude that most of the money must be wasted by incompetent officials? If narrowly based interest groups increasingly affect our politics, why shouldn't citizens increasingly conclude that the interests run the government? For fifteen years the citizenry has listened to a steady stream of promises but has seen very little in the way of follow-through. An increasing proportion of the electorate does not believe that elections make a difference, a fact that largely explains the much-discussed post-1960 decline in voting turnout.

Continued public disillusionment with the political process poses several real dangers. For one thing, disillusionment begets further disillusionment. Leadership becomes more difficult if citizens do not trust their leaders and will not give them the benefit of a doubt. Policy failure becomes more likely if citizens expect the policy to fail. Waste increases and government competence decreases as citizen disrespect for politics encourages a lesser breed of person to make careers in government. And "government by a few big interests" becomes more than a cliche ~ if citizens increasingly decide the cliche~ is true and cease participating for that reason.

Finally, there is the real danger that continued disappointment with particular government officials ultimately metamorphoses into disillusionment with government per se. Increasing numbers of citizens believe that government is not simply overextended but perhaps incapable of any further bettering of the world. Yes, government is overextended, inefficiency is pervasive, and ineffectiveness is all too common. But government is one of the few instruments of collective action we have, and even those committed to selective pruning of government programs cannot blithely allow the concept of an activist government to fall into disrepute.

The concept of democracy does not submit to precise definition, a claim supported by the existence of numerous nonidentical definitions. To most people democracy embodies a number of valued qualities. Unfortunately, there is no reason to believe that all such valued qualities are mutually compatible. At the least, maximizing the attainment of one quality may require accepting middling levels of another.

Recent American political thought has emphasized government of the people and by the people. Attempts have been made to [ensure] that all preferences receive a hearing, especially through direct expression of those preferences, but if not, at least through faithful representation. Citizen participation is the reigning value, and arrangements that foster widespread participation are much in favor.

Of late, however, some political commentators have begun to wonder whether contemporary thought places sufficient emphasis on government for the people. In stressing participation have we lost sight of accountability? Surely, we should be as concerned with what government produces as with how many participate. What good is participation if the citizenry is unable to determine who merits their support.

Participation and responsibility are not logically incompatible, but there is a degree of tension between the two, and the quest for either may be carried to extremes. Participation maximizers find themselves involved with quotas and virtual representation schemes, while responsibility maximizers can find themselves with a closed shop under boss rule. Moreover, both qualities can weaken the democracy they supposedly underpin. Unfettered participation produces Hyde Amendments and Immobilism. Responsible parties can use agenda power to thwart democratic decision—for more than a century the Democratic party used what control it had to suppress the racial issue. Neither participation nor responsibility should be pursued at the expense of all other values, but that is what has happened with participation over the course of the past two decades, and we now reap the consequences in our politics. . . .

The depressing thing is that no rays of light shine through the dark clouds. The trends that underlie the decline of parties continue unabated, and the kinds of structural reforms that might override those trends are too sweeping and/or outlandish to stand any chance of adoption.) Through a complex mixture of accident and intention we have constructed for ourselves a system that articulates interests superbly but aggregates them poorly. We hold our politicians individually accountable for the proposals they advocate, but less so for the adoption of those proposals, and not at all for overseeing the implementation of those proposals and the evaluation of their results. In contemporary America officials do not govern, they merely posture.

Going to Extremes, Losing the Center

W. John Moore

On the last day of the 1991-92 term, the U.S. Supreme Court issued perhaps its most eagerly anticipated decision of the decade, *Planned Parenthood of Southeastern Pennsylvania v. Casey.*

The Court's opinion created no legal milestone. *Roe v. Wade*, the 1973 ruling establishing a woman's fundamental right to abortion, "should be retained and once again confirmed," the Justices held. But they also said that states could impose restrictions on abortion, including a requirement that minors notify their parents before terminating a pregnancy. In short, the ruling was a compromise one that most Americans would accept, according to public opinion polls.

Activists on both sides of the abortion debate wasted no time in attacking, though. "Don't be fooled by the Court's smokescreen. What the Court did today is devastating for women," the National Abortion and Reproductive Rights Action League (NARAL) warned on the day of the decision. "Today, the Bush Court took away a woman's fundamental right to choose and invited every politician in America to interfere in what remains of this freedom."

NARAL's bitter opponent, the Chicago-based Americans United for Life, was just as unhappy. The Court has "taken two steps backward and turned a blind eye and a deaf ear to legal protection for children before birth. We are strongly disappointed that a majority of the Supreme Court reaffirmed abortion on demand" the anti-abortion group said in a press release.

The reaction of the two antagonists symbolizes interest-group politics in Washington, where a clash of conservative and liberal agendas has destroyed opportunities for consensus sought by the broader public. Eager to attack, seldom willing to compromise, these partisans disdain moderate solutions.

"You get a polarization of debate generated by elites which ordinary citizens find neither affects their interests nor addresses their concerns" said Thomas E. Mann, director of governmental studies at the Brookings Institution in Washington. "Interest groups have discovered that they can play on fears people have as a way to advance their own agendas.

Across the political spectrum, on a host of issues, interest groups have discovered that nothing rouses the faithful like a simple message denouncing your archenemy as evil incarnate. NARAL attacks Americans United for Life. Earth First! battles the timber industry. The Sierra Club blasts leaders of the "wise use" movement, who in turn demonize Interior Secretary Bruce E. Babbitt. People for the American Way chases the Christian Right across the countryside.

Extremism in the defense of ideology is no vice. Moderation in the pursuit of donor dollars is no virtue.

"Polarized rhetoric and extreme positions help arouse the faithful and stimulate membership and contributions" said William A. Galston, deputy assistant to President Clinton for domestic policy and previously a leading light of the centrist Democratic Leadership Council. "For systemic reasons, there is more short-term mileage to be gotten in narrower-focused intensity than in a broader approach."

But the interest groups' gain comes at a cost. A public seeking solutions in Washington discovers a government held hostage at times by interest-group rhetoric.

To some experts, the clash of ideas is democracy at work, proof positive of the beauty of pluralistic politics. University of Virginia sociologist James Davison Hunter, in Culture Wars: The Struggle to Define America (Basic Books, 1991), wrote that bitter disputes articulate issues at the heart of American culture. "But these differences are often intensified and aggravated by the way they are presented in public," Hunter added.

Campaign managers, political pundits, think-tank impresarios and the news media have helped perpetuate what Mann describes as an "attack on the middle."

Once upon a time, Washington think tanks went about their business quietly, with cadres of analysts using their expertise to influence policy. That kind of intellectual power remains a goal for most think tanks.

But as think tanks proliferate, the need to define an identity that's different from the competition's becomes paramount. The quest for money and attention leads to brasher statements and more-dramatic policy prescriptions, James A. Smith wrote in *The Idea Brokers: Think Tanks and the Rise of the New Policy Elite* (Basic Books, 1991). "When all of this is refracted through a media filter, it creates a perception of polarization," Smith said.

The news media, of course, thrive on conflict. There is CNN's Crossfire, a show based on the dubious premise that the truth somehow emerges from liberal and conservative soundbites. "For the media," Mann argues, "the road to truth is in finding two extremes and letting them clash. It is the new definition of fairness"

In his influential book, *Why Americans Hate Politics* (Simon & Schuster Inc., 1991), *Washington Post* political columnist E. J. Dionne Jr. argues that conservatives and liberals have ignored the majority of voters.

"Wracked by contradiction and responsive mainly to the needs of their various constituencies, liberalism and conservatism prevent the nation from settling the questions that most trouble it" Dionne wrote. "On issue after issue, there is consensus where the country should move or at least on what we should be arguing about; liberalism and conservatism make it impossible for that consensus to express itself."

But to succeed, politicians at least must persuade a majority of voters to support them. Washington interest groups are bound by no similar constraints. In fact, many groups are established to represent the viewpoint of a tiny portion of the populace that is absolutely passionate about a single issue—whether it be abortion, guns or the environment.

What an interest group lacks in size it can make up for with intensity. A group with an ideological agenda can't compromise without losing some of its constituents, who respond to fund-raising letters in part because they agree with the blistering rhetoric and absolutist positions staked out by the group.

"Few people are likely to send money to an organization because of its intense, flaming moderation" said R. Kent Weaver, a senior fellow at Brookings.

"A lot of this rhetoric is directed toward the 5 or 10 per cent of the people on each side who are major contributors," said Burdett Loomis, a political scientist at the University of Kansas (Lawrence).

As a result, Loomis added, interest groups succeed better at stopping perceived threats than in accomplishing legislative victories that may require compromise. The liberal People for the American Way, for example, made its name by leading the opposition to the nomination of Robert H. Bork to the Supreme Court. The group stopped Bork—and its contributions reached the highest level ever the next year.

Interest groups thrive on highlighting the differences between themselves and their foes and obscuring the similarities. The result is political discourse with all the civility of Bosnia. "The politics of bombast" as Brookings's Mann puts it.

The growth of single-issue or cause-oriented interest groups is a relatively recent development. Thirty per cent of such groups have formed since 1975; in 1986, at least 20 per cent of all interest groups and trade associations in Washington were in that category, according to an academic study that year.

Ironically, interest groups grow the fastest when their political prospects look the gloomiest. Consider the Fairfax (Va.) based National Rifle Association (NRA), long considered the undisputed champion of single-interest groups. Last year, the NRA failed to stop legislation that established a waiting period for handgun purchases; this spring, it suffered another blow when the House passed legislation that would ban assault rifles. But since the May 16 vote, the NRA has signed up 55,000 new members.

Clinton's support for gun control, which was crucial to the defeat of the gun lobby, has become the primary focus of the NRA's membership campaign. "Make no mistake: Bill Clinton is the American gun owner's worst nightmare," the NRA warned in a letter to prospective members last year. What was possibly Clinton's worse sin, according to the NRA.'? The President even "kissed [gun control advocate] Sarah Brady at rallies."

In the early 1980s, the environmental movement found itself confronting a hostile Administration determined to ease regulations on business. But environmental activists soon discovered a silver lining in the person of James G. Watt, President Reagan's Interior Secretary. Watt "was the devil figure for the environmentalists, like Jane Fonda and Teddy Kennedy used to be for the right" Weaver of Brookings said.

Watts visage on mailings was a magnet for money and support. The Wilderness Society prepared an eight-pound, two-volume compendium of press clips and critical cartoons in its *Watt Book*.

"In 1982, 95,000 new members joined our ranks largely because of the anti-environmental stance of James Watt," the Sierra Club said in a fund-raising letter a decade ago. The Sierra Club doubled its membership just during Watt's tenure. And membership and contributions kept growing during the 12-year Republican reign until the election of Clinton and Vice President Albert Gore Jr., a hero among environmentalists. In 1993, the Sierra Club's contributions dipped an estimated 6.8 per cent.

Other environmental groups have experienced similar drops in donations. The economic recession was part of the reason. But environmentalists attribute much of the falloff to the Gore factor. "There is this view that because Clinton has Gore on his team that he will do the fight thing on the environment. So contributions to most environmental groups have dropped or remained the same" said Graham Cox, vice president for public affairs at the National Audubon Society in New York City.

Some environmental groups have responded by discovering new enemies. The Sierra Club's latest foes are the partisans of what is called the "wise use" movement, conservative groups opposed to tough environmental restrictions on federal lands.

Environmental groups are not the only organizations that have discovered the downside to winning. After the pro-abortion rights Clinton-Gore team captured the White House, NARAL saw its monthly contributions drop by a third last year and its membership decline by 150,000.

"The worst thing that can happen to an interest group is that you win," said Ronald G. Shaiko, a-specialist on interest-group politics at the American University of Washington.

Meanwhile, conservative groups have enjoyed a resurgence. The American Conservative Union now says it has 500,000 members, a fivefold increase since the 1992 election. The increase follows years of decline during the Republican years, acknowledged Jeff Hollingsworth, the group's executive director. With Reagan's election, he said, "conservative activists may have felt that the dream came true."

Now, "the shock of a Clinton-Gore Administration has brought conservatism back to life," Hollingsworth said. If many political analysts argue that Clinton has governed as a centrist, Hollingsworth disagrees. "There's plenty of evidence that Bill Clinton talks moderate and liberals get all the action" he said.

That view certainly sells with conservatives: The President and Hillary Rodham Clinton headline almost every fund-raising letter mailed by a conservative organization to a carefully targeted audience. "These people are predisposed to loathing the Clintons," a conservative fund-raising expert conceded.

Opinion magazines with a conservative bent have pummeled the Clintons in story after story. Hillary Clinton graces (again) the June cover of *The American Spectator*, drawn as a witch astride a jet airplane. The story, *The Washington Post said*, is "the latest installment in that magazine's crusade to show that Hillary is the Antichrist of American politics." Inside, the subscription come-ons are even tougher.

The strategy works. According to figures compiled by the Audit Bureau of Circulations in Schaumburg, ILL., circulation at The American Spectator climbed from 72,468 in 1992 to 128,146 in 1993. Another conservative magazine, the weekly National Review, has also flourished in the Clinton year, with its circulation reaching 221,000 in 1993, up from 168,000 in 1992. Meanwhile, the left-wing bible, the Nation, saw its circulation drop approximately 5 per cent over the same period.

The mainstream news media share responsibility for catering to the extremes. Journalists often try to transform every discussion into a debate—leaving little time to analyze or provide perspective. Even shows for high-brow audiences, such as ABC News's Nightline or the Public Broadcasting System's MacNeil/Lehrer NewsHour, parade casts of dueling policy wonks. Woe to the analyst, critic or historian interested in context or complexity.

When talk radio pros decided that it was time to provide some balance to right-winger Rush Limbaugh, the man hired was lefty Jim Hightower, former head of the Texas Agriculture Commission—whose views are summed up in his immortal words, "There ain't nothin' in the middle of the road but yellow stripes and dead armadillos.

But the center is also the place to find most Americans, who are often unmoved by ideological concerns and unenthusiastic about interest groups. According to many political scientists, there is grave danger in Washington's basing policy only on pleas from ideological diehards.

The sum of all interest groups is not the national interest," the American University's Shaiko said. "And it never will be."

THE FEEDING FRENZY

Jeffrey H. Birnbaum

Few lobbyists entered the fray of Washington without first making sure they had a ready hoard of dollars to spread around. PAC and personal political contributions were expected of anyone who wanted to get his point across. Though money rarely bought votes outright, it did buy a lobbyist the chance to make his views known, a chance not everyone had. Access to the powers that be was rationed, and the size of one's political pocketbook was important to making the cut.

The importance of money in politics was openly acknowledged by both the lawmakers who took it and the lobbyists who doled it out. "Money is power," said Democratic Representative Bill Alexander of Arkansas. And the lobbyists who were able to provide money were able to wield more than their share of power. "Access to Congress can't be bought, but it can be acquired with the help of campaign contributions," said Democratic Senator Brock Adams of Washington State, in a marvelous example of doublespeak.

The influence of money was directly related to the central imperative of all elected officials: remaining in office. Washington insiders loved to recount the probably apocryphal tale of the senator who asked a lobbyist if he knew what the three most important things are to a member of Congress. The senator answered his own question: "Number one is getting reelected. Number two is getting reelected. And number three is getting reelected." Whatever a lobbyist could do to help the lawmaker stay in office, the lesson went, was certainly worth the effort.

One of the chief things a lobbyist could do was raise money for campaigns. The reason: Getting elected or reelected was astronomically expensive. Hundreds of thousands of dollars were needed just to win a seat in the House; millions of dollars were necessary for a Senate race, even in small states. And the only place to get that much money with relative ease was from political-action committees and Washington-based lobbyists.

Would-be lawmakers were taught this harrowing lesson openly in a seminar conducted by the House's Democratic Congressional Campaign Committee. According to a *Washington Post* article by Steve Sovern, a candidate for the House from Iowa, aspiring lawmakers were instructed that the only way they could win their elections was to join the campaign-money circuit that lobbyists controlled. At a seminar for candidates that Sovern attended during the 101st Congress, campaign consultant Frank Greer of Greer, Margolis, Mitchell advised, "The game of raising PAC money here in Washington will make the difference. Understand how the game is played. It's crucial to your being one of the few that will win."

Sovern was horrified when it was also made clear that the candidates had to do something in return for campaign contributions. Sovern quoted Democratic Representative Peter Hoagland of Nebraska as saying that a "business relationship" was formed between the PACs and the lawmakers they contributed to. What kind of relationship? "When you take PAC money," explained George Gould, a lobbyist for the letter carriers' union, "you are saying you're their friend."

Another way to look at campaign giving was that it placed lobbyists on an even plane with the lawmakers' own constituents. The people from back home did not need to give their lawmakers money. They could purchase their attention with the prospect of delivering votes. Washington-based lobbyists, in contrast, could not vote for legislators themselves, but they could provide the funds that bought the advertising and campaign support that got out the votes. Campaign contributions, in effect, permitted the lobbyists to buy their way into legislators' offices. . . .

Senator Adams, who also contributed to the handbook, went so far as to suggest that a lobbyist needed to give money to have any chance of being heard. "Some lobbyists make a good living organizing fundraisers, and volunteering for every member's fund-raising steering committee to develop access," he said. "Lobbyists arriving in Washington must either compete with those who already have access and proven track records or tie themselves to experienced lobbyists who are known and trusted and have probably been involved with political activities and fund-raising."

Some lobbyists believed that the constant pressure to give money amounted to nothing short of extortion. One lobbyist complained, "There are some congressmen you have to buy your way in. If you pay 'em, they'll see you; if you don't, you don't get in."

But that kind of extortion was a necessary evil. In *The Lobbying Handbook*, longtime lobbyist Joseph S. Miller is quoted as saying: "Because members and staff have their tin cups at the ready for campaign contributions, I often feel that they look upon me as a dollar sign, not as a person." But the pressing need for campaign money, he added, "means that those who can give money get access and are in a better position to move bills than those who can't."

In an interview, ex-Senator Long made clear that giving campaign money was an essential part of the Washington scene: "Members aren't going to have much time to visit with people who can't be bothered to attend a fund-raiser, who don't find it convenient to make an appropriate campaign contribution or urge a principal to make a contribution. They've got a word they use in the [lobbying] fraternity: They refer to people as players. All of the more effective lobbyists are known as players. The most effective tend to work on a bipartisan basis and contribute to campaigns. A lobbyist attends fund-raisers because he needs access, he needs to communicate with these people. He'll have a lot better chance to communicate if he's a player than if he's not a player."

Money, therefore, brought clout, as lobbyist Miller starkly recounted. In a paraphrase of Senator Long, Miller said: "The shades of gray are many between bribery and a contribution, and . . . it is difficult to determine whether money was given to support a campaign or because the contributor expected something in return. Neither party may state what that 'something' is, but both parties understand what's expected. We have come a long way since giving cash was the norm, but few people today doubt that strings are attached to campaign contributions.". . .

. . . A study of campaign reports filed with the Federal Election Commission showed that from 1972 through the end of 1989 members of the Senate alone raised more than $158 million in PAC donations. During that period, seventy-eight senators raised more than $1 million each, with five Democrats and five Republicans in the top ten. In 1988 alone, PACs contributed $31.9 million to the winners of Senate contests and $86.1 million to winners in the House. In 1989, the giving continued apace. According to *The Washington Post*, PACs contributed more than $57 million, 90 percent of which went to incumbents.

Fund-raising of one kind or another had become virtually a way of life for both lawmakers and lobbyists. Members of Congress, even those with safe seats, spent hours trying to shake the money tree. Boulder County, Colorado, Commissioner Josie Heath, a candidate for the Senate, told the *Post*: "You're just sort of shamelessly begging. That's what federal politics is about." And lobbyists devoted many of their work and after-work hours to either delivering checks, trying to get other lobbyists to deliver checks, or explaining to lawmakers why they couldn't deliver checks.

There was so much giving that lobbyists had to come up with inventive ways to collect more and more money. Increasingly, the nearly five thousand registered PACs built their coffers through "check-off" programs, which allowed people to contribute automatically through payroll deductions. And once the money was collected, lobbyists spent morning, noon, and night distributing it. Charles Babcock and Richard Morin of *The Washington Post* followed George Gould of the letter carriers' union, which was 1989's biggest PAC, as he attended as many as eleven fund-raisers in a single day. "If I drank," the lobbyist confessed, "I'd be incoherent by eight."

Few lobbyists attended that many fund-raisers, but almost all lobbyists were campaign givers, often through, or with the backing of, a PAC. Thevenot's National Realty Committee PAC, or REAL-PAC, gave $48,250 to fifty-one candidates during the 101st Congress. Juliano's Hotel Employees and Restaurant Employees International Union PAC, called TIP-PAC, gave $230,225 to more than two hundred candidates. And Ken Simonson and Tom Donohue's American Trucking Associations PAC gave $300,040 to 284 candidates. Even Eizenstat's and Kay's law firms established PACs that became major contributors. Eizenstat's firm's PAC gave $131,790 to 167 candidates in 1989 and 1990, and Kay's PAC contributed $91,106 to 142 candidates. In other words, they all covered a lot of ground. . . .

Often political money worked for lobbyists in subtle ways. It was not just a way to buy access and win friends; it also was the ticket to some of the biggest lobbying fests in Washington: political fund-raisers.

Thevenot found himself at one on Tuesday, October 24, the gala of the Democratic National Committee at Washington's historic Pension Building. The cavernous yet elegant structure is lined with three-story pillars, and that night it was packed to the rafters with black ties and glittering dresses. Lawmakers by the dozens and lobbyists by the hundreds mingled and chatted. The lobbyists paid $1,500 a head for the opportunity to do this hobnobbing, and the event cleared about $2.5 million for the Democrats' coffers. It was so crowded that the bars ran out of glasses during the cocktail hour, and security guards had to be called in to help close the bars down.

Thevenot made the best of his time there. In his wanderings through the throngs, he ran into Representative Norman Dicks of Washington State. Thevenot knew the congressman from when they both were Senate staffers, and they had stayed in touch through the years. Dicks asked Thevenot what he was up to, and the lobbyist happily explained his new Maglev coalition. Surely, Thevenot thought, a congressman from a region dominated by the Boeing Company would like to know about a new mode of transportation for which the aircraft maker might someday make components.

The table where Thevenot sat had been purchased by the PAC of one of his partner's clients, Wheelabrator Corporation, at the request of Senator Wyche Fowler of Georgia. It was the custom at these functions for lawmakers to contact potential contributors, often Washington lobbyists, and persuade them to buy a table where the lawmaker could sit. This time Thevenot's partner Bill Boardman was tapped. Thevenot himself had been contacted by other senators who had asked him to buy a table. But, he had to explain, a lobbyist could do only so much. His lobbying firm already had bought an entire table, and it was a good thing too. Thevenot's main corporate backer, the National Realty Committee, contributed to individual lawmakers and not to political parties.

Strategically situated then, Thevenot went about some serious schmoozing. A fund-raiser, he explained, "is an opportunity for people in my business to meet a lot of people, see a lot of people, be seen not only by members of Congress, but by potential clients who see you moving with the glitterati of the party. They observe how many of them you seem to know or seem to know you. The facility with which you move around in these circles makes an impression on them. It's kind of nice when you are standing there and someone whom you might want to, at some point, represent, sees a member come up, put his arm around your shoulder, and say, 'Wayne, how are you doin'?' That is part of the reason why you attend these things."

Thevenot found that he too was the object of lobbying. During dinner, Grace Bender, who once worked for Thevenot as an office manager, but had since become a Democratic party loyalist and fund-raiser, reminded him about a fund-raiser she was throwing in six days for Senator Jay Rockefeller of West Virginia. Thevenot agreed to attend. Saying no without good reason, he said, could be dangerous:

"A lot of it you do because you are asked to do it. A member calls you up and says, 'Will you do this?' and you say, 'No'? I'm not sure what kind of reception you would get if you were one of ten people asking to see him that week. Who would get the nod? It's a hell of a risk to take. And we're part of the process. I don't write the campaign-financing rules. But it's the system, and I'm not going to play the martyr and try to change it single-handedly. I'm just going to play it until they change it." . . .

CHAPTER 8

INTRODUCTION

Have you ever talked (or actually *listened*) to someone of a previous generation talk about the changes in the media? I know you tire of that "had to walk five miles through five feet of snow with no coat to get to school" stuff, but there really are major differences in the media as it exists today from 20 and more years ago. (Personally, I'm convinced that a major cause of obesity and divorce in the United States is the remote control!! Well, I digress.) The three selections I have chosen for you examine the media in three different ways.

There are more media outlets than ever before. It would seem that, accordingly, we would get more information, more in depth information, and a better explanation of the information we are given. Kiku Adatto reveals that from 1968 to 1988, during the peak election period of Labor Day to Election Day, the average media "sound bite" fell from 42.3 seconds to 9.8 seconds. However, this is not the only change that Adatto notes. Examine his article for the following:

1. What are the implications of the "sound bite" shrinkage noted above?

2. Note other changes which have occurred in the networks' coverage of election campaigns.

3. How could we better the public's ability to gain useful and accurate information concerning candidates and their positions on issues?

Kathleen Sullivan addresses the issue of the media's role in our government. What do we expect out of the media and how much of that is a reasonable expectation? Answer these questions:

1. Explain the contradictory views of the press noted by Sullivan. Which of these views do you think is most accurate?

2. In Sullivan's view, what should the government do about these criticisms of the press? Why?

THE INCREDIBLE SHRINKING SOUND BITE

Kiku Adatto

Standing before a campaign rally in Pennsylvania, the 1968 Democratic vice presidential candidate, Edmund Muskie, tried to speak, but a group of anti-war protesters drowned him out. Muskie offered the hecklers a deal. He would give the platform to one of their representatives if he could then speak without interruption. Rick Brody, the students' choice, rose to the microphone where, to cheers from the crowd, he denounced the candidates that the 1968 presidential campaign had to offer. "Wallace is no answer. Nixon's no answer. And Humphrey's no answer. Sit out this election!" When Brody finished, Muskie made his case for the Democratic ticket. That night Muskie's confrontation with the demonstrators played prominently on the network news. NBC showed fifty-seven seconds of Brody's speech, and more than a minute of Muskie's.

Twenty years later, things had changed. Throughout the entire 1988 campaign, no network allowed either presidential candidate to speak uninterrupted on the evening news for as long as Rick Brody spoke. By 1988 television's tolerance for the languid pace of political discourse, never great, had all but vanished. An analysis of all weekday evening network newscasts (over 280) from Labor Day to Election Day in 1968 and 1988 reveals that the average "sound bite" fell from 42.3 seconds in 1968 to only 9.8 seconds in 1988. Meanwhile the time the networks devoted to visuals of the candidates, unaccompanied by their words, increased by more than 300 percent.

Since the Kennedy-Nixon debates of 1960 television has played a pivotal role in presidential politics. The Nixon campaign of 1968 was the first to be managed and orchestrated to play on the evening news. With the decline of political parties and the direct appeal to voters in the primaries, presidential campaigns became more adept at conveying their messages through visual images, not only in political commercials but also in elaborately staged media events. By the time of Ronald Reagan, the actor turned president, Michael Deaver had perfected the techniques of the video presidency.

For television news, the politicians' mastery of television imagery posed a temptation and a challenge. The temptation was to show the pictures. What network producer could resist the footage of Reagan at Normandy Beach, or of Bush in Boston Harbor? The challenge was to avoid being entangled in the artifice and imagery that the campaigns dispensed. In 1988 the networks tried to have it both ways—to meet the challenge even as they succumbed to the temptation. They showed the images that the campaigns produced—their commercials as well as their media events. But they also sought to retain their objectivity by exposing the artifice of the images, by calling constant attention to their self-conscious design. . . .

When Bush kicked off his campaign with a Labor Day appearance at Disneyland, the networks covered the event as a performance for television. "In the war of the Labor Day visuals," CBS's Bob Schieffer reported, "George Bush pulled out the heavy artillery. A Disneyland backdrop and lots of pictures with the Disney gang." When Bruce Morton covered Dukakis riding in a tank, the story was the image, "In the trade of politics, it's called a visual," said Morton. "The idea is pictures are symbols that tell the voter important things about the candidate. If your candidate is seen in the polls as weak on defense, put him in a tank.

By 1988 television displaced politics as the focus of coverage. Like a gestalt shift, the images that once formed the background to political events—the setting and the stagecraft—now occupied the foreground. (Only 6 percent of reports in 1968 were devoted to theater criticism, compared with 52 percent in 1988.) And yet, for all their image-conscious coverage in 1988, reporters did not escape their entanglement. They showed the potent visuals even as they attempted to avoid the manipulation by "deconstructing" the imagery and revealing its artifice.

To be sure, theater criticism was not the only kind of political reporting on network newscasts in 1988. Some notable "fact correction" pieces offered admirable exceptions. For example, after each presidential debate, ABCs Jim Wooten compared the candidates' claims with the facts. Not content with the canned images of the politicians, Wooten used television images to document discrepancies between the candidates' rhetoric and their records. . . .

Another striking contrast between the coverage of the 1968 and 1988 campaigns is the increased coverage of political commercials. Although political ads played a prominent role in the 1968 campaign, the networks rarely showed excerpts on the news. During the entire 1968 general election campaign, the evening news programs broadcast only two excerpts from candidates' commercials. By 1988 the number had jumped to 125. In 1968 the only time a negative ad was mentioned on the evening news was when CBS's Walter Cronkite and NBC's Chet Huntley reported that a Nixon campaign ad—showing a smiling Hubert Humphrey superimposed on scenes of war and riot—was withdrawn after the Democrats cried foul. Neither network showed the ad itself.

The networks might argue that in 1988 political ads loomed larger in the campaign, and so required more coverage. But as with their focus on media events, reporters ran the risk of becoming conduits of the television images the campaigns dispensed. Even with a critical narrative, showing commercials on the news gives free time to paid media. And most of the time the narrative was not critical. The networks rarely bothered to correct the distortions or misstatements that the ads contained. Of the 125 excerpts shown on the evening news in 1988, the reporter addressed the veracity of the commercials' claims less than 8 percent of the time. The networks became, in effect, electronic billboards for the candidates, showing political commercials not only as breaking news but as stand-ins for the candidates, and file footage aired interchangeably with news footage of the candidates.

The few cases where reporters corrected the facts illustrate how the networks might have covered political commercials. ABC's Richard Threlkeld ran excerpts from a Bush ad attacking Dukakis's defense stand by freezing the frame and correcting each mistaken or distorted claim. He also pointed out the exaggeration in a Dukakis ad attacking Bush's record on Social Security, CBS's Leslie Stahl corrected a deceptive statistic in Bush's revolving-door furlough ad, noting: "Part of the ad is false .... Two hundred sixty-eight murderers did not escape . . . [T]he truth is only four first-degree murderers escaped while on parole.

Stahl concluded her report by observing, "Dukakis left the Bush attack ads unanswered for six weeks. Today campaign aides are engaged in a round of finger-pointing at who is to blame." But the networks also let the Bush furlough commercial run without challenge or correction. Before and even after her report, CBS ran excerpts of the ad without correction. In all, network newscasts ran excerpts from the revolving-door furlough ad ten times throughout the campaign, only once correcting the deceptive statistic.

It might be argued that it is up to the candidate to reply to his opponent's charges, not the press. But the networks' frequent use of political ads on the evening news created a strong disincentive for a candidate to challenge his opponent's ads. As Dukakis found, to attack a television ad as unfair or untrue is to invite the networks to run it again. In the final weeks before the election, the Dukakis campaign accused the Republicans of lying about his record on defense, and of using racist tactics in ads featuring Willie Horton, a black convict who raped and killed while on furlough from a Massachusetts prison. In reporting Dukakis's complaint, all three networks ran excerpts of the ads in question, including the highly charged pictures of Horton and the revolving door of convicts. Dukakis's response thus gave Bush's potent visuals another free run on the evening news. . . .

Along with the attention to commercials and stagecraft in 1988 came an unprecedented focus on the stage managers themselves, the "media gurus," "handlers," and "spin-control artists." Only three reports featured media advisers in 1968, compared with twenty-six in 1988. And the numbers tell only part of the story.

The stance reporters have taken toward media advisers has changed dramatically over the past twenty years. In The Selling of the President (1969), Joe McGinniss exposed the growing role of media advisers with a sense of disillusion and outrage. By 1988 television reporters covered image-makers with deference, even admiration. In place of independent fact correction, reporters sought out media advisers as authorities in their own right to analyze the effectiveness and even defend the truthfulness of campaign commercials. They became "media gurus" not only for the candidates but for the networks as well. . . .

So hypersensitive were the networks to television image-making in 1988 that minor mishaps—gaffes, slips of the tongue, even faulty microphones—became big news. Politicians were hardly without mishaps in 1968, but these did not count as news. Only once in 1968 did a network even take note of a minor incident unrelated to the content of the campaign. In 1988 some twenty-nine reports highlighted trivial slips.

The emphasis on "failed images" reflected a kind of guerrilla warfare between the networks and the campaigns. The more the campaigns sought to control the images that appeared on the nightly news, the more the reporters tried to beat them at their own game, magnifying a minor mishap into a central feature of the media event.

Early in the 1988 campaign, for example, George Bush delivered a speech to a sympathetic audience of the American Legion, attacking his opponent's defense policies. In a slip, he declared that September 7, rather than December 7, was the anniversary of Pearl Harbor. Murmurs and chuckles from the audience alerted him to his error, and he quickly corrected himself.

The audience was forgiving, but the networks were not. All three network anchors highlighted the slip on the evening news. Dan Rather introduced CBS's report on Bush by declaring solemnly, "Bush's talk to audiences in Louisville was overshadowed by a strange happening." On NBC Tom Brokaw reported, "He departed from his prepared script and left his listeners mystified." Peter Jennings introduced ABC's report by mentioning Bush's attack on Dukakis, adding, "What's more likely to be remembered about today's speech is a slip of the tongue."

Some of the slips the networks highlighted in 1988 were not even verbal gaffes or misstatements, but simply failures on the part of the candidates to cater to the cameras. In a report on the travails of the Dukakis campaign, Sam Donaldson seized on Dukakis's failure to play to ABC's television camera as evidence of his campaign's ineffectiveness. Showing Dukakis playing a trumpet with a local marching band, Donaldson chided, "He played the trumpet with his back to the camera." As Dukakis played, "Happy Days Are Here Again," Donaldson's voice was heard from off-camera calling, "We're over here, governor." . . .

The assumption that the creation of appearances is the essence of political reality pervaded not only the reporting but the candidates' self-understanding and conduct with the press. When Dan Quayle sought to escape his image as a highly managed candidate, he resolved publicly to become his own handler, his own "spin doctor. . . .The so-called handlers story, part of it's true," he confessed to network reporters. "But there will be no more handlers stories, because I'm the handler and I'll do the spinning." Surrounded by a group of reporters on his campaign plane, Quayle announced, "I'm Doctor Spin, and I want you all to report that."

It may seem a strange way for a politician to talk, but not so strange in a media-conscious environment in which authenticity means being master of your own artificiality. Dukakis too sought to reverse his political fortunes by seeking to be master of his own image. This attempt was best captured in a commercial shown on network news in which Dukakis stood beside a television set and snapped off a Bush commercial attacking his stand on defense. "I'm fed up with it," Dukakis declared. "Never seen anything like it in twenty-five years of public life. George Bush's negative television ads, distorting my record, full of lies, and he knows it." The commercial itself shows an image of an image—a Bush television commercial showing (and ridiculing) the media event where Dukakis rose in a tank. In his commercial, Dukakis complains that Bush's commercial showing the tank ride misstates Dukakis's position on defense.

As it appeared in excerpts on the evening news, Dukakis's commercial displayed a quintessentially modernist image of artifice upon artifice upon artifice: television news covering a Dukakis commercial containing a Bush commercial containing a Dukakis media event. In a political world governed by images of images, it seemed almost natural that the authority, of the candidate be depicted by his ability to turn of the television set. . . .

In a moment of reflection in 1988, CBS's political correspondents expressed their frustration with image-driven campaigns, "It may seem frivolous, even silly at times," said Schieffer, "But setting up pictures that drive home a message has become the No. I priority of the modern-day campaign. The problem, of course, is while it is often entertaining, it is seldom enlightening."

Rather shared his colleagues discomfort. But what troubled him about modern campaigns is equally troubling about television's campaign coverage. "With all this emphasis on the image," he asked, "what happens to the issues? What happens to the substance?"

THE ROLE OF THE MEDIA IN REPRESENTATIVE GOVERNMENT

Kathleen M. Sullivan

Criticism of the press's role in government lately has been sharp but contradictory. On the one hand, the press is attacked for having too big an effect on democratic deliberations. By ferreting out political or personal scandals, say the critics, the press drives good people away from politics. By choosing sensational news coverage to boost ratings, the press distorts the agenda for public policy-making. If the local nightly news dwells on brutal and graphic crime stories, politicians are forced to call for tough-on-crime measures even if the crime rate is dropping and the measures make bad crime policy. By covering political contests as horse races, critics assert, the press diverts attention from complex and serious policy issues. Voters learn more about what is at stake for politicians in an election than about what is at stake for them. The print media, faced with competition from twenty-four-hour news services, increasingly publishes biased analysis in place of facts. And the electronic media, by reducing political issues to sound bites of ten seconds or less, encourage political figures to engage in shrillness and mutual vilification rather than informed and dispassionate debate. On this view, the press is a powerful actor whose effects on politics have been largely negative.

On the other hand, the press is criticized equally harshly for weakness—for being too supine in the face of government. On this view, the press corps prizes access to politicians and their staffs so highly that it pulls its punches to avoid offending them. It is cowed by the government's own elaborate spin-control machinery, giving in to pressure to withhold unflattering stories. It is reactive in its coverage of political campaigns, trailing around obediently to cover carefully scripted appearances and raising tough issues about a candidate only when the candidate's opponent does. It is "scandal-shy," shirking exposure of sexual or financial wrongdoing that might harm politically powerful players, or might cause the public to disparage it as predatory. On this view, the institution that ought to serve as the watchdog of government has become a lapdog.

What should government do about these criticisms of the press? Absolutely nothing—at least absolutely nothing that aims at the content of media coverage of politics. That is because the press enjoys strong First Amendment protection for good reason. Some have likened the press to a fourth branch of government, providing the ultimate check and balance that prevents tyranny by the other three. The institutional press can monitor government more closely than individuals can, exposing public officials' errors and abuses to public criticism and making room for political dissent. A free press can also improve the quality of democratic decisionmaking. It disseminates not only facts but also ideas from diverse and mutually antagonistic sources. By enabling a variety of viewpoints to be aired on controversial public matters, it can inform and alter the making of public policy.

For these reasons, the Supreme Court has repeatedly held that press freedom should be "uninhibited, robust and wide-open," in Justice William Brennan's words. The Court has invalidated licensing schemes, prior restraints, gag orders, and special taxes imposed upon the press. It has held that public officials have to endure even "vehement, caustic, and sometimes unpleasantly sharp attacks" upon them unless the press deliberately or recklessly prints falsehoods. It has given the press substantial access rights to trials and other official proceedings, preventing government from operating in ways that are secretive or corrupt. In short, it has given the press substantial immunity from government restraint or retaliation.

What if the government tries to improve rather than censor the content of press coverage? Some contemporary press critics, for example, suggest that broadcasters and cable operators should be required to provide more or better public affairs programming, or free airtime for the expression of candidates' views. Others suggest that third party and independent candidates ought to be guaranteed more access to political coverage and televised debates. The government's few prior ventures into fine-tuning the content of the electronic media illustrate that this approach is seriously misguided. For some years the Federal Communications Commission required broadcasters to give free time for response to personal attacks or controversial political editorials. This so-called fairness doctrine could never have been imposed on the print media, which have broad editorial discretion as a matter of constitutional right. But the FCC viewed broadcast stations as a scarcer resource than printing presses and so held, with the Supreme Court's blessing, that they could be conscripted as conduits for the speech of others in order to maintain diversity of views.

The FCC has repealed the fairness doctrine, and Congress has failed to resurrect it by legislation. The reason is the death of scarcity; with more space on the electromagnetic spectrum and with the growth of satellite technology and cable, it could no longer be said that broadcasters held any choke-hold monopoly. But the reason may as well have been the failure of the fairness doctrine to serve its purposes: although rights of reply were meant to ensure vigorous debate on controversial issues, they in fact tended to encourage reticence and blandness as stations strove to avoid controversial statements that would trigger right-of-reply obligations. Forcing mainstream stations to carry a few, token adversarial viewpoints proved far less effective in increasing diversity of coverage than alternatives such as subsidizing public radio and television.

Any solution to existing problems in press coverage thus should come from the press itself rather than the government. There is much evidence that the press is responsive to public criticism, even to a fault. For instance, prompted by prominent public criticism of its sound-bite tendencies, every major broadcast and cable network devoted some amount of free airtime during the 1996 presidential campaign to lengthy, unedited statements by all the principal candidates. For another more dubious example, many local news outlets have experimented with "public journalism," which encourages ordinary citizens rather than journalists to set the agenda of issues for public affairs coverage. This movement seeks to emulate the success of talk radio and "town hall" television debate formats. While there is considerable merit to expanding the range of subject matter coverage, public journalists depart too far from valuable professional norms and customs when they make journalism a matter of mere market testing. One of the assumptions on which robust First Amendment protection rests is that the press governs itself by ethical norms of impartiality, independence, fairness, and objectivity that make it beholden neither to government nor to special interest constituencies. Compromising this independence might undermine the arguments for freedom from government regulation.

Arguments for government regulation of media content should therefore be rejected. They violate basic First Amendment principles. They threaten the press's watchdog role. But they also entirely miss a key point: the most important problem with the media in our current politics is not content but structure. The print and electronic media have always been privately owned, and it has long been true, as A. J. Liebling quipped, that "freedom of the press is guaranteed only to those who own one." But, just at the moment when we are experiencing the greatest decentralization of information the world has ever known across the global web of linked computers known as the Internet, we are also seeing an unprecedented wave of corporate concentration in the media industry. NBC is owned by General Electric, and, in a rash of recent mergers, the Disney Company took over ABC, Westinghouse took over CBS, and Time Warner merged with Turner Broadcasting, the home of the twenty-four-hour news service CNN. The corporate alliance of the news industry with giants of entertainment and defense raises serious questions. Will those who produce the news within such corporate structures be willing to bite the hand that feeds them? To pan their movies or to cover corporate scandals? To question the safety of their products or the wisdom of their procurement of government funds? To cover their political contributions? To devote coverage to the phenomenon of media concentration in itself? Some networks have already, in notorious incidents, pulled or apologized for negative coverage of the tobacco industry, in which their corporate owners held substantial financial interests. Of further concern is the possibility that concentrated media ownership will make the information delivered to the public increasingly centrist, homogeneous, and bland. Some radio stations and commentators have already been dropped, post-merger, because they were perceived as too far outside the political mainstream.

The First Amendment poses far less an obstacle to government regulation of media structure than media content. The free speech and press guarantees have never exempted the press from the reach of content-neutral laws, including, most relevantly, antitrust laws. The Supreme Court has held, for example, that cable operators may be required to carry local broadcast stations if their control over the cable conduit and their vertical integration with cable programmers poses a competitive threat to the broadcast system. The reason is that such a law aims at the economic structure of the industry, not at any programming the systems carry. If a television is, as one FCC commissioner once remarked, a "toaster with pictures," the government is as free to regulate the toaster as it is bound to leave the protected content of the pictures alone.

Yet government has lately shied away from addressing seriously the problems of media oligopoly and cross-ownership posed by the recent wave of concentration. This hands-off approach should be reexamined. Closer scrutiny of deals under existing antitrust laws would be desirable. The solution might be to separate conduits from content—to require corporations to choose between making programs and carrying them. Or the solution might be to tax the use of the public broadcast spectrum and to direct the resulting revenues toward expanding publicly subsidized radio and television stations, so long as government leaves them editorial control. Of course, there are countervailing arguments: some say that large-scale media companies are needed to do battle in an increasingly global competition; others suggest that freedom of expression on the Internet undermines the ability of the corporate media to homogenize ideas or exert ideological domination, so that the problem is self-limiting.

These questions are quite complex, but one thing about them is straightforward: the First Amendment does not place any gag order on asking them. Freedom of speech and press entails some limits on economic regulation; special taxation of the press, for example, has rightly been held to be censorship by other means. But the First Amendment is misread when invoked as a bar to all regulation of media market structure. Government need not treat all the institutions of the press as if they were lone orators on soapboxes. The misguided focus on fine-tuning press content has diverted attention from this more important structural debate.

CHAPTER 9

INTRODUCTION

Were you eligible to vote in the last election? Did you vote? Why or why not? Did your closest friends and/or your family members vote? This final chapter deals with the concept of participation. The overall lack of participation by Americans in the simplest activities of their political system, such as voting, has been well discussed. Why do Americans participate at such low levels? Is our level of participation really as bad as it seems? Political scientist Thomas Patterson has been dealing with this issue for years and has written an excellent article.

1. Why does Patterson argue that participation has decreased?

2. Why do some argue that the diminishment in participation is overstated and not as serious a problem as some believe?

3. What do YOU think?

The second article in this chapter is drawn from a book called Bowling Alone. This work deals with what seems to be a diminishing level of social interactions in our society. In this excerpt, which is a chapter that summarizes a section of his book, he examines possible factors which may be contributing to this phenomenon.

1. What are the factors which may be leading to this lack of cohesion in our society?

2. How well does Putnam support or debunk these factors?

THE INCREDIBLE SHRINKING ELECTORATE

Thomas E. Patterson

I've lost interest in voting.

—twenty-six-year-old Pennsylvania voter

I just don't vote.

—twenty-five-year-old North Carolina resident

I don't have any time, and I'm not interested anyway.

—forty-year-old Washington resident

I don't see any reason to vote.

—thirty-year-old Wisconsin resident

SAM ROBERTS, a Miami resident, was kicking himself. A Gore supporter, he had not voted in the 2000 presidential election. "I should have voted" Roberts told a reporter. "Had planned to but didn't get around to it. Dumb."

With the outcome of the 2000 election hanging by the thread of a few hundred votes in Florida, citizen regret was widespread. Nearly half of adult Americans had not voted, and a CNN poll indicated most of them wished they had.

Even if more people go to the polls in the next election, and the terrorist attacks of September 11, 2001, could have that effect, the long-term prospects are anything but bright. The voting rate has fallen in nearly every presidential election for four decades. An economic recession and Ross Perot's spirited third-party bid sparked a healthy 5 percent increase in 1992, but turnout in 1996 plunged to 49 percent, the first time since the 1920s that it had slipped below 50 percent.

Many expected turnout to rise in 2000. The Clinton-Dole race four years earlier was one-sided from the start. The contest between A1 Gore and George W. Bush, however, looked to be the tightest since 1960, when John F. Kennedy won by the slim margin of 100,000 votes. "Close elections tend to drive up voter interest" said CNN's political analyst Bill Schneider. Turnout did rise, but only slightly: a mere 51 percent of U.S. adults voted in 2000.

That was a far cry from the 63 percent turnout for the Kennedy-Nixon race of 1960, which became the benchmark for evaluating participation in subsequent elections. In every presidential election for the next twenty years, turnout fell. It rose by 1 percentage point in 1984, but then dropped 3 points in 1988. Analysts viewed the trend with alarm, but the warning bells really sounded in 1996, when more Americans stayed home than went to the polls on Election Day. In 1960, 68.8 million adults voted and 40.8 million did not. In 1996, 96.3 million came out and 100.2 million passed.

The turnout trend in the midterm congressional elections has been no less alarming. The voting rate was nearly 50 percent on average in the 1960s, barely stayed above 40 percent in the 1970s, and has averaged 37 percent since then. After a recent midterm vote the cartoonist Rigby showed an election clerk eagerly asking a stray cat that had wandered into a polling place, "Are you registered?"

The period from 1960 to 2000 marks the longest ebb in turnout in the nation's history. If in 2000, as in 1960, 63 percent of the electorate had participated, nearly 25 million more people would have voted. If that many queued up at a polling booth in New York City, the line would stretch all the way to Los Angeles and back, twice over.

Fewer voters are not the only sign that Americans are less interested in political campaigns. Since 1960, participation has declined in virtually every area of election activity, from the volunteers who work on campaigns to the viewers who watch televised debates. The United States had 100 million fewer people in 1960 than it did in 2000 but, even so, more viewers tuned to the October presidential debates in 1960 than did so in 2000.

Few today pay even token tribute to presidential elections. In 1974, Congress established a fund to underwrite candidates' campaigns, financed by a checkoff box on personal income tax returns that allowed citizens to assign $1 (later raised to $3) of their tax liability to the fund. Initially, one in three taxpayers checked the box. By the late 1980s, only one in five marked it. Now, only one in eight does so.

What could possibly explain such trends? Why are citizens drawing back from election politics? Why is the voter vanishing?

American politics has many strange aspects, but few so mysterious as the decline in electoral participation. Two decades ago, the political scientist Richard Brody observed that the declining rate was at odds with existing theories about voting behavior.

One such theory held that rising education levels would spawn higher participation. In 1960, college-educated Americans were 50 percent more likely to vote than those who had not finished high school. With college graduates increasing steadily in number, the future of voting in America looked bright. "Education not only tends to imbue persons with a sense of citizen duty, it also propels them into political activity," the political scientist V. O. Key wrote. In 1960, half of the adult population had not finished high school and fewer than 10 percent had graduated from college. Today, 25 percent hold a college degree and another 25 percent have attended college. Yet, turnout has declined.

The voting rate of African Americans deepens the mystery. In 1960, only 29 percent of southern blacks were registered to vote. An imposing array of barriers—poll taxes, rigged literacy tests, and courthouse intimidation—kept them from registering. Jim Crow laws ruled southern politics, as did segregationist appeals. Ross Barnett was elected Mississippi's governor in 1959 to the tune of a race-baiting song that included a line saying he would oppose integration with forceful intent. When George Wallace first ran for governor of Alabama, he was beaten by an out-and-out racist candidate, prompting Wallace to vow: "I'll never be outniggered again." He kept his word and won handily when he ran in 1962. Only 22,000 of Mississippi's 450,000 blacks—a mere 5 percent—were registered to vote. North Carolina had the South's highest level of black registration but, even there, only 38 percent were enrolled.

The force of the civil rights movement swept the registration barriers aside. The Twenty-Fourth Amendment, ratified in 1964, prohibits states from requiring citizens to pay "any poll tax or other tax" before they can vote in federal elections. The Voting Rights Act of 1965 empowered the U.S. attorney general to send federal examiners to supervise registration in the seven southern states where literacy tests had been imposed and where fewer than 50 percent of eligible adults were registered. Within half a year, black registration in the states of Alabama, Georgia, Louisiana, Mississippi, and South Carolina rose by 40 percent. The Voting Rights Act also suspended the use of literacy tests, which were banned completely five years later. President Lyndon Johnson told southern officials not to resist electoral change: "To those who seek to avoid action by their National Government in their own communities, who want to and seek to maintain purely local control over elections, the answer is simple: open your polling places to all your people."

Many southern blacks saw their names on polling lists for the first time in their lives. African-American registration rose to 43 percent in 1964 and to more than 60 percent by 1970. In the process, black turnout in the region doubled. Southern whites reacted by also voting in larger numbers, mostly for racial conservatives. In 1960, participation in the South was 30 percentage points below that of the rest of the country. Today, it is less than 5 points lower. Nationally, the voting rate of African Americans is now nearly the same as that of whites. Why, then, has the overall rate declined?

The women's vote adds to the mystery. Although women gained the right to vote in 1920, they were slow to exercise it. Even as late as 1960, turnout among women was nearly 10 percentage points below that of men. American society was changing, however. The tradition-minded women born before suffrage were giving way to generations of women who never doubted that the vote belonged to them as much as it did to men. Today, women vote at the same rate as men. But the overall rate has fallen.

The relaxation of registration laws in recent years also provides reason to think that the turnout rate should have gone up, not down. Unlike Europe, where governments take responsibility to get citizens registered and where participation exceeds 80 percent, the United States places the burden of registration on the individual. For a long period, this arrangement was a boon to officials who wanted to keep the poor and uneducated from voting. States devised schemes that hampered all but the stable homeowner. In most states, residents had to live at the same address for as long as a year before they were eligible to register, and had to re-register if they moved only a few doors away. Registration offices were open for limited hours and were sometimes located at inconvenient or hard-to-find places. Many states closed their rolls a year before an election. By the time people got around to thinking about going to the polls, the deadline had long since passed. Many districts were also quick to purge the rolls of nonvoters, requiring them to re-register if they wanted to exercise their right to vote.

For years, the League of Women Voters sought to persuade Congress and the states to reduce registration barriers. Many scholars also believed that registration reform was the answer to the turnout problem. Studies indicated that participation among America's registered voters was nearly identical to that of European voters. The political scientists Raymond Wolfinger and Steven Rosenstone estimated that eased registration requirements could boost presidential election turnout by as much as 9 percent.

Registration laws have been relaxed. No state today is allowed to impose a residency requirement that exceeds thirty days for a federal election. Six states—Idaho, Maine, Minnesota, New Hampshire, Wisconsin, and Wyoming—allow residents to register at the polls on Election Day. The Motor Voter Act, passed by Congress in 1993, has even shifted some of the registration burden to the states. They must offer registration to citizens who seek services at public assistance agencies, such as food stamp and Medicare offices, or who apply for driver's licenses. States can also offer registration at unemployment offices and other public facilities, such as libraries and schools. Moreover, the act requires states to allow registration by mail and prohibits them from arbitrarily purging nonvoters from the rolls.

Millions of Americans have enrolled through the Motor Voter Act. Most of them would have registered anyway under the old system, but the Federal Election Commission estimates that the legislation has added at least 10 million registrants to the rolls since 1993. With so many additional registrants, why did turnout drop by 5 million voters between 1992 and 2000?

The political scientists Michael McDonald and Samuel Popkin claim that the turnout decline is a "myth." "There is no downward trend [since 1972] in the national turnout rate," they say. Their argument is built on the fact that the U.S. Census Bureau bases its official turnout figures on the total adult population. This population includes individuals who are ineligible to vote, including noncitizens, prison inmates, and convicted felons. Their numbers have increased substantially since 1960. As a result of liberalized immigration laws, the United States in recent decades has experienced its largest influx of immigrants since World War I. Noncitizens were 2 percent of the adult population in 1960 and today account for 7 percent. Tougher drug and sentencing laws have also increased the number of ineligible voters. The nation now has a higher percentage of its population behind bars than any other country in the world. Roughly 3.5 million are disqualified from voting because they are incarcerated or a convicted felon. This is a sizeable increase from 1960, when fewer than 500,000 were ineligible to vote for these reasons.

When voting rates are adjusted for ineligible adults, the picture improves. Between 1960 and 2000 turnout among eligible voters declined by 9 points (from 64 to 55 percent), compared with the Census Bureau's population-based figure of 12 points (63 to 51 percent). Even by this revised estimate, however, the voting rate is disturbingly low. If turnout in 2000 had been 9 points higher, 18 million more Americans would have gone to the polls—a number equal to the combined turnout in the twenty-four states of Alaska, Arizona, Arkansas, Delaware, Hawaii, Idaho, Iowa, Kansas, Maine, Mississippi, Montana, Nebraska, Nevada, New Hampshire, New Mexico, North Dakota, Oklahoma, Rhode Island, South Carolina, South Dakota, Utah, Vermont, West Virginia, and Wyoming. By any measure, that's a lot of missing voters.

The revised figures, however, reveal a potentially significant pattern. The decline among eligible voters is concentrated between 1960 and 1972. Since then, turnout among eligible voters in both the presidential and the congressional midterm elections has fallen only slightly, leading McDonald and Popkin to conclude that the appearance of steadily declining turnout is an illusion." If they are right, concern about electoral participation is overstated. There would still be the puzzling question of why the gains in education and registration have not produced the 15-20 percent rise in turnout that voting theories would have predicted? However, fears that the participation problem might worsen would seem unfounded.

Unfortunately, a closer look at turnout trends—and, as will be evident later in this chapter, other participation trends—indicates that the flight from electoral politics is not illusory. For one, disenfranchised citizens in 1960 were not limited to noncitizens, prison inmates, and convicted felons. Southern blacks may in theory have been eligible to vote, but most of them were effectively barred from participating, as were the many poor southern whites who could not afford the poll tax or pass a literacy test. Thus, the clearest picture of what's been happening with turnout in recent decades emerges from a look at nonsouthern states only. There, turnout among eligible voters exceeded 70 percent in 1960. By 1972, it had dropped to 60 percent, and, in 1996, barely topped 50 percent. The non-South voting rate is now near the level of the 1820s, a time when many eligible voters could not read or write and had to travel by foot or on horseback for hours to get to the nearest polling place.

Since the 1970s voting rates have also fallen in presidential primaries. Nearly 30 percent of adults in states with presidential primaries voted in these contests in 1972 and 1976. Since then, the primary election turnout has fallen sharply. It was just 17 percent in the 2000 presidential primaries and 13 percent in 1996 (when only the Republicans had a contested race).

Turnout in congressional primaries has also been on a downward trajectory. It fell from 30 percent in 1970 to 20 percent in 1986. Since then, the average has been closer to 15 percent.

Voting rates for statewide and local elections are not readily available, but fragmentary evidence points to a sharp decline here as well. In Connecticut, for example, turnout in municipal elections fell from 53 to 43 percent between 1989 and 1997. After surveying a number of states and cities, Jack Doppelt and Ellen Shearer concluded in 1999 that turnout had become "an embarrassment." They reported no locations where voting numbers had risen significantly and plenty where the numbers had dropped to historic lows. For example, the combined turnout for two statewide 1998 Texas primaries, a regular one and a runoff election, was 14 percent of registered voters. Only 3 percent showed up for the runoff.

The first elections after the September 11, 2001, terrorist attacks did not disrupt the trend. In the two highest-profile statewide races—those for governor in Virginia and in New Jersey—turnout fell from its level four years earlier. It dropped by 5 percentage points in Virginia and by 10 points in New Jersey. Even in New York State, where residents had been urged to come out in local elections in order to show the world that democracy was stronger than ever, voting was down. Syracuse had its lowest turnout in seventy-six years, Binghamton its lowest in thirty years, and Buffalo apparently its lowest ever. Even in New York City, only 36 percent of registered voters (about 25 percent of the adult population) went to the polls.

It is too early to know the impact that the World Trade Center and Pentagon attacks will have on political involvement. Americans might stage a triumphant return to the polls in upcoming elections. But any claim that their interest in voting has not flagged since the 1970s is based on incomplete evidence.

Does a diminished appetite for voting affect the health of American politics? Is society harmed when the voting rate is low or in decline? As the *Chicago Tribune* said in an editorial, it may be "humiliating" that the United States, the oldest continuous democracy, has nearly the lowest voting rate in the world. But does it have any practical significance?

Some observers take comfort in low-turnout elections. They say the country is better off if less interested and less knowledgeable citizens stay home on Election Day. In a 1997 cover story in *The Atlantic Monthly*, Robert Kaplan wrote that "apathy, after all, often means that the political situation is healthy enough to be ignored. The last thing America needs is more voters—particularly badly educated and alienated ones—with a passion for politics.

The gist of this age-old argument is that low turnout protects society from erratic or even dangerous shifts in public opinion. Irregular voters are not as well informed as habitual voters and are therefore more likely to get carried away by momentary passions. If these voters participate heavily, it is argued, outcomes could vary greatly from one election to the next, resulting in disruptive policy shifts. In his essay "In Defense of Nonvoting" the columnist George Will says "good government" rather than voting is "the fundamental human right." He notes that high turnout and massive vote swings contributed to the political chaos that brought down Germany's Weimar Republic, enabling the Nazis to seize power. Will claims that America's declining voting rate is a healthy development.

America's voters, however, have not acted whimsically. Except for an interlude in the 1780s, when the Articles of Confederation governed the United States, erratic voting has not been a persistent source of political instability.

America's voters have typically recoiled at the prospect of radical change. William Jennings Bryan's "Cross of Gold" speech enthralled the 1896 Democratic convention delegates, but his nomination prompted large numbers of swing voters to abandon the Democratic Party in fear of free coinage of silver. "Thou Shalt Not Steal" blared an anti-Bryan editorial in the *Chicago Tribune*. When Barry Goldwater, the Republican nominee in 1964, exclaimed that "extremism in defense of liberty is no vice" he got buried in one of the greatest landslides in presidential history. Hard-core Republicans backed him, but other voters went sharply in the other direction. Eight years later, the Democratic nominee, George McGovern, took positions on Vietnam and income security that alarmed many, and he lost both the election and the swing vote by even wider margins than Goldwater.

Small and obstinate electorates rather than large and whimsical ones have been America's affliction. During the South's Jim Crow era, low-turnout, whites-only elections helped sustain segregation. Even today, electoral dysfunction typically stems from small electorates. As turnout in recent congressional primaries declined, hard-core partisans (the "wing nuts") became an increasingly larger proportion of those voting, which contributed to the more frequent defeat of moderate candidates. In turn, Congress became a more divided and rancorous institution.

U.S. elections are hardly at a crisis point. Swing voters still decide the outcome of national elections, and the drop in turnout has not threatened the legitimacy of elected officials. Nevertheless, elections are now less adaptive. As electorates shrink, they tend to calcify. If huge shifts in the vote are antithetical to sound government, so, too, are tiny ones. They signal a polity with a reduced capacity to respond to changing needs.

Elections have also become less representative. Politics is prone to what the political scientists Sidney Verba, Kay Lehman Schlozman, and Henry Brady call "participatory distortion." Citizens of higher income, education, and age are greatly overrepresented in nearly every political activity, from contacting legislators to contributing money. Voting is the least distorted activity. For a long period, in fact, election analysts claimed that turnout was irrelevant because voters and nonvoters thought alike. "Most electoral outcomes" Ruy Teixeira concluded in 1992, "are not determined in any meaningful way by turnout."

This argument is still heard, but the evidence for it is less convincing than it was even a decade ago. Who votes does matter. As the electorate has shrunk, it has come to include proportionally more citizens who are older, who have higher incomes, or who hold intense opinions on such issues as gun control, labor rights, and abortion. On balance, these tendencies have worked slightly to the Republicans' advantage, which, in close races, can tip the balance. Polls indicated that if all eligible adults had voted in 2000, the Democrats would have captured the presidency and both houses of Congress. Turnout also affected the outcome of the 1994 midterm election that launched the "Republican Revolution" in Congress. Surveys showed that nonvoters preferred Democratic congressional candidates by a substantial margin.

If turnout among those of lower education and income were substantially higher, the GOP would not necessarily have lost the 1994 and 2000 elections. Republican candidates would run on broader platforms if more people voted regularly. So, too, would Democratic candidates, who have increasingly directed their appeals at special interests and higher-income voters. Campaign platforms have always been tailored to those who vote. As the political scientists Steven Rosenstone and John Mark Hansen note: "The idle go unheard: They do not speak up, define the agenda, frame the issues, or affect the choices leaders make."

The increasing number of nonvoters could be a danger to democracy. Although high participation by itself does not trigger radical change, a flood of new voters into the electorate could possibly do it. It's difficult to imagine a crisis big and divisive enough to prompt millions of new voters to suddenly flock to the polls, especially in light of Americans' aversion to political extremism. Nevertheless, citizens who are outside the electorate are less attached to the existing system. As the sociologist Seymour Martin Lipset observed, a society of nonvoters "is potentially more explosive than one in which most citizens are *regularly* involved in activities which give them some sense of participation in decisions which affect their lives."

Voting can strengthen citizenship in other ways, too. When people vote, they are more attentive to politics and are better informed about issues affecting them. Voting also deepens community involvement, as the philosopher John Stuart Mill theorized a century ago. Studies indicate that voters are more active in community affairs than nonvoters are. Of course, this association says more about the type of person who votes as opposed to the effect of voting. But recent evidence, as Harvard University's Robert Putnam notes, "suggests that the act of voting itself encourages volunteering and other forms of good citizenship."

Going to the local polling place and voting does not require a lot of time. In most locations, it takes about as long to drive to a video store and rent a couple of movies. Other forms of electoral participation, such as canvassing or paying careful attention to election news, can be far more time consuming. How involved are citizens in these more demanding forms of participation?

When it comes to joining groups or helping in campaigns, Americans have a stronger tradition of participation than Europeans. Since the publication of Alexis de Tocqueville's *Democracy in America*, the United States has been admired for its political activism. "A nation of joiners" was Tocqueville's characterization of the United States. But it is losing this distinction in election campaigns. Millions still put bumper stickers on their cars, wear campaign buttons, display lawn signs, attend campaign rallies, or work on a campaign, but their numbers are falling. In 1972, 12 percent of Americans attended a campaign rally or speech and more than 6 percent worked for a party or candidate. By the 1980s, citizens were a third less likely to engage in these activities and, today, are only half as likely. The number who contribute money to a candidate or party has also decreased by nearly 50 percent since the 1970s.

Attention to election news has also declined. Campaign coverage has never been more plentiful, or so widely ignored. In 1960, nearly 50 percent claimed to have watched a "good many" election programs. That figure has fallen to fewer than 30 percent. Attention to newspaper coverage of campaigns has decreased even more sharply.

Although they are still a major attraction, even the October presidential debates get less attention than before. Except for the Super Bowl, the Summer Olympics, and the Academy Awards, the debates are the most watched events on television. Like those other contests, the debates are, as Alan Schroeder writes, "human drama at its rawest." Conflict, risk, and suspense are all elements of drama, and the debates offer them on a level unmatched by other campaign events. They have regularly produced surprising performances. Ronald Reagan demonstrated an unexpected command of the issues in 1980 and, just as unexpectedly, addled his way through a 1984 debate, concluding his performance with a time-capsule anecdote to which he forgot the ending.

Although the October debates still attract tens of millions of viewers, the numbers have been falling steadily. The four Kennedy-Nixon debates each attracted roughly 60 percent of all households with television sets. When debates resumed with Carter and Ford in 1976, viewers again flocked to their TVs, as they also did for the single Reagan-Carter face-off in 1980. Since then, except for the Clinton-Bush-Perot encounters in 1992, debate audiences have been declining. Only 46 percent of the country's television households watched the two Reagan-Mondale debates in 1984. Barely more than 36 percent saw the Bush-Dukakis debates in 1988. The Clinton-Dole debates in 1996 averaged 29 percent.

The debate audiences in 2000 were widely expected to exceed that level. The Bush-Gore contest was much tighter than the Clinton-Dole race, and large numbers of voters had not yet settled on a candidate. "In just thirty-five days, Americans will choose a new president," said CBS's Dan Rather on the night of the first debate. "What's about to happen . . . could have a big impact on whether it will be Democrat Al Gore or Republican George Bush. . . . [T]he race is tight. Yet, the audience rating for the three Bush-Gore debates was no higher than for the three Clinton-Dole debates. The third debate in 2000 had a 26 per-cent rating—the lowest ever.

The audiences for primary election debates are also shrinking. Large numbers of Americans saw Robert Kennedy and Eugene McCarthy face off in 1968 and watched Hubert Humphrey and McGovern debate in 1972. The 1980 Republican debate in New Hampshire that thrust Ronald Reagan back into the lead for the GOP nomination also attracted a sizeable audience. In contrast, the two dozen primary debates in 2000 drew, on average, 1.8 million viewers—about a fifth of the audience of the typical prime-time program. None of these debates attracted even as many as 5 million viewers. If the debates had been a new television series, they would have been cancelled after the initial episode. The first Democratic debate in 2000 went head-to-head with a World Wrestling Federation match: the wrestlers had four times as many viewers as the candidates. Even then, WWF's *SmackDown!* with 7.2 million viewers was rated ninety-first among the week's television shows.

The convention audience is also dwindling. At one time, Americans could hardly get their fill of the televised national party conventions. They were so popular that they became even a marketing tool. "Buy a television, watch the conventions" suggested a 1952 RCA ad. Another RCA ad said: "With the aid of television, we had what amounted to the greatest town meeting ever held. . . . Sixty million people had front-row seats and got a better picture of what was going on than any delegate or any reporter on the convention floor.

In 1952, the typical television household watched 25 hours of convention coverage, often in the company of friends and neighbors. Even as late as 1976, the typical household viewed the conventions for 11 hours. Since then the ratings have hit the skids. By 1996, the average had fallen to less than 4 hours. A new low was reached in 2000: 3 hours of convention viewing for the typical household. In 1976, 28 percent of television households had their sets on and tuned at any given moment to the convention coverage. Only 13 percent were watching in 2000, down from 17 percent in 1996.

Throughout the 2000 campaign, as part of our Vanishing Voter Project, we monitored Americans' attention to the campaign through weekly national surveys. By the time Election Day arrived, we had conducted 80,000 interviews in fifty-two weeks, the most comprehensive study ever conducted of election interest. Our polls paint a disturbing picture of involvement in the world's foremost democracy. During the typical week, four times as many respondents said they were paying "just some," "only a little," or "no" attention to the campaign as said they were paying "a great deal" or "quite a bit" of attention.

The 2000 election was slow to engage Americans. By Thanksgiving 1999, the candidates had been campaigning nonstop for two months, and four primary debates had already been held. Nevertheless, the campaign might just as well have been taking place in Siberia. Americans sat around their holiday dinner tables talking about everything but George Bush, John McCain, Bill Bradley, and Al Gore. Only one in twenty adults reported having talked about the campaign on Thanksgiving Day—and that included conversations of any length with anybody, not just extended discussions with family members over turkey and trimmings.

Interest rose during the period of the Iowa caucuses and the New Hampshire primary, and it continued to grow through early March's decisive Super Tuesday primaries, fueled in part by McCain's drawing power. The number who said they were paying close attention nearly doubled. Even then, many were tuned out. In the week after New Hampshire's GOP primary, only 47 percent could name McCain as the winner. Four percent claimed Bush had won, and 49 percent said they did not know.

After Super Tuesday, interest dropped sharply. By the end of April, three in four said they were paying almost no attention to the campaign. Americans were so uninvolved during the late-spring and early-summer months that many forgot some of what they had learned about the candidates' policy positions earlier in the campaign.

Not until the August conventions did people again start to pay closer attention. The news that Gore had selected Joseph Lieberman as his running mate—the first Jewish candidate to run on a major-party ticket—was known to 66 percent of Americans within forty-eight hours of the announcement. The October debates also sparked interest, as did the news four days before the election that Bush had been arrested in 1976 for driving while intoxicated. Within a day, 75 percent were aware of the incident. But these were unusual moments. In only two weeks out of fifty-two did the number of adults who said they were paying "very close" or "quite a bit of" attention reach 40 percent.

An inattentive public is an uninformed one. As the 2000 campaign entered its final week, only one issue position—Gore's stand on prescription drugs—was familiar to a majority of Americans. During the past half century there has been a revolution in higher education and in mass communication. Citizens have never had so much information available to them or been better equipped to handle it. Research indicates, however, that Americans today are no better informed about election politics than they were fifty years ago. The high school-educated public of 1948 knew as much about Harry Truman's and Thomas Dewey's positions on price controls and the Taft-Hartley Act as the media-saturated, college-educated public of 2000 knew about Gore's and Bush's stands on prescription drugs and tax cuts.

Ironically, it was not until after Election Day that the public became keenly interested in the 2000 campaign. The unfolding drama in Florida captured imaginations in a way that the campaign itself never did. Interest had peaked just before Election Day when 46 percent were paying "a great deal" or "quite a bit" of attention. During the following week, as it became clear that the Florida vote would decide the outcome, nearly 80 percent were paying close attention. For a period, a majority acted as if election politics really mattered, talking about it with interest, and absorbing each new twist in the Florida vote count?

Except for the black community and some die-hard partisans, however, the Florida wrangling was cause for neither anger nor anxiety. Citizens were captivated by the story but not wedded to the result. Only 10 percent believed the situation was "a constitutional crisis" and, within two weeks, half said the dispute had "gone on too long already." The public's response was a stark contrast to how Americans had reacted in 1876, the last time a president was chosen by post-election wheeling and dealing. Then they had taken to the streets, and more than a few fistfights broke out. Wider civil unrest was averted only when a political deal was brokered to end the Civil War Reconstruction. Nothing remotely like that was required to keep the peace in 2000. "There will be no mobs gathering to shout 'Gore or blood' or 'Bush or blood'" the *New York Times*'s Adam Clymer wrote. "Nobody cares that much."

What is going on here? Why are Americans less engaged by political campaigns today than a few decades ago? And is the situation likely to change anytime soon?

Some commentators say participation follows a natural cycle and will rise again soon, just as it did after downturns in the 1890s, 1920s, and 1940s. "Historians will almost certainly remember our time,' says the *Boston Globe*'s David Shribman," as the preface to a new period of political activism, agitation, and passion?

But this argument overlooks the persistence of the current trend and the special nature of those earlier periods. Turnout dropped sharply in the 1890s before stabilizing a few elections later. That era, however, was defined by deliberate efforts to suppress voting. Democratic-controlled southern legislatures used poll taxes, literacy tests, and the grandfather clause in order to prevent African Americans from registering. "The costs of voting were deliberately made so high," writes the political scientist Walter Dean Burnham, "that probably half of the white electorate was effectively disenfranchised along with almost all of the [blacks]."

Turnout in the South was 65 percent in the 1880s. By the early 1900s, it had fallen to 30 percent. In the North, Republican-controlled legislatures imposed registration requirements only on big-city residents, most of whom were working-class Democrats. The ballot fraud perpetrated by urban political-machines declined as a result but so did the voting rate of eligible voters.

Turnout also fell sharply in the 1920s, the first decade in which women were allowed to vote. Men had long been out of arguments for keeping the vote from women. Senator Wendell Phillips had said in 1898: "One of two things is true: either woman is like man—and if she is, then a ballot based on brains belongs to her as well as to him. Or she is different, and then man does not know how to vote for her as she herself does." Finally, in 1920, ratification of the Nineteenth Amendment gave women what they had been seeking for decades.

Nevertheless, women were slow to take advantage of suffrage, and the overall turnout rate fell sharply. Turnout had been 62 percent in 1916. It was a mere 49 percent in 1920. In Illinois, the only state where ballots for the two sexes were counted separately, women's voting rate in 1920 was 27 percentage points lower than that of men. "It was not to be expected that the adult women who suddenly find themselves in possession of the franchise should be as conscientious in its exercise as men who from childhood had been encouraged to think politically," wrote Arthur M. Schlesinger and Erik McKinley Eriksson in "The Vanishing Voter" a 1924 article in *The New Republic*.

Turnout also fell sharply in 1944 and 1948, but, in this case, too, there were special circumstances: world war and its aftermath. In Britain as well as in the United States, people were so preoccupied by the war effort that partisan politics was a secondary concern. No analyst has fully explained why this had to be the case or why the wartime governing parties in both England and the United States suffered stinging defeats in postwar legislative elections. By the 1950s, voting rates in Britain and America had returned to normal. Except for 1944 and 1948, turnout was near or above 60 percent in every U.S. presidential election between 1936 and 1968.

The recent downturn in voting has lasted longer than the earlier ones and has occurred despite the upward pressure of advances in education, registration, and civil rights. The latest period does not closely resemble any past period, and there is no end clearly in sight. What might possibly explain it?

Politics has had to compete with more things for people's time and attention. Life today offers distractions on a scale unimaginable even a few decades ago, not only from cable television and the Internet but also in career and lifestyle choices. This development has been felt in European democracies as well, which have also experienced declining participation rates, although on a much smaller scale than in the United States.

The decline is also attributable in part to the march of time. The civic-minded generation raised during the Depression and the Second World War has been gradually replaced by the more private-minded X and Y generations that lived through childhood and adolescence without having experienced a great national crisis. Today's young adults are less politically interested and informed than any cohort of young people on record. The voting rate of adults under thirty was 50 percent in 1972. It was barely above 30 percent in 2000.

The participation decline, however, is not due entirely to generational replacement. Changes in the electoral system, political parties, the news media, and the conduct of campaigns-many of which are the consequence of deliberate policy choices—have contributed to the decrease in turnout and involvement. An explanation of these developments is the focus of this book, which will also offer a few modest suggestions on what might be done to address the problem.

For one, the electoral system needs fixing. Although the Florida debacle in 2000 revealed defects in how ballots are cast and counted, the participation problem does not reside at the tail end of the campaign. What happened to ballots in Florida and elsewhere is an inexcusable failure of election officials to safeguard the integrity of the vote. Nevertheless, because Americans were not aware of the problem until after Election Day, it cannot possibly explain why only half of them showed up at the polls or why only a sixth of them voted in the primaries or why three-fourths of them ignored daily events on the campaign trail.

The front end of the campaign is where the real participation problems start. Three decades ago, against the backdrop of the Vietnam protests, the presidential selection system was changed in order to place the voters in control of the nominating process. In its report, *Mandate for Reform*, the McGovern-Fraser Commission said: "popular participation is the way . . . for people committed to orderly political change to fulfill their needs and desires within our traditional political system." The commission might have accomplished its goal if the reformed system had been properly designed. Instead, the reform produced a presidential campaign that starts far too early and lasts far too long, that runs on big money and responds to special interests, that has sapped the national party conventions of their energy and purpose, and that wears down the public as it grinds its way month after month toward November. If ever there was an election system designed to drive an electorate into submission, the year-long system of electing presidents is it.

Although some observers place the blame for declining participation squarely on citizens—they are portrayed as lazy and indifferent to their responsibilities—that argument . . . is refuted by the adverse changes that have taken place in U.S. politics during the past four decades. Ordinary citizens have been buffeted by developments they do not control and only vaguely comprehend, and which have diminished their stake, interest, and confidence in elections.

The great tools of democracy—its electoral institutions and media organizations—have increasingly been used for private agency. Personal ambition now drives campaigns, and profit and celebrity now drive journalism. Candidates, public officials, and journalists operate in a narrow professional world that is largely of their own making and that is remote from the world of the public they serve.

To be sure, ordinary Americans share some of the blame for their lapse in participation. It's always easier to leave the work of democracy to others. But most of the fault lies elsewhere, and citizens cannot be expected to rededicate themselves merely because they are told their democracy needs them. Stronger leadership is required. Officials, candidates, and the media have failed in their responsibility to give Americans the type of politics that can excite, inform, and engage them—and that will fully and fairly reflect their will. The political scientist E. E. Schattschneider said it best: "Democracy was made for the people, not the people for Democracy."

WHAT KILLED CIVIC ENGAGEMENT? SUMMING UP

Robert D. Putnam

We are about ready to sum up our conclusions about the complex of factors that lies behind the erosion of America's social connectedness and community involvement over the last several decades. First, however, we must review the evidence for and against several additional suspects.

First, the American family structure has changed in several important and potentially relevant ways over the last several decades. The downturn in civic engagement coincided with the breakdown of the traditional family unit—mom, dad, and the kids. Since the family itself is, by some accounts, a key form of social capital, perhaps its eclipse is part of the explanation for the reduction in joining and trusting in the wider community. What does the evidence show?

Evidence of the loosening of family bonds is unequivocal. In addition to the century-long increase in divorce rates (which accelerated from the mid-1960s to the mid-1970s and then leveled off), and the more recent increase in single-parent families, the incidence of one-person households has more than doubled since 1950, in part because of the rising number of widows living alone. According to the General Social Survey, the proportion of all American adults who are currently married from 74 percent in 1974 to 56 percent in 1998, while the proportion of adults who have children at home fell from 55 percent to 38 percent. The Census Bureau reports that the fraction of adults who are both married and have kids at home—the archetypal Ozzie and Harriet family—was sliced by more than one-third from 40 percent in 1970 to 26 percent in 1997.

It is a commonplace of cocktail conversation that we meet people through our spouses and our children. To what extent has the transformation of American family structure and home life over the last thirty years (fewer marriages, more divorces, fewer children, more people living alone) contributed to the decline of civic engagement? The surprising answer is "Probably not much."

Marriage and children do change the kinds of social networks to which one belongs. Both marriage and children increase time spent in community organizations and at home and decrease time spent in informal socializing with friends. Only two types of organizational affiliations, however, are sufficiently strongly related to marital and parental status to make a real difference in the aggregate: church- and youth-related activities.

Americans who are married and those with children are much more likely to be involved in religious activities, including church membership, church attendance, and church-related social activities. As I will explain momentarily, it is not clear which is cause and which effect, but the link is strong. Not surprisingly, parents are also more involved in school and youth groups (PTA, Scouts, and so on), and they are more likely to "attend public meetings on town or *school* affairs" (emphasis added). Finally, since church- and youth-related activities are the two most common sites for volunteering in America, parents are more likely to volunteer than people of the same age and social status who are single and childless.

On the other hand, neither marital nor parental status boosts membership in other sorts of groups. Holding other demographic features constant, marriage and children are *negatively* correlated with membership in sports, political, and cultural groups, and they are simply unrelated to membership in business and professional groups, service clubs, ethnic organizations, neighborhood associations, and hobby groups. Married people attend *fewer* club meetings than demographically matched single people.

Married people are slightly (but only slightly) more likely to give and attend dinner parties, to entertain at home, and to take an active role in local organizations. On the other hand, married people are *less* likely to spend time informally with friends and neighbors. Married people tend to be homebodies. As the marriage rate declined, therefore, the main effect on social life should have been to move social activities from the home into more public settings, but there should have been no generic effects on civic engagement as such. Interest in politics is actually slightly higher among single and childless adults than among married people and parents, other things being equal. Having kids is more important in inducing local involvement (leadership, meetings, volunteering), as we have seen. Parenthood is marginally more important than marriage per se as an entree to community life, but the effect does not appear to extend beyond school- and youth-related activities themselves.

Divorce per se is negatively related to involvement in religious organizations but appears to be unrelated (positively or negatively) to other forms of civic involvement, formal or informal. Compared to demographically matched never married people, divorced people don't entertain friends less often (though they do give slightly fewer dinner parties), don't volunteer less, don't attend club meetings less often, don't work on fewer community projects, and actually sign slightly more petitions, attend slightly more public meetings, and write to Congress slightly more often. Divorce itself does not seem to be seriously implicated in the general trend toward civic disengagement.

The traditional family unit is down (a lot) and religious engagement is down (a little), and there is probably some link between the two. However, the nature of that link is quite unclear. It might be that the dissolution of the traditional family has led to lower religious involvement, or it might be that lower religious involvement has led to greater acceptance of divorce and other non-traditional family forms. In other words, the decline of the traditional family may have contributed to the decline of traditional religion, but the reverse is equally possible. In any event, the evidence is *not* consistent with the thesis that the overall decline in civic engagement and social connectedness is attributable to the decline in the traditional family. On the contrary, to some extent the decline in family obligations ought to have freed up time for more social and community involvement.

If we could rerun the last thirty or forty years, holding the traditional family structure constant—which we can do statistically by giving extra weight to the married people and parents who appear in our surveys—we might produce more religious participation and we surely would produce more involvement in school and youth groups. For those two reasons, that bit of hypothetical social engineering would modestly increase the average level of volunteering. (Ironically, volunteering is one of the few forms of civic engagement for which there is no decline to explain.) *However*, tinkering with family structure in this way would have virtually no effect on membership or activity in secular organizations (from Kiwanis to the NAACP to the AMA), nor would it halt the decline in political activities such as voting or party work. It would tend to *decrease* the time we spend with friends and neighbors even more than we have in fact witnessed. In short, apart from youth- and church-related engagement, *none* of the major declines in social capital and civic engagement that we need to explain can be accounted for by the decline in the traditional family structure. In my view, there are important reasons for concern about the erosion of traditional family values, but I can find no evidence that civic disengagement is among them.

Race is such a fundamental feature of American social history that nearly every other feature of our society is connected to it in some way. Thus it seems intuitively plausible that race might somehow have played a role in the erosion of social capital over the last generation. In fact, the decline in social connectedness and social trust began just after the greatest successes of the civil rights revolution of the 1960s. That coincidence suggests the possibility of a kind of civic "white flight," as legal desegregation of civic life led whites to withdraw from community associations. This racial interpretation of the destruction of social capital is controversial and can hardly be settled within the compass of these brief remarks. Nevertheless the basic facts are these.

First, racial differences in associational membership are not large. At least until the 1980s, controlling for educational and income differences, blacks belonged to more associations on average than whites, essentially because they were more likely than comparably situated whites to belong to both religious and ethnic organizations and no less likely to belong to any other type of group. On the other hand, as we saw in chapter 8, racial differences in social trust are very large indeed, even taking into account differences in education, income, and so on. Clearly these racial differences in social trust reflect not collective paranoia, but real experiences over many generations.

Second, the erosion of social capital has affected all races. This fact is inconsistent with the thesis that "white flight" is a significant cause of civic disengagement, since African Americans have been dropping out of religious and civic organizations and other forms of social connectedness at least as rapidly as white Americans. In fact, the sharpest drop in civic activity between the 1970s and the 1990s was among college-educated African Americans. Even more important, among *whites* the pace of civic disengagement has been un-correlated with racial intolerance or support for segregation. Avowedly racist or segregationist whites have been no quicker to drop out of community organizations during this period than more tolerant whites. The decline in group membership is essentially identical among whites who favor segregation, whites who oppose segregation, and blacks.

Third, if civic disengagement represented white flight from integrated community life after the civil rights revolution, it is hard to reconcile with the generational differences described in chapter 14. Why should disengagement be hardly visible at all among Americans who came of age in the first half of the century, when American society was objectively more segregated and subjectively more racist than in the 1960s and 1970s? If racial prejudice were responsible for America's civic disengagement, disengagement ought to be especially pronounced among the most bigoted individuals and generations. But it is not.

This evidence is not conclusive, but it does shift the burden of proof onto those who believe that racism is a primary explanation for growing civic disengagement over the last quarter century, however virulent racism continues to be in American society. Equally important, this evidence also suggests that reversing the civil rights gains of the last thirty years would do nothing to reverse the social capital losses.

Circumstantial evidence, particularly the timing of the downturn in social connectedness, has suggested to some observers that an important cause—perhaps even *the* cause—of civic disengagement is big government and the growth of the welfare state. By "crowding out" private initiative, it is argued, state intervention has subverted civil society. This is a much larger topic than I can address in detail here, but a word or two is appropriate.

On the one hand, some government policies have almost certainly had the effect of destroying social capital. For example, the so-called slum clearance policies of the 1950s and 1960s replaced physical capital but destroyed social capital, by disrupting existing community ties. It is also conceivable that certain social expenditures and tax policies may have created disincentives for civic-minded philanthropy. On the other hand, it is much harder to see which government policies might be responsible for the decline in bowling leagues, family dinners, and literary clubs.

One empirical approach to this issue is to examine differences in civic engagement and public policy across different political jurisdictions to see whether swollen government leads to shriveled social capital. Among the U.S. states, however, differences in social capital appear essentially uncorrelated with various measures of welfare spending or government size. Citizens in free-spending states are no more engaged than citizens in frugal ones. Cross-national comparison can also shed light on this question. Among the advanced Western democracies, social trust and group membership are, if anything, *positively* correlated with the size of government; social capital appears to be highest of all in the big-spending welfare states of Scandinavia. This simple analysis, of course, cannot tell us whether social connectedness encourages welfare spending, whether the welfare state fosters civic engagement, whether both are the result of some other unmeasured factor(s). Sorting out the underlying causal connections would require much more thorough analysis. However, even this simple finding is not easily reconciled with the notion that big government undermines social capital.

* * *

If big government is not the primary cause of declining civic engagement in contemporary America, how about big business, capitalism, and the market? Thoughtful social critics have long feared that capitalism would undermine the preconditions for its own success by eroding interpersonal ties and social trust. Many of the grand masters of nineteenth-century social theory, from Georg Simmel to Karl Marx, argued that market capitalism had created a "cold society," lacking the interpersonal warmth necessary for friendship and devaluing human ties to the status of mere commodities. The problem with this generic theory of social disconnectedness is that it explains too much: America has epitomized market capitalism for several centuries, during which our stocks of social capital and civic engagement have been through great swings. A constant can't explain a variable.

One version of economic determinism, however, may have more validity—the gradual but accelerating nationalization and globalization of our economic structures. The replacement of local banks, shops, and other locally based firms by far-flung multinational empires often means a decline in civic commitment on the part of business leaders. As Wal-Mart replaces the corner hardware store, Bank of America takes over the First National Bank, and local owners are succeeded by impersonal markets, the incentives for business elites to contribute to community life atrophy. Urbanist Charles Heying has shown, for example, how such "corporate delocalization" in the last third of the twentieth century tended to strip Atlanta of its civic leadership. The social cohesion and civic commitment of Atlanta's elite rose from the 1930s to a peak in the 1960s and then declined to the 1990s, very much the same trajectory as our other measures of social capital. Heying offers suggestive evidence of similar trends in places as diverse as Chicago, Philadelphia, Dayton, and Shreveport. One of Boston's top developers complained to me privately about the demise of "the Vault," a celebrated cabal of local business leaders. "Where are the power elite when you need them?" he said. "They're all off at corporate headquarters in some other state."

I have no doubt that global economic transformations are having an important impact on community life across America. The link is most direct, however, as regards larger philanthropic and civic activities. It is less clear why corporate delocalization should affect, for example, our readiness to attend a church social, or to have friends over for poker, or even to vote for president. Nevertheless, the connection between civic disengagement and corporate disengagement is worth exploring.

Let us sum up what we have learned about the factors that have contributed to the decline in civic engagement and social capital traced in section II.

First, pressures of time and money, including the special pressures on two-career families, contributed measurably to the diminution of our social and community involvement during these years. My best guess is that no more than 10 percent of the total decline is attributable to that set of factors.

Second, suburbanization, commuting, and sprawl also played a supporting role. Again, a reasonable estimate is that these factors together might account for perhaps an additional 10 percent of the problem.

Third, the effect of electronic entertainment—above all, television—in privatizing our leisure time has been substantial. My rough estimate is that this factor might account for perhaps 25 percent of the decline.

Fourth and most important, generational change—the slow, steady, and ineluctable replacement of the long civic generation by their less involved children and grandchildren—has been a very powerful factor. The effects of generational succession vary significantly across different measures of civic engagement-greater for more public forms, less for private *schmoozing*—but as a rough rule of thumb we concluded in chapter 14 that this factor might account for perhaps half of the overall decline.

Slightly complicating our accounting for change is the overlap between generational change and the long-term effects of television. Not all of the effects of television are generational—even members of the long civic generation who are heavy TV watchers reduce their civic involvement—and not all of the effects of generational succession can be traced to television. (We speculated that the fading effects of World War II are also quite important, and other factors too may be lurking behind the "generational effect.") Nevertheless, perhaps 10-15 percent of the total change might be attributed to the joint impact of generation and TV—what we might term in shorthand "the TV generation."

All of these estimates should be taken with a few grains of salt, partly because the specific effects vary among different forms of community involvement. Generation is more important in explaining the decline of churchgoing, for example, and less important in explaining the decline in visiting with friends. . . . Work, sprawl, TV, and generational change are all important parts of the story, but important elements in our mystery remain unresolved.